AQA Law for AS

Fourth Edition

Jacqueline Martin

Editor: Denis Lanser

HODDER EDUCATION

AN HACHETTE UK COMPANY

Orders: please contact Bookpoint Ltd, 130 Milton Park, Abingdon, Oxon
OX14 4SB. Telephone: (44) 01235 827720. Fax: (44) 01235 400454. Lines are
open from 9.00 – 5.00, Monday to Saturday, with a 24 hour message
answering service. You can also order through our website
www.hoddereducation.co.uk

If you have any comments to make about this, or any of our other titles,
please send them to educationenquiries@hodder.co.uk

British Library Cataloguing in Publication Data
A catalogue record for this title is available from the British Library

ISBN: 978 1 4441 1049 4

First Edition Published 2002
Second Edition Published 2005
Third Edition Published 2008
This Edition Published 2010
Impression number 10 9 8 7 6 5
Year 2014 2013 2012

Hachette UK's policy is to use papers that are natural, renewable and
recyclable products and made from wood grown in sustainable forests. The
logging and manufacturing processes are expected to conform to the
environmental regulations of the country of origin.

Illustrations by Peter Lubach
Cover photo © Alan Crosthwaite/Alamy
Typeset by Dorchester Typesetting Group Ltd
Printed and bound in Dubai for Hodder Education, an Hachette UK
Company, 338 Euston Road, London NW1 3BH

Contents

Preface

This book is aimed at the AQA specification for AS Law. The topics are covered in the order in which they appear in that specification.

The first chapter is an introductory one. It deals with the differences between civil and criminal law and gives a brief introduction to human rights. I have included this chapter as it is important that students grasp that civil and criminal cases are dealt with in different ways and in different courts. Brief introductions to human rights and European law have been included as they affect so many aspects of our legal system.

The order of topics then starts with those set out for Unit 1 of the AS, Law Making and the Legal System. These are Acts of Parliament, including influences on Parliamentary law-making, delegated legislation, statutory interpretation, judicial precedent, civil courts, alternative dispute resolution, criminal courts, lay magistrates, juries, the legal profession, funding and the judiciary. The book then covers the topics needed for Unit 2, the Concept of Liability, starting with an introduction to concepts in criminal law and offences against the person, then criminal procedure and sentencing. The final two chapters are on the tort of negligence and the law of contract. Within each of these chapters are sections on civil procedure and damages in the context of the relevant area of law.

Throughout the text I have used the previous edition of *AQA Law for AS*, which many teachers of AQA AS Law are already familiar with, as the basis for this textbook. I have kept to the principles of explaining points simply and clearly, but at the same time providing some depth for the more able students. As well as covering the factual material, each chapter contains critical analysis at a level suitable for AS students.

The text is broken up into manageable 'bites' with the use of sub-headings. There are also diagrams and charts to help students with their understanding of topics. Key facts charts are included for each topic to enable students to have an overview of the topics. These charts are also helpful as revision aids.

Newspaper articles, cases and other 'live' material are provided in most chapters to illustrate the legal system at work today. Many of these items are also used as a basis for activities and exercises for students to do. There are also application tasks for students based on scenario-style questions. In this fourth edition 'Test yourself' questions have been added in each chapter. These can be done by using the book to find the answers and test understanding of a new topic or they can be used as revision questions to test student's recall of topics.

Examination questions from the specimen paper, January 2009 or June 2009 examination papers for the new specification for AQA AS Law are also given at the end of most chapters. In addition, examiner tips have been added after the questions to help students understand what is required of an answer in the AS examinations.

My thanks go to Denis Lanser for reading the whole of this manuscript when it was in draft and for making valuable comments thereon.

Jacqueline Martin

Acknowledgements

The authors and publishers would like to thank the following for the use of photographs in this volume:

© rnl – Fotolia.com p16; © SIMON WALKER/ Rex Features p24; © Richard Sowersby/Rex Features p37; © Alex Segre/Rex Features p79; © Photofusion Picture Library/Alamy p95; © Stockdisc/Corbis p134; © Peter Dazeley/Photographer's Choice/Getty Images p139; Courtesy of Citizens Advice p159; © TOBY MELVILLE/Reuters/Corbis p166; © PA Wire/Press Association Images p172; © Dan Atkin/Alamy p219; © PhotoAlto/Alamy p245.

The authors and publishers would like to thank the following for the use of copyright material:

AQA examination materials are reproduced by permission of the Assessment and Qualifications Alliance; Courier Media Group Limited p 3;

© Telegraph Media Group Limited 2009 p4; Daily Mail pp4, 5, 98 and 218; © The Times 2007/nisyndication.com p4; © The Times 1995/nisyndication.com p6; © The Times 1995/nisyndication.com p7-8; © The Times 2007/nisyndication.com p140; reproduced by permission of the Supreme Court of the United Kingdom p171; © The Times 2006/nisyndication.com p176; extracts on p 222 from 'Taking Responsibility' by Finola Farrant and Joe Leverson from New Law Journal by permission of LexisNexis Butterworths; © Crown copyright material is reproduced with permission of the Controller of HMSO.

Every effort has been made to trace and acknowledge ownership of copyright. The publishers will be glad to make suitable arrangements with any copyright holders whom it has not been possible to contact.

Table of Acts of Parliament

Table of Cases

Introduction to Law

Murderer jailed for life

Burglar caught

Headlines like these in newspapers are what many people think of when 'law' is mentioned. The other main source of information for the ordinary person is television programmes such as The Bill and Crimewatch. The headlines and these TV programmes all involve criminal cases.

This does not give a complete picture of the law. In fact, the law deals with a very wide variety of different cases and situations. As well as all the criminal cases that we hear so much of, the law also deals with what is called civil law.

The AQA AS specification you are studying requires you to understand the different ways in which civil and criminal cases are dealt with. This is part of Unit 1. For Unit 2 you have to study some aspects of criminal law and one area of civil law. This can be either contract law or the law of negligence in tort.

1.1 Civil law

Civil law is about private disputes between individuals and/or businesses. There are several different types of civil law. Some important areas of civil law are:

- contract law;
- law of tort;
- family law;
- employment law;
- company law.

These all deal with different matters.

Contract cases

Consider the following situations:

(a) a family complain that their package holiday did not match what was promised by the tour operator and that they were put into a lower grade of hotel than the one they had paid for;
(b) a woman has bought a new car and discovers that the engine is faulty;
(c) a man who bought a car on hire-purchase has failed to pay the instalments due to the hire-purchase company.

All these situations come under the law of contract. There are also many other situations in which contracts may be involved. A contract is an agreement between two or more people and that agreement can be enforced by the courts.

If a court case is successfully taken for breach of contract, the court will try to put the parties into the position they would have been if the contract had not been broken. This is usually done by ordering the person who broke the contract to pay a sum of money in compensation to the

---

paying for a package holiday

---

buying a car

---

making a hire-purchase agreement

Figure 1.1 Examples of contracts

other person. This sum of money is called an award of damages. In a very small number of contracts the court may order the person in breach to carry out the contract. This is called specific performance.

Tort cases

Now look at the next list. These also involve disputes between individuals and/or businesses, but there is no contract or agreement between them:

(a) a child pedestrian crossing a road is injured by a car whose driver is travelling too fast (the tort of negligence);
(b) a family complain that their health is being affected by the noise and smoke from a factory which has just been built near their house (the tort of nuisance);
(c) a man complains that a newspaper has written an untrue article about him which has damaged his reputation (the tort of defamation).

Incident	Type of tort
Injury caused by car hitting pedestrian	Negligence
Being affected by noise	Nuisance
Untrue article in newspaper	Defamation

Figure 1.2 Examples of torts

All these cases come under the law of tort. This area of law recognises that there are situations where one person owes a legal responsibility to another. If there is a breach of this responsibility, then the person affected can make a claim under the law of tort. If successful the court will award them damages, which means a sum of money in compensation for any injury to them, their property or their reputation. Where there is a situation which is continuing (such as in (b) above), it is also possible for the court to order the person causing the problem not to do certain things. The examples above show possible breaches of different torts.

Other types of civil law

Other divisions of civil law concentrate on specific topics. Family law covers all disputes that may arise within families. A major part of this is divorce law and who should have the day-to-day care of any children of the family. Employment law covers all aspects of employment: for example, any disputes about unfair dismissal or redundancy come under this area of law. Company law is very important in the business world: it regulates how a company should be formed, sets out the formal rules for running a company, and deals with the rights and duties of shareholders and directors.

As well as these areas of civil law, there are also laws relating to land, to copyright, to marine law and many other topics. So it can be seen that civil law covers a wide variety of situations.

1.2 Criminal law

Criminal law sets out the types of behaviour which are forbidden at risk of punishment. A person who commits a crime is said to have offended against the State and so the State has the right to prosecute them. This is so even though there is often an individual victim of a crime as well. For example, if a defendant commits the crime of burglary by getting into someone's house and stealing money and other property, the State will prosecute the defendant for that burglary. But there is also an individual, the person living in the house, who is the victim of the crime. If the State does not prosecute then that individual has the right to prosecute. This happens only rarely in cases where the victim is an individual, but it is common in cases such as shoplifting where the business that owns the shop will often prosecute.

The criminal courts have the right to punish those who break the criminal law. So, at the end of a case where the defendant is found guilty, that defendant will be given a punishment. Such punishments include imprisonment, a community sentence such as unpaid work, a fine, or a ban from driving.

Any individual victim of the crime will not necessarily be given compensation, though where possible the courts do make a compensation order as well as punishing the offender.

Activity

On this page and the next page there are five newspaper articles. Three are about civil cases and two are about criminal cases. Read the articles and answer the questions at the end.

After you have done this activity read section 1.3 to get a clearer understanding of the differences between the way civil and criminal cases are dealt with in the courts.

Source A

Woman sentenced over benefit fraud worth £3,000

A West Kingsdown woman who used false information to claim more than £3,000 in benefits she was not entitled to has been prosecuted.

Heather Binns pleaded guilty to three charges of benefit fraud at Sevenoaks Magistrates' Court following a tip-off from a member of the public.

Mrs Binns claimed she was a lone parent in receipt of Income Support when she was actually living with a partner who was in full-time employment.

She has now been given a community sentence and ordered to do 50 hours' unpaid work to be completed over a 12-month period and ordered to pay £100 costs.

Adapted from an article in the Sevenoaks Chronicle *and www.thisiscourier.co.uk, 21 June 2007*

Source B

Couple sue wedding photographer

A newly-married couple have successfully sued their wedding photographer after paying £1,450 for a 'woefully inadequate' service.

Marc and Sylvia Day were presented with a disc full of pictures from the big day with heads chopped off, inattentive guests and random close-ups of vehicles.

The cutting of the cake was missed and of the 400 images they were sent, only 22 met with their approval.

They have now been awarded compensation by a judge after winning a case for breach of contract against the photographer.

Deputy District Judge Keith Nightingale, found in favour of the Days at Pontefract county court and criticised Mr Bowers for providing 'inappropriate' photos and a 'woefully inadequate' service.

He ordered him to pay back £500 from the £1,450 to the Days with £450 in damages, £100 for their loss of earning and £170 in court fees.

Adapted from an article by Paul Stokes in The Daily Telegraph, *5 October 2009*

Source C

Life in jail for shot that rang out

An armed robber whose bullet deflected off the mobile phone in a jeweller's pocket has been jailed for life for attempted murder.

. . . Darren Price, 25, survived being shot by Sean Henry, who ran out of Amore jewellers in Horsham, West Sussex, with £50,000 of diamond rings.

Henry, 35, who was out of jail on licence at the time of the offence in September 2005, was found guilty by a jury of attempted murder, robbery and possession of a gun after a three-week trial at Hove Crown Court. He was ordered to serve at least 15 years.

Adapted from an article in The Times, *29 June 2007.© The Times 2007/ nisyndication.com*

Source D

Father-of-two awarded £600,000 after wife died following NHS blunders

A man whose wife died after a series of NHS blunders following childbirth yesterday gave a harrowing account of his family's suffering.

Ben Palmer said that his children, Harry, five, and Emily, two, still cry every night for their mother, Jessica, nearly three years after her death.

Mrs Palmer, 35, died less than a week after Emily's birth in June 2004 after medical staff repeatedly failed to spot that she had developed blood poisoning.

Yesterday a judge ordered that the hospital trusts involved pay the family £600,000 in damages.

Speaking after the hearing at London's High Court, Mr Palmer, 36, said: 'My wife died a horrific death six days after giving birth to our daughter. This should not have happened'.

Taken from an article in the Daily Mail, *13 March 2007*

Source E

Ex-partners reach deal on splitting £3m lottery jackpot

A former couple battling in the courts over a £3 million National Lottery jackpot-win have agreed to settle their case.

High Court judge Mr Justice Kitchin adjourned the hearing until this afternoon when he is expected to approve the terms of the settlement.

Maureen Todd, 55, took 53-year-old Desmond Congdon to court after he ran out on her 15 months after winning the lottery.

Before the win in 2004 he had moved into her home in Melksham, Wiltshire and promised to marry her.

They signed an agreement that the win would be shared between them but she claimed he took most of the money on what she said was a worldwide gambling spree . . .

After discussions outside court today, Bernard Weatherill QC, representing Mrs Todd, told the judge: 'The parties have been able to discuss terms to prevent the case from continuing'.

Taken from an article in the Daily Mail,
17 May 2007

Questions

1. Identify which of these articles is referring to civil cases and which to criminal cases. (If you wish to check that you are right before continuing with the rest of the questions, turn to the start of Appendix 1 at the back of the book.)
2. Look at the articles which you have identified as civil cases and state in which courts the cases were dealt with.
3. Look at the articles which you have identified as criminal cases and state in which courts the defendants were tried.
4. In one criminal case, the defendant pleaded guilty. Who made the decision about whether the defendant was guilty in the other case?
5. Were all the civil cases decided by a judge? If not, explain why.
6. What did the people taking the civil case receive as a result of winning their case?
7. In the criminal cases the defendants received punishment. List the different punishments used in the cases.
8. Two of the articles on civil cases show there was a long time between the event for which the claim is made and the actual award of damages. How long was that time?

1.3 Differences between civil and criminal law

There are many differences between civil cases and criminal cases. The newspaper articles on the previous pages show some of these differences. There are other differences as well and it is important to understand fully the distinctions between civil and criminal cases.

1.3.1 Purpose of the law

Civil law upholds the rights of individuals and the courts can order compensation in an effort at putting the parties in the position they would have been if there had not been any breach of the civil law.

Criminal law is aimed at trying to maintain law and order. So, when a person is found guilty of an offence, that offender will be punished. There is also the aim of trying to protect society and this is the justification for sending offenders to prison.

1.3.2 Person starting the case

In civil cases the person starting the case is the individual or business which has suffered as a result of the breach of civil law.

Criminal cases are taken on behalf of the State, and so there is a Crown Prosecution Service responsible for conducting most cases. However, there are other State agencies which may prosecute certain types of offence, for example the Environment Agency who prosecute pollution cases.

The person starting the case is given a different name in civil and criminal cases. In civil cases they are called the claimant, while in criminal cases they are referred to as the prosecutor.

1.3.3 Courts

The cases take place in different courts. In general, civil cases are heard in the High Court or the County Court. The High Court deals with more serious cases while the county court deals with cases of lower value. (Note that some civil matters, especially family cases, can be dealt with in the magistrates' courts – see 9.5 for further details.)

In both the High Court and the county court a judge will try the case. It is very rare to have a case tried by a jury in a civil matter. See Chapter 12 for details of when a jury might be used in a civil case.

Criminal cases will be tried in either the magistrates' courts or the Crown Court. The magistrates' courts deal with less serious offences and the case is tried by a panel of lay magistrates or by a single legally qualified district judge. Serious offences are tried in the Crown Court. The case is tried by a judge sitting with a jury. The judge decides points of law and the jury decide the verdict of guilty or not guilty.

1.3.4 Standard of proof

Criminal cases must be proved 'beyond reasonable doubt'. This is a very high standard of proof, and is necessary since a conviction could result in the

Example

Judgment overtakes Brink's-Mat accused 11 years later

Eleven years after a man was acquitted of the £26 million Brink's-Mat bullion robbery, a High Court judge ruled that he was involved and must repay the value of the gold.

Anthony White, acquitted at the Old Bailey in 1984 of taking part in Britain's biggest gold robbery, was ordered to repay the £26,369,778 value and £2,188,600 in compensation. His wife Margaret was ordered to pay £1,084,344. Insurers for Brink's-Mat had sued the couple for the value of the proceeds.

Mr Justice Rimmer told Mr White that his acquittal did not mean that the Old Bailey jury had been satisfied he was innocent; only that he was not guilty according to the standard of proof required in criminal cases . . .

The case against the Whites is the latest and almost the last in a series of actions since the 1983 robbery brought by insurers for Brink's-Mat against people either convicted or suspected of taking part in the robbery.

Using the lower standards of proof in civil courts and in actions for seizure of assets, lawyers believe that they will recoup at least £20 million.

Taken from an article by Stewart Tendler in The Times, *2 August 1995. © The Times 1995/nisyndication.com*

defendant serving a long prison sentence.

Civil cases have to be proved 'on the balance of probabilities'. This is a much lower standard of proof, where the judge decides who is more likely to be right. This difference in the standard of proof means that it is possible for a defendant who has been acquitted in a criminal case to be found liable in a civil case based on the same

	CIVIL CASES	CRIMINAL CASES
Purpose of the law	To uphold the rights of individuals	To maintain law and order; to protect society
Person starting the case	The individual whose rights have been affected	Usually the State through Crown Prosecution Service
Legal name for that person	Claimant	Prosecutor
Courts hearing cases	County court or High Court Some cases dealt with in tribunals	Magistrates' Court or Crown Court
Standard of proof	The balance of probability	Beyond reasonable doubt
Person/s making the decision	Judge Very rarely a jury	Magistrates in magistrates' courts OR A judge and jury at the Crown Court
Decision	Liable or not liable	Guilty (convicted) or not guilty (acquitted)
Powers of the court	Usually an award of damages, also possible: injunction, specific performance of a contract, rescission or rectification	Prison, community sentence fine, discharge, driving ban

Figure 1.3 Differences between civil and criminal cases

facts. Such situations are not common, but one is illustrated in the article in the previous column.

1.3.5 Outcome of case

A defendant in a civil case is found liable or not liable. A defendant in a criminal case is found guilty or not guilty. Another way of stating this in criminal cases is to say that the defendant is convicted or acquitted.

At the end of a civil case anyone found liable will be ordered to put right the matter as far as possible. This is usually done by an award of money in compensation, known as damages, though the court can make other orders such as an injunction to prevent similar actions in the future or an order for specific performance where the defendant who broke a contract is ordered to complete that contract.

At the end of a criminal case a defendant found guilty of an offence may be punished.

1.4 Double liability

It is possible for the same incident to give rise to both civil and criminal liability. This occurs most often where someone is injured as a result of another person's bad driving. The driver can then be prosecuted in the criminal courts for a driving offence and the injured person can also claim against the driver in the civil courts. This next newspaper article shows a case where this happened.

Example

Record £8.5 million for woman hit by car

A 22-year-old woman who suffered serious brain damage in a road accident nine years ago has been awarded £8.5 million, believed to be a record for a personal injury case (Frances Gibb writes).

Leanne Evans was hit by a 79-year-old driver on a pelican crossing in Birmingham when she was 13. The driver was fined £75 and convicted of careless driving.

Leanne now needs round-the-clock attention from eight carers, has severe memory impairment and uses a wheelchair.

Her father, Ivor Evans, said: 'We are very pleased for Leanne. This award will at least give her a limited quality of life and allow her to enjoy some of the things that every other 22-year-old likes to do, like going to pop concerts, going to the theatre and having a holiday, as well as making sure she has all the medical care that she needs'.

Frances Gibb, The Times, *15 March 2007.*
© *The Times 2007/nisyndication.com*

In this article the criminal case was the one in which the driver was convicted of careless driving. The civil case is the one in which the injured girl was awarded £8.5 million pounds.

Activity

Look through newspapers to find articles about court cases. When you have found an article use your knowledge about civil and criminal cases to decide what type of case it is.

If you are having difficulty finding civil cases, try searching for the phrase 'High Court' or 'county court' in newspapers online. The following have good search engines:

www.dailymail.co.uk
www.telegraph.co.uk.

1.5 Human rights and the English legal system

The Human Rights Act 1998 incorporated the European Convention on Human Rights into our law. This is important as it has affected many areas of the English legal system. This section explains key rights under the Convention and also gives a brief summary of some of the effects on our legal system.

1.5.1 The European Convention on Human Rights

The Convention sets out the rights that the people of Europe should have. These are:

- the right to life (Article 2), though it is recognised that states may impose the death penalty for certain crimes;
- the right not to be tortured or subjected to inhumane or degrading treatment (Article 3);
- slavery is forbidden (Article 4);
- the right to liberty (Article 5), although limitations on this right are permitted so that people who are lawfully arrested or held in custody for trial or given a prison sentence by a court can be detained;
- the right to a fair trial (Article 6);
- the right not to be punished except according to law (Article 7);
- the right to respect for private and family life (Article 8).

The Convention also sets out freedoms which people should be able to enjoy. These include:

- freedom of thought, conscience and religion;
- freedom of expression; and
- freedom of assembly and association.

1.5.2 Effect on the English legal process

Before the Convention was incorporated into our law by the Human Rights Act 1998, anyone who wanted to complain of a breach of human rights had to take their case to the European Court of Human Rights. If the United Kingdom was found to be in breach of the Convention, the Government did not have to change the law. However, in some cases they did do so. An example is *T v United Kingdom; V v United Kingdom* (1999) (see Criminal trials below).

Since the Convention was incorporated, people can rely on the rights it gives in our courts. In addition, there have been some changes in our legal system in order to comply with the Convention. Some of these are explained below. These points are not the only way in which the English legal system has been affected by the European Convention on Human Rights. However, they give some illustration of how wide ranging the effect has been on our legal system.

Civil cases

An appeal route for small claims cases was created. Previously there had been no appeal for small claims cases. This would have breached Article 6 of the Convention – the right to a fair trial.

Criminal trials

In the case of *T v United Kingdom; V v United Kingdom* (1999), the European Court of Human Rights had ruled that there was a breach of Article 6. In the case a boy of 10 and a boy of 11 were tried for murder in the Crown Court. The European Court of Human Rights held the formality of a Crown Court trial would have made it difficult for the boys to understand what was happening. This meant that the trial was not fair and there was a breach of the European Convention.

Following this decision, trials of juveniles at the Crown Court were altered to make the trial process less formal.

Sentencing

Where an offender is sentenced to prison for life, it is usual to set a minimum period which must be served before the offender can be considered for parole. This minimum sentence used to be set by the Home Secretary (a Government minister). The European Court of Human Rights held that this was a breach of the European Convention. This has been changed so that judges are now responsible for setting any minimum period.

Judicial appointment

Part-time judges in this country used to be appointed for a period of three years. After this time they could then be appointed for further periods of three years. In addition the appointment was by the Lord Chancellor (a Government minister). The length of appointment was changed to five years as it was thought that the shorter period meant that there was a risk of the judges not being sufficiently independent from the Government. This would have been a breach of the European Convention.

1.5.3 Effect on sources of law

As well as affecting our legal system, the Human Rights Act 1998 sets out three important matters for the way our law is made and interpreted. These affect the making of Acts of Parliament, decisions on points of law by judges and the way in which judges interpret new laws. Each of these is explained below.

Acts of Parliament

When a new potential Act of Parliament (known as a Bill) is put before Parliament, there must be a statement as to whether it is compatible with Convention rights or not.

Precedent

Section 2(1)(a) of the Human Rights Act 1998 states that our courts must take into account any judgment or decision of the European Court of Human Rights. This means that judges, when deciding a case, must look at human rights cases, as well as our own English law.

Statutory interpretation

Section 3 of the Act states that, so far as it is possible to do so, all legislation (that is Acts of Parliament and other laws made in this country) must be given effect so that it is compatible with the European Convention. For example, if the wording of an Act of Parliament has two possible meanings, then the meaning which fits with the European Convention is the one that must be used.

1.6 European Union Law

Britain joined the European Union on 1 January 1973 (it was at that time called the European Economic Community). Since this date EU law has had an effect on our law. The main effects are on the laws in relation to trade, work and employment law, and equality.

1.6.1 European Union treaties

The European Communities Act 1972, which was passed by the British government of the day in order for us to join the EU, says that EU treaties are automatically part of our law. The Act states that EU treaties are:

> **"** without further enactment to be given legal effect or used in the UK. **"**

So, once a treaty has been signed by all member States, that treaty becomes part of our law.

1.6.2 Regulations and directives

In addition the EU can make two other types of law. These are regulations and directives.

Regulations

Regulations are 'binding in every respect and directly applicable in each Member State'. This means that EU regulations do not have to be adopted in any way by the individual states. They automatically become law in each member country.

This 'direct applicability' point was tested in *Re Tachographs: Commission v United Kingdom* (1979), where a regulation requiring mechanical recording equipment to be installed in lorries was issued. The UK government of the day decided not to implement the regulation, but to leave it to lorry owners to decide whether or not to put in such equipment. When the matter was referred to the European Court of Justice it was held that Member States had no discretion in the case of regulations. The regulation was law in Britain.

Directives

Directives are an important method by which the laws within Member States are made uniform. There have been directives covering many topics including company laws, banking, insurance, health and safety of workers, equal rights, consumer law and social security.

Member States pass their own laws to bring directives into effect. This has to be done within a time limit set by the European Commission. If Britain or another Member State does not pass its own law to bring the EU directive into effect in its own country, then the European Court of Justice has ruled that the directive will have direct effect. This ruling allows individuals in the country to rely on the EU directive if they are bringing an action against their own State.

This happened in *Marshall v Southampton and South West Hampshire Area Health Authority* (1986). Miss Marshall was required to retire at the age of 62 when men doing the same work did not have to retire until age 65. Under the Sex Discrimination Act 1975 in English law this was not discriminatory. However, she was able to succeed in an action for unfair dismissal by relying on the Equal Treatment Directive 76/207. This directive had not been fully implemented in the United Kingdom but the European Court of Justice held that it was sufficiently clear and imposed obligations on the Member State. This ruling allowed Miss Marshall to succeed in her claim against her employers because her employers were 'an arm of the state'; i.e. they were considered as being part of the State.

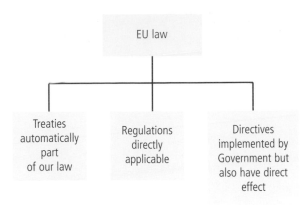

Figure 1.4 The different types of EU law

1.6.3 European Court of Justice

The role of the European Court of Justice is to ensure that EU law is applied uniformly in all Member States. It does this in two ways. The first is that it hears cases to decide whether Member States have failed to fulfil obligations under the Treaties. An example of such a case is *Re Tachographs: Commission v United Kingdom* (1979) in 1.6.2 above.

The second way is by the European Court of Justice hearing references from national courts for preliminary rulings on points of European law. This function is a very important one, since any ruling made by the European Court of Justice is then binding on courts in all Member States. This ensures that the law is indeed uniform throughout the European Union. An example of a case being referred to the European Court of Justice by a British court is *Marshall v Southampton and South West Hampshire Area Health Authority* (1986) (see 1.6.2).

Test Yourself

1. Give an example of a civil case.
2. What is the purpose of the civil law?
3. Which two courts try civil cases?
4. Give an example of a criminal case.
5. What is the purpose of the criminal law?
6. Which two courts try criminal cases?
7. What is meant by 'double liability'?
8. Name three rights that are given by the European Convention on Human Rights.
9. Explain one way in which the English Legal System has been affected by human rights.
10. What types of cases does the European Court of Justice hear?

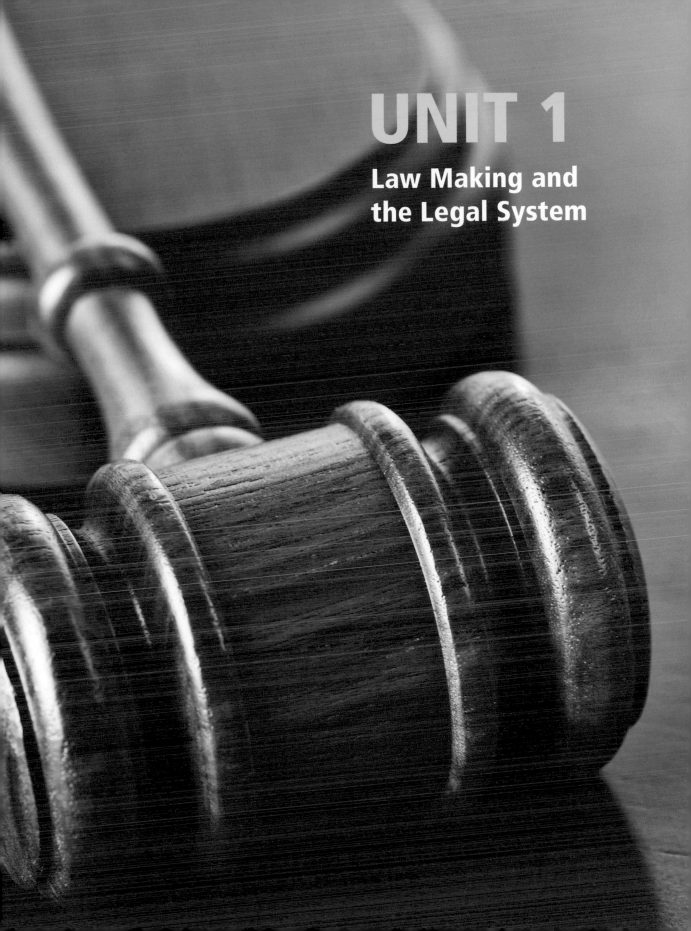

UNIT 1

Law Making and the Legal System

Chapter 2

Parliament

2.1 Parliament

A key principle in a democracy is that laws should be made by the elected representatives of society. In the United Kingdom this means that major laws are made by Parliament. Parliament consists of the House of Commons and the House of Lords.

2.1.1 House of Commons

The members of the House of Commons are elected by the public. The country is divided into constituencies and each of these votes for one Member of Parliament (MP).

There must be a general election at least once every five years, though such an election can be called sooner by the Prime Minister. In addition, there may be individual by-elections in constituencies where the MP has died or retired during the current session of Parliament.

The government of the day is formed by the political party which has a majority in the House of Commons, and it is the government which has the main say in formulating new Acts of Parliament.

2.1.2 House of Lords

The House of Lords is a non-elected body. Before 1999, there were over 1,100 members of the House of Lords of whom 750 were hereditary peers. The rest consisted of life peers (people who have been given a title for their service to the country), judges and bishops.

In 1999 the Labour Government reviewed membership of the House of Lords and decided that it should consist of some nominated members (like the life peers) and some elected members. In particular they decided that an inherited title should not automatically allow that person to take part in the law-making process. Temporary changes were made to the membership of the House of Lords so that it consisted of:

- 92 hereditary peers;
- life peers;
- the most senior bishops in the Church of England.

This was meant to be a temporary solution while the government consulted on the final make-up of the House of Lords. However, there has not yet been agreement on how many of the House of Lords should be elected and how many should be nominated (and by whom). As a result the reform of the House of Lords has not been completed.

Note that the 12 most senior judges used to sit in the House of Lords, but they no longer do so. They are now separate from Parliament and sit as the Supreme Court (see 13.2.1).

2.2 Influences on Parliament

2.2.1 Law Commission

The Law Commission was set up in 1965. It considers areas of law which are believed to be in need of reform. The actual topics may be referred

The Houses of Parliament

to it by the Lord Chancellor on behalf of the government, or it may itself select areas in need of reform and seek governmental approval to draft a report on them. It concentrates on what is sometimes called 'lawyers' law' or 'pure law'. In other words it is concerned with specific areas of law, such as contract law, land law or criminal law.

The Law Commission works by researching the area of law that is thought to be in need of reform. It then publishes a consultation paper seeking views on possible reform. The consultation paper will describe the current law, set out the problems and look at options for reform (often including explanations of the law in other countries).

Following the response to the consultation paper, the Commission will then draw up positive proposals for reform. These will be presented in a report which will also set out the research that led to the conclusions. There will often be a draft Bill attached to the report with the intention that this is the exact way in which the new law should be formed. Such a draft Bill must, of course, go before Parliament and go though the necessary Parliamentary stages if it is to become law.

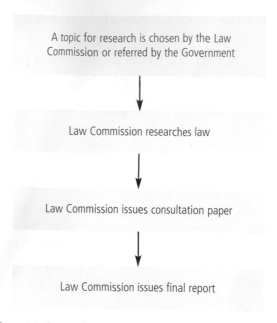

Figure 2.1 The way the Law Commission works

Codification

The Law Commission also puts forward proposals to codify law. The purpose of this is to bring together all the law on one topic into one Act.

This makes the law simpler and easier to find. The Law Commission spent many years writing a draft criminal code which aimed to include the main general principles of criminal law. The draft Criminal Code was first published in 1985. However, the Government has never implemented it. In 2008, the Law Commission stated that it would be concentrating on smaller areas of the code, as there was more chance that the Government would be prepared to make such reforms of the law.

Repeal

Another of the Law Commission's roles is to identify old Acts which are no longer used, so that Parliament can repeal these Acts. The Law Commission has been very successful in this. By 2009 over 2,000 old and out-of-date Acts had been repealed as a result of their work as well as parts of thousands of other Acts. In their 2009 proposals for repealing old Acts, they list six Acts from 1697 relating to workhouses for the poor.

@ Internet Research

Look at the Law Commission's website (www.lawcom.gov.uk) and make a list of three areas of law which the Law Commission is currently researching.

Advantages

The main advantages of having the Law Commission issue reports on areas of law are:

1. areas of law are researched by legal experts;
2. the Law Commission consults before finalising its proposals;
3. whole areas of law can be considered, not just small issues;
4. if Parliament enacts the reform of a whole area of law, then the law is in one Act, such as the Land Registration Act 2002 (see below) and it is easier to find and to understand.

Examples of laws that the government has enacted following a report by the Law Commission include:

- Land Registration Act 2002 which was important for anyone selling or buying a house, flat or any other building or land, as it modernised and simplified the method of registering land;
- Fraud Act 2006 which reformed the law on fraud and deception offences;
- Corporate Manslaughter and Corporate Homicide Act 2007 which makes companies and other organisations criminally liable for deaths caused through bad working practices.

Disadvantages

The main disadvantage is that the Law Commission has to wait for the government to bring in the reforms it proposes. The Government is often slow to enact reforms and some Law Commission reports have not yet been made law.

Each year in its annual report, the Law Commission highlights the number of reports which are still awaiting implementation by Parliament.

A major area of criminal law that is still awaiting reform is non-fatal offences against the person. (This is an area of law you have to study for Unit 2 of the AS.) In 1993 the Law Commission issued a report, *Offences Against the Person* (Law Com No 218) recommending reform to this area of law. Five years later, in 1998, the government issued a consultation paper which included a draft Bill on this area of law. However, the government did not proceed with the Bill and the reforms proposed by the Law Commission have never been made.

Another example of law where the proposals for reform have not been made is in the civil law of negligence. In 1998 the Commission issued a report, *Liability for Psychiatric Illness* (Law Com No 249) suggesting changes to the law where a person suffers psychiatric illness because of another person's negligence. This reform to the law has not been made by the government.

These two examples show how slow Parliament can be over taking action on the Law Commission's proposals. Clearly the Law Commission can only be effective if the government and Parliament are prepared to find time to enact reforms.

There is a problem with the amount of time available in Parliament. A lot of time has to be given to financial matters such as the budget and taxation; foreign policy and issues such as the war in Iraq; events in this country such as terrorist attacks; health and education. So only a limited time is left for 'pure' law reform.

Other disadvantages

The Government may accept the Law Commission's recommendations in principle. However, when reforming the law, the Government may not follow all the recommendations. In addition, as a Bill goes through Parliament, changes to the wording may be made so that the final law is very different to that proposed by the Law Commission. This can cause the law to be less satisfactory than the original proposals.

The Government does not have to consult the Law Commission on changes to the law. This can mean that major changes are made without the benefit of the Law Commission's legal knowledge and extensive research.

2.2.2 Political influence

When there is a general election all the political parties publish a list of the reforms they would carry out if they were elected as the next government. This is called the party's manifesto, and it is one of the ways in which the party tries to persuade people to vote for them.

The party that has the most members of Parliament after a general election becomes the government. This party then has the whole life of the Parliament (this can be up to five years) to bring in the reforms they promised in their manifesto. Most of the reforms will gradually be put before Parliament to pass as an Act of Parliament.

Throughout any session of Parliament, the government has the major say on what new laws will be put before the House of Commons and the House of Lords for debate.

At the opening of each session of Parliament (usually about once a year) the government announces its plans for new laws in that session. This is done in the Queen's speech. This speech is written for the Queen by the Prime Minister and other senior ministers. This is shown in the speech as the Queen will usually use the words 'my Government will …'.

Advantages

Each political party has its proposals for reform ready so that if they are elected as the government they know what they wish to do.

The fact that the government has a majority in the House of Commons means that virtually every law it proposes will be passed. This makes the law-making process efficient.

Disadvantages

If a different party is elected at the next general election, they may decide to repeal or alter some of the laws that the previous government passed. This is because their policies are likely to be quite different from the previous government. Changes in the law in this way can be costly and open to criticism.

2.2.3 European Union law

As Britain is a member of the European Union, the government has to bring into effect any new laws passed by the European Union. This may be done by passing an Act of Parliament. For example, the Sex Discrimination Act 1975 and the Sex Discrimination Act 1986 were enacted in order to bring our laws on discrimination into line with EU law.

Most EU laws are, however, brought into effect through delegated legislation (see section 3.1.1).

This is good as the law in these areas is uniform through all the EU member countries. However, some aspects of EU Law are unpopular in Britain. For example, the EU originally ruled that all goods had to be sold using metric measurements, such as kilograms. Many people in this country objected to this as Britain had up to then used what are called 'imperial' measurements. For weighing items this means using pounds and ounces, not kilograms.

2.2.4 Public opinion/media

Where there is strong public opinion about a change to the law, the government may bow to such opinion. This is more likely towards the end of a term of government when there will be a general election soon and the government wants to remain popular with the majority of people.

Media

The term media means the ways in which information is supplied to the public. It includes television and radio, newspapers and magazines.

The media play a large role in bringing public opinion to the government's attention. Where an issue is given a high profile on television and in the newspapers, then it also brings it to the attention of other members of the public and may add to the weight of public opinion. This is an advantage of a free press. They are able to criticise government policy or bring any other issue to the attention of the government.

An example of the media highlighting bad practice was seen in 2009 over Members of Parliament's expenses claims. Expenses claims made by various MPs were detailed in a national newspaper. Some of the claims were for quite large amounts of money and some were even for items which the MP had not paid for. This caused a public outrage at the system of MPs' expenses. Parliament then had to reform the whole system.

However, there is also the disadvantage that in some cases this can be seen as the media manipulating the news and creating public opinion.

In addition, specific events may also play a role in formulating the law. A particularly tragic example was the massacre in 1996 of 16 young children and their teacher in Dunblane by a lone gunman with a legally owned gun. An enquiry into the ownership of guns was set up and a

pressure group organised a petition asking for guns to be banned. Eventually Parliament banned private ownership of most handguns.

The disadvantage of government responding too quickly to high-profile incidents (a 'knee-jerk reaction') is that the law may be poorly drafted. This was seen with the Dangerous Dogs Act 1991 where the wording in the Act has led to many disputed cases in the courts.

2.2.5 Pressure groups

These are groups which have a particular interest. They try to bring matters they are interested in to the attention of the general public and the government. There are two types of pressure group: sectional and cause. Sectional pressure groups exist to represent the interests of a particular group of people. They often represent work groups or professions. Examples include the Law Society which represents solicitors' interests, the British Medical Association which represents doctors and trade unions which represent workers in different types of job.

Cause pressure groups exist to promote a particular cause. There are many different types of 'cause' pressure group. Examples include environmental groups such as Greenpeace, animal welfare groups, human rights groups, such as Amnesty and ASH, the anti-smoking group.

Pressure groups may cause the government to reconsider the law on certain areas. This was seen in 2000 when the government finally agreed to reduce the age of consent for homosexual acts in private to 16. Another example of the government bowing to public opinion and the efforts of the pressure group, the League against Cruel Sports, was the passing of the Hunting Act 2004 which banned hunting foxes with dogs. In 2007 strict laws against smoking in public places were introduced because of public opinion and medical opinion.

Sometimes pressure groups will campaign against a proposed change to the law. This was seen when the government tried to restrict the right to trial by jury. Pressure groups such as Justice and Liberty campaigned against this as they thought the changes infringed human rights.

Influence		Advantages	Disadvantages
Law Commission	An independent body to review the law and propose reform	• law researched by legal experts • consults before finalising proposals • whole areas of law can be considered, not just small issues	Parliament slow to implement some reforms Only limited time is available in Parliament for 'pure' law reform
Political	Each political party will have its own policies. When a party is elected as the government, these policies will be a major influence on the laws they introduce into Parliament	Each political party has its proposals for reform ready if it is elected A government majority in the House of Commons means that virtually every law it proposes will be passed	New Governments may repeal or alter laws passed by previous Governments
European Union	Britain joined the EU in 1973. Since then EU laws have to be given effect here	Creates uniformity in laws in all EU countries	Not always popular with the public
Public opinion/media	Strong public opinion can lead to a change in the law The media play an important role in highlighting issues of public concern	Brings public opinion to the government's attention	Media manipulating the news and creating public opinion Responding too quickly to high-profile incidents may lead to poorly drafted law
Pressure groups	Groups which have a particular interest and bring issues to the attention of the general public and the government	Raise important issues Wide range of issues is drawn to the attention of the government	Trying to impose their ideas on the majority Pressure groups may have conflicting interests

Figure 2.2 Influences on Parliamentary law-making

Lobbying

Some pressure groups try to persuade individual Members of Parliament to support their cause. This is called lobbying (because members of the public can meet MPs in the lobbies (small hallways) through which MPs go to get to the House of Commons). If a pressure group is successful, it may persuade an MP to ask questions in Parliament about a particular problem. It is also possible that a backbench MP may use the Private Members Bill session (see section 2.4.1) to introduce a Bill trying to reform the law in the way that the pressure group wants. However, it is very unlikely that such a Bill will be passed by Parliament unless there is widespread support for it.

Advantages

Pressure groups often raise important issues. Environmental groups have made the government much more aware of the damage being done to our environment by greenhouse gases and other pollutants.

A wide range of issues is drawn to the attention of the government as there are so many pressure groups with different aims and issues.

Disadvantages

It can be argued that pressure groups are seeking to impose their ideas, even where the majority of the public do not support their views.

There are also occasions when two pressure groups have conflicting interests and want opposing things. This was seen when the ban against fox hunting was considered. The League against Cruel Sports wanted it banned, but the Countryside Alliance wanted it to be allowed to continue.

@ Internet Research

Look up websites of pressure groups such as Liberty (www.liberty-human-rights.org.uk) or Justice (www.justice.org.uk) or Greenpeace (www.greenpeace.org.uk). (These are only suggestions. You can find many other websites by searching.) Choose one pressure group and write a brief summary of any changes in the law it is suggesting or any success in changing the law that it has had.

2.3 The pre-legislative procedure

Each government minister has a department of civil servants and advisers. The particular ministry which is responsible for the area in which a change in the law is being considered will draft ideas for change.

These ideas may be published as a consultation paper. This will outline possible changes, often with alternatives, and anyone can then send in comments on those ideas. Usually pressure groups or groups with a particular interest in the matter will respond to the consultation paper, but members of the public are also entitled to respond. All consultation papers are published on the website of the ministry issuing them.

2.3.1 Green and White papers

On major matters a Green Paper may be issued by the Minister with responsibility for that matter. A Green Paper is a consultative document on a topic in which the government's view is put forward with proposals for law reform. Interested parties are then invited to send comments to the relevant government department, so that a full consideration of all sides can be made and necessary changes made to the government's proposals. Following this the government will publish a White Paper with its firm proposals for new law.

Test Yourself

1. Explain what the Law Commission is and how it works.
2. Give two examples of law reform which resulted from the Law Commission's work.
3. Give two advantages of the Law Commission.
4. Give two disadvantages of the Law Commission.
5. What is meant by a 'sectional' pressure group? Give an example.
6. What is meant by a 'cause' pressure group? Give an example.
7. Explain how pressure groups may try to influence Parliament.
8. Give two advantages of pressure groups.
9. Give two disadvantages of pressure groups.
10. Give two other influences on Parliament (other than the Law Commission and pressure groups.

Consultation before any new law is framed is valuable as it allows time for mature consideration. Governments have been criticised for sometimes responding in a 'knee-jerk' fashion to incidents and, as a result, rushing law through that has subsequently proved to be unworkable.

2.4 Formal legislative process

Major legislation is usually made through Acts of Parliament. Acts of Parliament are also known as statutes. There is a very long and formal process which has to be followed before an Act of Parliament becomes law.

2.4.1 Introducing an Act of Parliament

The great majority of Acts of Parliament are introduced by the government and these are initially drafted by lawyers in the Civil Service who are known as parliamentary counsel to the Treasury. The government department which is responsible for the new law gives instructions as to what is to be included and the intended effect of the proposed law.

Bills

When the proposed Act has been drafted it is published, and at this stage it is called a Bill. It will only become an Act of Parliament if it successfully completes all the necessary stages in Parliament. Where it is a Bill put forward by the government it will be introduced into Parliament by a government minister. For example, the Minister of Justice (or an MP in that department) will introduce any Bills about the justice system, while the Minister for the Department for the Environment, Food and Rural Affairs (or an MP in that department) will introduce any Bills on issues about the environment.

Even at this early stage there are difficulties, as the draftsmen face problems in trying to frame the Bill. It has to be drawn up so that it represents the government's wishes, while at the same time using correct legal wording so that there will not be any difficulties in the courts applying it. It must be unambiguous, precise and comprehensive. Achieving all this is not easy, and there may be unforeseen problems from the language used, as discussed in the section on statutory interpretation.

In addition, there is usually a pressure on time, as the government will have a timetable of when they wish to introduce the draft Bill into Parliament.

Private Members' Bills

As well as Bills being introduced into Parliament by the government, it is possible for individual (private) Members of Parliament to introduce a Bill. These MPs are those who are not government ministers. They can be from any political party. They are also known as 'backbenchers' because they do not sit in the front row in the actual House of Commons. (The government ministers sit in the front row.) There are two ways a private MP can introduce a Bill. These are:

- by ballot;
- through the 'ten-minute' rule.

Ballot

The Parliamentary process allows for a ballot each Parliamentary session in which 20 private members are selected who can then take their turn in presenting a Bill to Parliament. The time for debate of private members' Bills is limited, usually only being debated on Fridays, so that only the first six or seven members in the ballot have a realistic chance of introducing a Bill on their chosen topic.

Ten-minute rule

Backbenchers can also try to introduce a Bill through the 'ten-minute' rule, under which any MP can make a speech of up to ten minutes supporting the introduction of new legislation. This method is rarely successful unless there is no opposition to the Bill, but some Acts of Parliament have been introduced in this way, for example the Bail (Amendment) Act 1993 which gave the prosecution the right to appeal against

Type of Bill	Explanation	Example
Government Bill	Introduced by the Government	Legal Services Act 2007
Private Member's Bill	Introduced by a private MP	Household Waste Recycling Act 2003
Public Bill	Involves matters of public policy and affects the general public	Legal Services Act 2007
Private	Affects a particular person, organisation or place	Whitehaven Harbour Act 2007
Hybrid	Introduced by the Government but affects a particular person, organisation or place	Crossrail Act 2008

Figure 2.3 Types of bill

the granting of bail to a defendant. Members of the House of Lords can also introduce private members' Bills.

Relatively few private members' Bills became law, but there have been some important laws passed as the result of such Bills. A major example was the Abortion Act 1967 which legalised abortion in this country. More recent ones include the Marriage Act 1994 which allows people to marry in any registered place, not only in Register Offices or religious buildings, and the Household Waste Recycling Act 2003 which places local authorities under a duty to recycle waste.

Public Bills

Most Bills introduced into Parliament involve matters of public policy which will affect either the whole country or a large section of it. These Bills are known as Public Bills. Most government Bills are in this category. For example the Constitutional Reform Act 2005, the Tribunals, Courts and Enforcement Act 2007 and the Legal Services Act 2007 all started as Public Bills.

Private Bills

A small number of Bills are designed to pass a law which will affect only individual people or corporations. These do not affect the whole community. They are known as Private Bills. A recent example of such a Bill was the Whitehaven Harbour Bill which was passed by Parliament and is now the Whitehaven Harbour Act 2007. This transferred all rights and obligations in respect of the harbour from three separate companies to the Whitehaven Harbour Commissioners.

Hybrid Bills

These are a cross between Public Bills and Private Bills. They are introduced by the Government, but if they become law they will only affect a particular person, organisation or place. A recent example is the Crossrail Act 2008 which was introduced into Parliament as a hybrid Bill. This Act allows for the construction of underground rail links in London and will affect people in the area.

2.4.2 Role of the House of Commons

As the members of the House of Commons are democratically elected, most Bills are introduced into the House of Commons first. If the House of Commons votes against a Bill, then that is the end of the Bill.

During the course of a Bill through the House

Inside the Houses of Parliament

of Commons, there will be debates on issues of the policy behind the law as well as on the specific details of the Bill.

The government will have a majority in the House of Commons, so that it is likely that policies supported by the government will become law.

2.4.3 Role of the House of Lords

The House of Lords acts as a check on the House of Commons. All Bills go through the House of Lords and they can vote against proposed changes to the law. In some cases this may alert the House of Commons to a problem with the proposal and it will be dropped or amended.

However, the power of the House of Lords is limited by the Parliament Acts 1911 and 1949. These allow a Bill to become law even if the House of Lords rejects it, provided that the Bill is reintroduced into the House of Commons in the next session of Parliament and passes all the stages again there. So the House of Lords can only delay a law by up to one year.

The principle behind the Parliament Acts is that the House of Lords is not an elected body. Its function is to refine and add to the law rather than oppose the will of the democratically elected House of Commons. In fact there have only been four occasions when this procedure has been used to by-pass the House of Lords after they had voted against a Bill. These were for the:

- War Crimes Act 1991;
- European Parliamentary Elections Act 1999;
- Sexual Offences (Amendment) Act 2000;
- Hunting Act 2004.

Following the passing of the Hunting Act 2004 under the use of the Parliament Acts, there was a challenge as to whether the Act was constitutionally valid. This was in *R (Jackson and others) v Attorney General* (2005). The challenge was on the basis that the Parliament Act 1949 could not be used as it had increased the House of Commons' power without the agreement of the House of Lords. It was held that the Parliament Act 1949 merely placed limits on the power of the unelected House of Lords. It did not increase the power of the House of Commons. Therefore the Hunting Act 2004 had been validly enacted and was law.

2.4.4 The Parliamentary process

In order to become an Act of Parliament, the Bill will usually have to be passed by both Houses of Parliament, and in each House there is a long and complex process. A Bill may start in either the House of Commons or the House of Lords, with the exception of finance bills which must start in the House of Commons. All Bills must go through the following stages.

1. **First Reading**

   This is a formal procedure where the name and main aims of the Bill are read out. Usually no discussion takes place, but there will be a vote on whether the House wishes to consider the Bill further.

   The vote may be verbal, that is the Speaker of the House asks the members as a whole how they vote and the members shout out 'Aye' or 'No'. If it is clear that nearly all members are in agreement, either for or against, there is no need for a more formal vote.

   If it is not possible to judge whether more people are shouting 'Aye' or 'No' there will be a formal vote in which the members of the House vote by leaving the Chamber and then walking back in through one of two special doors on one side or the other of the Chamber. There will be two 'tellers' positioned at each of these two voting doors to make a list of the Members voting on each side. These tellers count up the number of MPs who voted for and against and declare these numbers to the Speaker in front of the members of the House.

2. **Second Reading**

   This is the main debate on the whole Bill in which MPs debate the principles behind the Bill. The debate usually focuses on the main principles rather than the smaller details. Those MPs who wish to speak in the debate

must catch the Speakers' eye, since the Speaker controls all debates and no-one may speak without being called on by the Speaker. At the end of this a vote is taken in the same way as for the First Reading; obviously there must be a majority in favour for the Bill to progress any further.

3. **Committee Stage**

   At this stage a detailed examination of each clause of the Bill is undertaken by a committee of between 16 and 50 MPs. This is usually done by what is called a Standing Committee, which, contrary to its name, is a Committee chosen specifically for that Bill.

   In such a committee the government will have a majority and the opposition and minority parties are represented proportionately to the number of seats they have in the House of Commons.

   The members of Parliament nominated for each Standing Committee will usually be those with a special interest in or knowledge of the subject of the Bill which is being considered. For finance Bills the whole House will sit in committee.

4. **Report Stage**

   At the Committee stage amendments to various clauses in the Bill may have been voted on and passed, so this report stage is where the committee report back to the House on those amendments. (If there were no amendments at the Committee stage, there will not be a 'Report' stage – instead the Bill will go straight on to the Third Reading.) The amendments will be debated in the House and accepted or rejected. Further amendments may also be added. The Report stage has been described as 'a useful safeguard against a small Committee amending a Bill against the wishes of the House, and a necessary opportunity for second thoughts'.

5. **Third Reading**

   This is the final vote on the Bill. It is almost a formality since a Bill which has passed through all the stages above is unlikely to fail at this late stage. In fact in the House of Commons there will only be an actual further debate on the Bill as a whole if at least six MPs request it. However, in the House of Lords there may sometimes be amendments made at this stage.

6. **The House of Lords**

If the Bill started life in the House of Commons it is now passed to the House of Lords where it goes through the same five stages outlined above. If the House of Lords makes amendments to the Bill, then it will go back to the House of Commons for them to consider those amendments. If the Bill started in the House of Lords then it passes to the House of Commons.

7. **Royal Assent**

The final stage is where the monarch formally gives approval to the Bill and it then becomes an Act of Parliament. This is now a formality and, under the Royal Assent Act 1967, the monarch will not even have the text of the Bills to which she is assenting; she will only have the short title. The last time that a monarch refused assent was in 1707, when Queen Anne refused to assent to the Scottish Militia Bill.

These stages in the Parliamentary procedure are shown in a flow chart in Figure 2.4.

Commencement of an Act of Parliament

Following the Royal Assent the Act of Parliament will come into force on midnight of that day, unless another date has been set. However, very few Acts are implemented immediately. Instead the Act itself states the date when it will commence or passes responsibility on to the appropriate minister to fix the commencement date. In the latter case the minister will bring the Act into force by issuing a commencement order.

This can cause problems as it can be necessary to keep checking which sections have been brought into force. It may be that some sections or even a whole Act will never become law. An example of

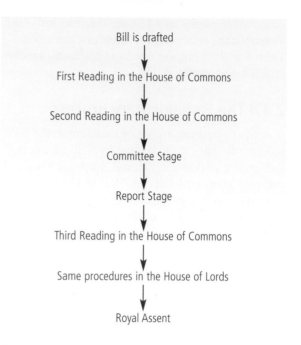

Figure 2.4 Flow chart of the passing of an Act of Parliament starting in the House of Commons

this is the Easter Act 1928, which was intended to fix the date of Easter Day. Although this Act passed all the necessary Parliamentary stages, and was given the Royal Assent, it has never come into force.

2.5 Example of an Act of Parliament

On page 28 is a reproduction of the Law Reform (Year and A Day Rule) Act 1996. This shows what an Act of Parliament looks like. The name of the Act is given immediately under the Royal coat of arms and underneath the name 1996 CHAPTER 19 means that it was the 19th Act to be passed in 1996.

Next follows a short statement or preamble about the purpose of the Act. Then there is a formal statement showing that the Act has been passed by both Houses of Parliament and received the Royal Assent; this is included in all Acts. After this comes the body of the Act, which is set out in sections; this is an unusually short Act as it has only three sections.

Section 1 abolishes the 'year and a day rule'. Note that the Act actually refers to it in those terms; this is because the rule was a part of the common law and was never written down in any statute. Section 2 sets out when the consent of the Attorney-General is needed before a prosecution can be started. The last section gives the name by which the Act may be cited and it also sets out that the Act does not apply to cases in which the incident which led to death occurred before the Act was passed.

Section 3(3) is concerned with the commencement of the Act; this sets the commencement date for section 2 at two months after the Act is passed. As section 1 is not specifically mentioned, the normal rule that an Act comes into effect on midnight of the date on which it receives the Royal Assent applies to that section.

@ Internet Research

1. Look up a recent Act of Parliament on the Internet. You can find Acts on www.opsi.gov.uk. Try to find the commencement section.
2. Look up any Bill that is currently going through Parliament. These are on www.parliament.uk. What stage in the parliamentary process has the Bill you have chosen reached?

2.6 Advantages of law making in Parliament

The main advantage of parliamentary-made law is that it is made by our elected representatives. This means it is democratic. Also, as there has to be a general election at least once every five years, the public can vote out any government if it has not performed as the public expected.

Another advantage is that Acts of Parliament can reform whole areas of law in the one Act. An example is in the criminal law with the Fraud Act 2006 which abolished all the old offences of deception and fraud and created a newer and, hopefully, simpler structure of offences. Judges can only change the law on very small areas of law as they can only rule on the point of law in the case they are deciding.

Acts of Parliament can also set broad policies and give the power to others to make detailed regulations. This is known as delegated legislation (see Chapter 3). This is an advantage because the general structure is laid down by Parliament but it allows greater detail in the law than if it was just contained in an Act of Parliament.

Also before a Bill is presented to Parliament there will have been consultation on the proposed changes to the law. This allows the government to take into consideration objections to the proposals. Also, as all Bills have to go through the lengthy process in both Houses of Parliament, the new law will be thoroughly discussed in Parliament.

Law made by Parliament is also certain as it cannot be challenged under the doctrine of Parliamentary supremacy (see section 2.8).

2.7 Disadvantages of law making in Parliament

Although there are major advantages to having law made in Parliament, there are also some disadvantages. One is that Parliament does not always have time to deal with all the reforms that are proposed. This is particularly true of reform of 'lawyers' law' such as criminal law or the law of contract.

An example of law that is still awaiting reform is the law on assaults and other offences against the person. The Law Commission proposed changes to the law on offences against the person in 1993. Reform was needed because the old law dated back to an Act of 1861 which was very difficult to understand. In 1997 the government accepted that there was a need for reform and published a draft Bill in 1998. However, this was not put before Parliament and the law has not yet been reformed.

ELIZABETH II   c. **19**

Law Reform (Year and a Day Rule) Act 1996

1996 CHAPTER 19

An Act to abolish the "year and a day rule" and, in consequence of its abolition, to impose a restriction on the institution in certain circumstances of proceedings for a fatal offence. [17th June 1996]

B E IT ENACTED by the Queen's most Excellent Majesty, by and with the advice and consent of the Lords Spiritual and Temporal, and Commons, in this present Parliament assembled, and by the authority of the same, as follows:—

1. The rule known as the "year and a day rule" (that is, the rule that, for the purposes of offences involving death and of suicide, an act or omission is conclusively presumed not to have caused a person's death if more than a year and a day elapsed before he died) is abolished for all purposes.

Abolition of "year and a day rule".

2.—(1) Proceedings to which this section applies may only be instituted by or with the consent of the Attorney General.

Restriction on institution of proceedings for a fatal offence.

(2) This section applies to proceedings against a person for a fatal offence if—

    (a) the injury alleged to have caused the death was sustained more than three years before the death occurred, or

    (b) the person has previously been convicted of an offence committed in circumstances alleged to be connected with the death.

(3) In subsection (2) "fatal offence" means—

    (a) murder, manslaughter, infanticide or any other offence of which one of the elements is causing a person's death, or

    (b) the offence of aiding, abetting, counselling or procuring a person's suicide.

Figure 2.5 The Law Reform (Year and a Day Rule) Act 1996

2   c. **19**   *Law Reform (Year and a Day Rule) Act 1996*

(4) No provision that proceedings may be instituted only by or with the consent of the Director of Public Prosecutions shall apply to proceedings to which this section applies.

(5) In the application of this section to Northern Ireland—

(a) the reference in subsection (1) to the Attorney General is to the Attorney General for Northern Ireland, and

(b) the reference in subsection (4) to the Director of Public Prosecutions is to the Director of Public Prosecutions for Northern Ireland.

Short title, commencement and extent.

3.—(1) This Act may be cited as the Law Reform (Year and a Day Rule) Act 1996.

(2) Section 1 does not affect the continued application of the rule referred to in that section to a case where the act or omission (or the last of the acts or omissions) which caused the death occurred before the day on which this Act is passed.

(3) Section 2 does not come into force until the end of the period of two months beginning with the day on which this Act is passed; but that section applies to the institution of proceedings after the end of that period in any case where the death occurred during that period (as well as in any case where the death occurred after the end of that period).

(4) This Act extends to England and Wales and Northern Ireland.

© Crown copyright 1996

PRINTED IN THE UNITED KINGDOM BY MIKE LYNN
Controller and Chief Executive of Her Majesty's Stationery Office
and Queen's Printer of Acts of Parliament

Figure 2.5 The Law Reform (Year and a Day Rule) Act 1996 continued

Even where the Government introduces a Bill into Parliament the process of becoming an Act with all the different reading, committee and report stages can take several months.

The Government is in control of the Parliamentary timetable and allows very little time for private members' Bills. Even when a private member does manage to introduce a Bill, it can be easily voted out by the Government as they have the majority in the House of Commons. The result is that very few private members' Bills become law.

Another disadvantage is that Acts of Parliament are often very long and complex. This can make them difficult to understand. In fact many of the cases that go to the House of Lords on appeals are about what the words in an Act of Parliament mean.

The law can become even more complicated where one Act amends another so that it is necessary to consult two or more Acts to find out exactly what the law is.

2.8 Parliamentary supremacy

The most widely recognised definition of Parliamentary supremacy was given by Dicey in the nineteenth century. He made three main points:

1. Parliament can legislate on any subject-matter.
2. No Parliament can be bound by any previous

Parliament, nor can a Parliament pass any Act that will bind a later Parliament.

3. No other body has the right to override or set aside an Act of Parliament.

Parliamentary supremacy is also referred to as Parliamentary sovereignty.

Legislating on any subject-matter

There are no limits on what Parliament can make laws about. It can make any law it wants. For example, in the past Parliament changed the rule on who should succeed to the throne. This was in 1700 when Parliament passed the Act of Settlement which stated that the children of King James II (who were the direct line of the monarchy) could not succeed to the throne.

Parliament can also change its own powers. It did this with the Parliament Acts 1911 and 1949 which placed limits on the right of the House of Lords to block a Bill by voting against it (see section 2.4.3).

Cannot bind successor

Each new Parliament should be free to make or change what laws they wish. They cannot be bound by a law made by a previous Parliament. They can repeal any previous Act of Parliament.

There are, however, some laws that become such an important part of the British constitution that they cannot realistically be repealed. For example, the Act of Settlement in 1700 changed the line of succession to the throne. It affected who was entitled to become King or Queen. Realistically, after 300 years, this can not now be repealed.

Another example where it would be impractical to repeal the law is the Statute of Westminster 1931. Before 1931 The United Kingdom had the right to make law for Dominion countries (now Commonwealth countries). Section 4 of the Statute of Westminster stated that no future United Kingdom statute should extend to law in those countries unless the countries requested and consented to the legislation. These countries included Australia, Canada and New Zealand.

Technically, the Statute of Westminster 1931 could be repealed and the UK could pass a law extending to one or more of these countries, but obviously none of those countries would accept such a law. So, it is impracticable to repeal the Statute of Westminster.

There are other modern limitations which have been self-imposed by Parliament. These are dealt with in section 2.8.1 below.

Cannot be overruled by others

This rule is kept to even where the Act of Parliament may have been made because of incorrect information. This was shown by *British Railways Board v Pickin* (1974). A private Act of Parliament, the British Railways Act 1968, was enacted by Parliament. Pickin challenged the Act on the basis that the British Railways Board had fraudulently concealed certain matters from Parliament. This alleged fraud had led to Parliament passing the Act which had the effect of depriving Pickin of his land or proprietary rights. The action was struck out because no court is entitled to go behind an Act once it has been passed. A challenge cannot be made to an Act of Parliament even if there was fraud.

2.8.1 Limitations on Parliamentary supremacy

There are now some limitations on Parliament's supremacy but all these limits have been self-imposed by previous Parliaments. The main limitations are through:

- membership of the European Union;
- the effect of the Human Rights Act 1998;
- devolution.

Effect of membership of the EU

The United Kingdom joined the European Union in 1973. In order to become a member, Parliament passed the European Communities Act 1972. Although, as Parliament passed that Act, it is theoretically possible for a later Parliament to pass an Act withdrawing from the European Union,

Key facts

Influences on Parliamentary law making	• Law Commission reports • political influence, party policy, manifesto • EU law • public opinion/media • pressure groups
Pre-legislative procedure	• consultation papers • Green papers • White papers
Parliamentary procedure	• first reading • second reading • committee stage • report stage • third reading • same procedure in other House • Royal Assent
Advantages	• democratic • allows full reform of major areas • sets policies • consultation before Bill is presented to Parliament • discussion in both Houses during process to pass Act
Disadvantages	• limited Parliamentary time may prevent some laws from being reformed • Acts can be long and complex • wording may be difficult and lead to court case on interpretation of meaning
Parliamentary supremacy (sovereignty)	• can legislate on any subject-matter • cannot bind successor • cannot be overruled by others • limitations due to EU membership, Human Rights Act 1998 and devolution

Figure 2.6 Key Facts chart on Acts of Parliament

political reality means that this is very unlikely. Membership of the EU affects so much of our law and political system.

Membership of the EU means that EU laws take priority over English law even where the English law was passed after the relevant EU law. This was shown by the Merchant Shipping Act 1988 which set down rules for who could own or manage fishing boats registered in Britain. The Act stated that 75 per cent of directors and shareholders had to be British. The European Court of Justice ruled that this was contrary to European Union law under which citizens of all member states can

work in other member states. The Merchant Shipping Act 1988 could not be effective so far as other EU citizens were concerned.

Effect of Human Rights Act 1998

This states that all Acts of Parliament have to be compatible with the European Convention on Human Rights. It is possible to challenge an Act on the ground that it does not comply with the Convention. Under s 4 of the Human Rights Act, the courts have the power to declare an Act incompatible with the Convention.

This happened in *H v Mental Health Review Tribunal* (2001). When a patient was making an application to be released, the Mental Health Act 1983 placed the burden of proof on the patient to show that he should be released. Human rights meant that it should be up to the state to justify the continuing detention of such a patient. The court made a declaration that the law was not compatible with human rights. Following this declaration of incompatibility, the Government changed the law.

However, a declaration of incompatibility does not mean that the Government has to change the law. Also, if Parliament wishes it can pass a new Act which contravenes the European Convention on Human Rights.

Devolution

The Scotland Act 1998 and the Wales Act 1998 have devolved (handed down) certain powers to the Scottish Assembly and to the Welsh Assembly. As a result they can make laws on some matters for their own countries without having to get Parliament's approval. This means that Parliament's supremacy has been lost in these areas.

It is theoretically possible that a future Parliament could repeal the Scotland Act 1998 and the Wales Act 1998, but it seems unlikely as such a move would be very unpopular and would lose support for any political party which proposed it.

Test Yourself

1. What type of Paper may be issued by the Government before a new Bill is introduced into Parliament?
2. Who introduces the majority of Bills into Parliament?
3. By what two methods can a private MP introduce a Bill into Parliament?
4. Explain what is meant by a public Bill.
5. When a Bill is introduced into the House of Commons what stages does it have to pass before it goes to the House of Lords?
6. Which Acts limit the House of Lords' powers in respect of Bills?
7. Give three advantages of the Parliamentary system of law-making.
8. Give three disadvantages of the Parliamentary system of law-making.
9. Briefly explain what is meant by Parliamentary supremacy.
10. What are the limitations on Parliamentary supremacy?

Examination questions

(a) Explain what is meant by the doctrine of Parliamentary supremacy and briefly explain one limitation on this doctrine.   (10 Marks)

(b) Briefly explain the roles of the House of Commons, House of Lords and the monarch in the formal process of statute law creation.   (10 Marks)

(c) Discuss the advantages of the process of law making in Parliament.   (10 Marks)

AQA Law 1 Specimen Paper

Examiner's tip

Know the examiners' approach to marking

For part (a) of the question above the AQA mark scheme states that, to get into the top mark band, you must deal with the two issues (doctrine of Parliamentary supremacy and a limitation on it) in the following way:

max 10: two sound

max 9: one sound, one clear

max 8: one sound, one some **or** two clear.

Sound means that:

- The material will be predominantly accurate and contain material relevant to the Potential Content;
- The material will be supported by generally relevant authority and/or examples;
- It will generally deal with the Potential Content in a manner required by the question.

As a consequence, the essential features of the Potential Content are dealt with competently and coherently.

Clear means that:

- The material is broadly accurate and relevant to the Potential Content;
- The material will be supported by some use of relevant authority and/or examples;
- The material will broadly deal with the Potential Content in a manner required by the question.

As a consequence, the underlying concepts of the Potential Content will be present, though there may be some errors, omissions and/or confusion which prevent the answer from being fully rounded or developed.

NB These definitions of sound and clear are important as they are used for marking on every question. The full mark scheme can be found on AQA's website **www.aqa.org.uk**.

Now answer the question trying to make sure that you deal with both issues in a sound way. Use the information in sections 2.8 and 2.8.1 for your answer.

Chapter 3

Delegated Legislation

Delegated legislation is law made by some person or body other than Parliament, but with the authority of Parliament. That authority is usually laid down in a 'parent' Act of Parliament known as an enabling Act. The enabling Act creates the framework of the law and then delegates power to others to make more detailed law in the area.

3.1 Types of delegated legislation

There are three different types of delegated legislation:

- Orders in Council;
- statutory instruments;
- bylaws.

Figure 3.1 shows these in diagram form.

3.1.1 Orders in Council

The Queen and the Privy Council have the authority to make Orders in Council. The Privy Council is made up of the Prime Minister and other leading members of the government. So this type of delegated legislation effectively allows the government to make laws without going through Parliament.

Orders in Council can be made on a wide range of matters, especially:

- giving legal effect to European Directives;
- transferring responsibility between Government departments, e.g. when the Ministry of Justice was created, the powers of the previous Department of Constitutional Affairs and some of the powers of the Home Office were transferred to this new ministry;
- bringing Acts (or parts of Acts) of Parliament into force.

In addition, the Privy Council has power to make law in emergency situations under the Civil Contingencies Act 2004. This power will usually only be exercised in times of emergency when Parliament is not sitting.

Orders in Council can also be used to make other types of law. For example, in 2003, an Order in Council was used to alter the Misuse of Drugs Act 1971 so as to make cannabis a class C drug. Five years later, the Government decided that it had been a mistake to downgrade cannabis and another Order in Council was issued changing

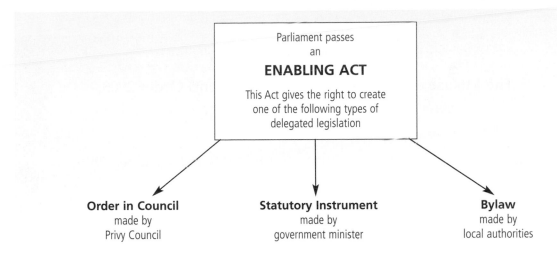

Figure 3.1 Different types of delegated legislation

cannabis back to a class B drug (see Figure 3.2).

There must be an enabling Act allowing the Privy Council to make Orders in Council on the particular topic. For the change of category of cannabis, the enabling Act was the Misuse of Drugs Act 1971.

Another enabling Act giving power to make Orders in Council is the Constitutional Reform Act 2005. This allows the Privy Council to alter the number of judges in the Supreme Court.

3.1.2 Statutory instruments

The term 'statutory instruments' refers to rules and regulations made by government ministers. Ministers

@ Internet Research

Look up recent Orders in Council on the Privy Council website at www.privy-council.org.uk.

From the Home page you should be able to find recent Orders in Council by going to the Privy Council Meetings page and from there to 'Latest orders'.

Look to see which enabling Acts have allowed recent orders to be made. The Enabling Act is usually given on the left-hand side of the list of orders.

and government departments are given authority to make regulations for areas under their particular responsibility. There are about 15 Departments in the Government. Each one deals with a different area of policy and can make rules and regulations in respect of matters it deals with. So the Minister for Work and Pensions will be able to make regulations on work-related matters, such as health and safety at work, while the Minister for Transport will be able to deal with necessary road traffic regulations.

Statutory instruments can be very short, covering one point such as making the annual change to the minimum wage. However, other statutory instruments may be very long with detailed regulations which were too complex to include in an Act of Parliament.

Examples of statutory instruments which include a lot of detail are:

- the Chemicals (Hazard Information and Packaging for Supply) Regulations 2009. This statutory instrument was made by the Minister for Work and Pensions under powers given in the European Communities Act 1972 and the Health and Safety at Work etc Act 1974;
- police codes of practice in relation to such powers as stop and search, arrest and detention. These were made by the Minister for Justice under powers in the Police and Criminal Evidence Act 1984.

2008 No. 3130

DANGEROUS DRUGS

The Misuse of Drugs Act 1971 (Amendment) Order 2008

Made	*10th December 2008*
Coming into force	*26th January 2009*

At the Court at Buckingham Palace, the 10th day of December 2008

Present,

The Queen's Most Excellent Majesty in Council

In accordance with section 2(5) of the Misuse of Drugs Act 1971 a draft of this Order has been laid before Parliament after consultation with the Advisory Council on the Misuse of Drugs and approved by a resolution of each House of Parliament.

Accordingly, Her Majesty, in exercise of the powers conferred upon Her by sections 2(2) and 2(4) of that Act, is pleased, by and with the advice of Her Privy Council, to order as follows:

Citation, commencement and revocation

1.—(1) This Order may be cited as the Misuse of Drugs Act 1971 (Amendment) Order 2008 and shall come into force on 26th January 2009.

(2) The Misuse of Drugs Act 1971 (Modification) (No. 2) Order 2003 is revoked.

Amendments to the Misuse of Drugs Act 1971

2.—(1) Schedule 2 to the Misuse of Drugs Act 1971 (which specifies the drugs which are subject to control under that Act) is amended as follows.

(2) In Part 2 (Class B drugs)—

(a) in paragraph 1(a), after"Amphetamine"insert—

"Cannabinol

Cannabinol derivatives

Cannabis and cannabis resin";

(b) after paragraph 2 insert—

"**2A.** Any ester or ether of cannabinol or of a cannabinol derivative."; and

(c) in paragraph 3, for"or 2"substitute", 2 or 2A".

(3) In Part 3 (Class C drugs) the following words are repealed —

(a) in paragraph 1(a),"Cannabinol","Cannabinol derivatives"and"Cannabis and cannabis resin"; and

(b) in paragraph 1(d),"or of cannabinol or a cannabinol derivative".

Judith Simpson
Clerk of the Privy Council

Figure 3.2 Example of an order in Council

Definition of delegated legislation	Law made by bodies other than Parliament, but with the authority of Parliament through an enabling or parent Act		
	Types of delegated legislation	**Made by**	**Examples**
	Orders in Council	Made by Queen and Privy Council	The Misuse of Drugs Act 1971 (Amendment) Order 2008
	Statutory Instruments	Made by government ministers	Codes of Practice under PACE
	By-laws	Made by local authorities or public corporations	Local parking regulations

Figure 3.3 Types of delegated legislation

Statutory instruments are a major way of making law, as over 3,000 are made each year.

3.1.3 By-laws

These can be made by local authorities to cover matters within their own area, for example, a County Council can pass laws affecting the whole county while a District or Town council can only make by-laws for its district or town. Many local by-laws will involve traffic control, such as parking restrictions. Other by-laws may be for such matters as banning drinking in public places or

Alcohol-free zones are created by by-laws

banning people from riding cycles in local parks.

By-laws can also be made by public corporations and certain companies for matters within their jurisdiction, which involve the public. This means that bodies such as the British Airports Authority and the railways can enforce rules about public behaviour on their premises.

3.2 Control of delegated legislation

As delegated legislation in many instances is made by non-elected bodies and, since there are so many people with the power to make delegated legislation, it is important that there should be some control over delegated legislation. Control is exercised by Parliament and by the courts. In addition there may sometimes be a Public Enquiry before a law is passed on an especially sensitive matter, such as planning laws which may affect the environment.

3.2.1 Control by Parliament

Enabling Act

Parliament has the initial control over what powers are delegated as the enabling Act sets out the limits within which any delegated legislation must be made. For example, the Act will state which government minister can make the regulations. It

Look at the following two sources and answer the questions below.

Source A

2009 No. 606
HEALTH AND SAFETY
The Health and Safety Information for Employees (Amendment) Regulations 2009

Made	*10th March 2009*
Laid before Parliament	*16th March 2009*
Coming into force	*6th April 2009*

The Secretary of State, in exercise of the powers conferred by sections 15(1), (2), (3)(a), (4) and (9) of, and paragraph 15(1) of Schedule 3 to, the Health and Safety at Work etc. Act 1974 ("the 1974 Act"), and for the purpose of giving effect without modifications to proposals submitted to him by the Health and Safety Executive under section 11(3) of the 1974 Act after the carrying out by the said Executive of consultation in accordance with section 50(3) of that Act, hereby makes the following Regulations:

Citation, commencement and interpretation

1.—(1) These Regulations may be cited as the Health and Safety Information for Employees (Amendment) Regulations 2009 and shall come into force on 6th April 2009.

(2) In these Regulations "the 1989 Regulations" means the Health and Safety Information for Employees Regulations 1989.

Amendment of the 1989 Regulations

2.—(1) The 1989 Regulations are amended as follows.

(2) In regulation 3(3) for "nine months" substitute "five years".

(3) After regulation 5(1)(b) insert the following—

"; or (c) information as to how any of his employees may obtain the information referred to in (a) and (b) above.".

(4) After regulation 5(3)(b) insert the following—

"; or (c) information as to how any of his employees may obtain the information referred to in (a) and (b) above.".

Extension outside Great Britain

3. These Regulations shall apply to and in relation to premises and activities outside Great Britain to the same extent as provided for in regulation 2(5) of the 1989 Regulations.

Jonathan Shaw
Parliamentary Under Secretary of State
Department for Work and Pensions
10th March 2009

Source B

Alcohol free zones in Knowsley

Alcohol free zones are being set up in Knowsley to tackle crime and anti social behaviour caused by binge drinking. The Safer Knowsley Partnership, which includes Merseyside Police and Knowsley Council, is taking the measure after successfully securing the borough's first Designated Public Place Orders back in 2008.

The orders have been approved in Wignall Park, Court Hey Park, Stadtmoers, Millennium Green and Henley Park, and will come into force on 16th July 2009. The orders will make it an offence for anyone to drink alcohol after being required by a police officer not to do so.

Police have the power to confiscate and dispose of alcohol and it is an arrestable offence to fail to co-operate, without reasonable excuse, with a police officer's request. The ban does not affect drinking in any licensed premises.

Reducing crime and disorder

Knowsley Council's Licensing Committee approved the orders on 25th June 2009. This is part of the Safer Knowsley Partnership's on-going commitment to reduce alcohol related crime and disorder and anti social behaviour.

Taken from Merseyside Police website July 2009

Questions

1. What type of delegated legislation is Source A?
2. Which Act is the enabling Act which allowed this delegated legislation to be made?
3. Which government department was responsible for producing the regulations?
4. To which type of delegated legislation does Source B refer?
5. Who made the orders referred to in the source?
6. What effect do these orders have?

will also state the type of laws to be made and whether they can be made for the whole country or only for certain places. The Act can also set out whether the government department must consult other people before making the regulations.

Parliament also retains control over the delegated legislation as it can repeal the powers in the enabling Act at any time. If it does this then the right to make regulations will cease.

Delegated Powers Scrutiny Committee

There is a Delegated Powers Scrutiny Committee in the House of Lords which considers whether the provisions of any Bills going through

Parliament delegate legislative power inappropriately. It reports its findings to the House of Lords before the Committee stage of the Bill, but it has no power to amend Bills.

It is sensible that checks are made on what powers are proposed to be delegated. If the powers in the original enabling Act are appropriate, then the delegated legislation is more likely to be properly drawn up.

However, there also need to be checks to make sure that powers are not being used wrongly. Parliament has the following ways of checking on delegated legislation:

- affirmative resolution;
- negative resolution;

● Joint Select Committee on Statutory Instruments (Scrutiny Committee).

In addition there are special controls for any delegated legislation made under the Legislative and Regulatory Reform Act 2006 (see section 3.2.2).

Affirmative resolutions

A small number of statutory instruments will be subject to an affirmative resolution. This means that the statutory instrument will not become law unless specifically approved by Parliament. The need for an affirmative resolution will be included in the enabling Act. For example, an affirmative resolution is required before new or revised police Codes of Practice under the Police and Criminal Evidence Act 1984 can come into force. One of the disadvantages of this procedure is that Parliament cannot amend the statutory instrument; it can only be approved, annulled or withdrawn.

Negative resolutions

Most other statutory instruments will be subject to a negative resolution, which means that the relevant statutory instrument will be law unless rejected by Parliament within 40 days. The main problem with this procedure is that very few of the statutory instruments will be looked at. They are available for MPs to consider, but, as there are so many statutory instruments, it is likely that only a few will be looked at.

Questions

Individual Ministers may also be questioned by MPs in Parliament on the work of their departments, and this can include questions about proposed regulations.

Scrutiny Committee

A more effective check is the Joint Select Committee on Statutory Instruments, usually called the Scrutiny Committee. This committee reviews all statutory instruments and, where necessary, will draw the attention of both Houses

of Parliament to points that need further consideration. However, the review is a technical one and not based on policy. The main grounds for referring a statutory instrument back to the Houses of Parliament are that:

● it imposes a tax or charge – this is because only an elected body has such a right;
● it appears to have retrospective effect which was not provided for by the enabling Act;
● it appears to have gone beyond the powers given under the enabling legislation;
● it makes some unusual or unexpected use of those powers;
● it is unclear or defective in some way.

The Scrutiny Committee can only report back its findings; it has no power to alter any statutory instrument.

The two main problems are, first, that the review is only a technical one limited to the points set out above. Secondly, even if the Committee discovers a breach of one of these points, the Committee cannot alter the regulations or stop them from becoming law. The Committee can only draw the attention of Parliament to the matter.

3.2.2 The Legislative and Regulatory Reform Act 2006

This Act sets procedure for the making of statutory instruments which are aimed at repealing an existing law in order to remove a 'burden'. For the purpose of the Act 'burden' means any of the following:

(a) a financial cost;
(b) an administrative inconvenience;
(c) an obstacle to efficiency, productivity or profitability; or
(d) a sanction, criminal or otherwise, which affects the carrying on of any lawful activity.

Any minister making a statutory instrument under the powers of this Act must consult various people and organisations. These include:

● organisations which are representative of interests substantially affected by the proposals;

- the Welsh Assembly in relation to matters upon which the Assembly exercises functions;
- the Law Commission where appropriate.

Orders made under this power of this Act must be laid before Parliament. There are three possible procedures:

1. **negative resolution procedure**
   where the Minister recommends that this procedure should be used, it will be used unless within 40 days one of the Houses of Parliament objects to this;
2. **affirmative resolution procedure**
   this requires both Houses of Parliament to approve the order: even though the Minister has recommended this procedure Parliament can still require the super-affirmative resolution procedure to be used;
3. **super-affirmative resolution procedure**
   under this the Minister must have regard to:

- any representations;
- any resolution of either House of Parliament;
- any recommendations by a committee of either House of Parliament who are asked to report on the draft order.

This super-affirmative resolution procedure gives Parliament more control over delegated legislation made under the Legislative and Regulatory Reform Act 2006. It is important that this is the position as the Act gives Ministers very wide powers to amend Acts of Parliament.

3.2.3 Control by the courts

Delegated legislation can be challenged in the courts on the ground that it is *ultra vires*, that is, it goes beyond the powers that Parliament granted in the enabling Act. The validity of delegated legislation may be challenged through the judicial review procedure, or it may arise in a civil claim between two parties.

Any delegated legislation which is ruled to be *ultra vires* is void and not effective. This was illustrated by *R v Home Secretary, ex parte Fire Brigades Union* (1995) where changes made by the Home Secretary to the Criminal Injuries Compensation scheme were held to have gone beyond the power given to him in the Criminal Justice Act 1988.

The courts will presume that unless an enabling act expressly allows it, there is no power to do any of the following:

- make unreasonable regulations – in *Strickland v Hayes Borough Council* (1896) a by-law prohibiting the singing or reciting of any obscene song or ballad and the use of obscene language generally, was held to be unreasonable and so *ultra vires*, because it was too widely drawn in that it covered acts done in private as well as those in public;
- levy taxes;
- allow sub-delegation.

It is also possible for the courts to hold that delegated legislation is *ultra vires* because the correct procedure has not been followed. For example in the *Aylesbury Mushroom* case (1972) the Minister of Labour had to consult 'any organisation . . . appearing to him to be representative of substantial numbers of employers engaging in the activity concerned'. His failure to consult the Mushroom Growers' Association, which represented about 85 per cent of all mushroom growers, meant that his order establishing a training board was invalid as against mushroom growers. However, it was valid in relation to others affected by the order, such as farmers, as the Minister had consulted with the National Farmers Union.

In *R v Secretary of State for Education and Employment, ex parte National Union of Teachers* (2000) a High Court judge ruled that a statutory instrument setting conditions for appraisal and access to higher rates of pay for teachers was beyond the powers given under the Education Act 1996. In addition, the procedure used was unfair as only four days had been allowed for consultation.

Statutory Instruments can also be declared void if they conflict with European Union legislation.

	Advantages	Disadvantages
CONTROL BY PARLIAMENT		
Enabling Act	Parliament sets limits Parliament can amend or repeal Act	The powers in the Act may be very wide
Delegated Powers Scrutiny Committee	Looks at proposed powers before they are enacted Should ensure that only appropriate powers are given	Can only report – cannot amend Bill
Affirmative resolution	Means Parliament must agree with the regulations	Time-consuming: cannot be used for all SIs
Negative resolution	Gives MPs the opportunity to check SIs before they come into force	Unlikely that many SIs will be looked at under this procedure
Scrutiny Committee	Ensures ● do not impose taxes or ● go beyond the powers ● are not retrospective ● make unusual or unexpected use of powers ● are unclear or defective	Only a technical check – cannot check substance of the SI. Committee can only report to Parliament – it cannot make changes
CONTROL BY THE COURTS		
Judicial review Doctrine of *ultra vires*	Anyone affected by the delegated legislation can ask for a judicial review Court can declare delegated legislation void	It is expensive to take court proceedings Can normally only do this if the correct procedure has not been followed OR if the delegated legislation goes beyond the power given by the enabling Act

Figure 3.4 Advantages and disadvantages of controls over delegated legislation

3.3 Advantages of delegated legislation

Saves Parliamentary time

Parliament does not have time to consider and debate every small detail of complex regulations. Making such regulations through delegated legislation saves Parliamentary time.

Need for technical expertise

Parliament may not have the necessary technical expertise or knowledge required; for example health and safety regulations in different industries need expert knowledge, while local parking regulations need local knowledge.

Modern society has become very complicated and technical, so that it is impossible that members of Parliament could have all the

Key facts

		Comment or Case
Advantages of delegated legislation	● knowledge and expertise ● saving of Parliamentary time ● allows consultation ● can be made quickly ● can be changed more quickly than Acts of Parliament	
Disadvantages of delegated legislation	● undemocratic ● risk of sub-delegation ● large volume ● lack of publicity	
Control by Parliament	● Negative resolution ● Affirmative resolution ● Scrutiny Committee ● Super-affirmative resolution	Becomes law unless within 40 days there is an objection Must be approved by both Houses of Parliament Reviews and can draw Parliament's attention to problems, but cannot amend Only for SIs made under Legislative and Regulatory Reform Act 2006
Control by the courts	Judicial review to decide: ● if it is beyond the powers given in the enabling Act ● unreasonable ● failed to follow correct procedure	*R v Home Secretary, ex parte Fire Brigades Union* (1995) *Strictland v Hayes* (1896) *Aylesbury Mushroom case* (1972)

Figure 3.5 Key facts chart for delegated legislation

knowledge needed to draw up laws on controlling technology, ensuring environmental safety, dealing with a vast array of different industrial problems or operating complex taxation schemes. It is thought that it is better for Parliament to debate the main principles thoroughly, but leave the detail to be filled in by those who have expert knowledge of it.

Allows consultation

Ministers can have the benefit of further consultation before regulations are drawn up. Consultation is particularly important for rules on technical matters, where it is necessary to make sure that the regulations are technically workable.

Allows quick law-making

As already seen the process of passing an Act of Parliament can take a considerable time and in an emergency Parliament may not be able to pass law quickly enough. Orders in Council, especially, can be made very quickly.

Easy to amend

Delegated legislation can be amended or revoked easily when necessary so that the law can be kept up to date. This is useful where monetary limits have to change each year as, for example, the minimum wage or the limits for legal aid. Ministers can also respond to new or unforeseen

Test Yourself

1. What is an enabling Act?
2. Who can make Orders in Council?
3. Who can make bylaws?
4. What is the other type of delegated legislation?
5. Name three ways in which Parliament can control delegated legislation.
6. Give three advantages of these controls.
7. Give three disadvantages of these controls.
8. When can the courts declare that delegated legislation is void?
9. Give three advantages of using delegated legislation.
10. Give three disadvantages of using delegated legislation.

situations by amending regulations made through a statutory instrument. This is another reason why use of delegated legislation is sometimes preferred to an Act of Parliament.

3.4 Disadvantages of delegated legislation

1. The main criticism is that delegated legislation takes law making away from the democratically elected House of Commons and allows non-elected people to make law. This is acceptable provided there is sufficient control, but, as already seen, Parliament's control is fairly limited. This criticism cannot be made of by-laws made by local authorities since these are elected bodies and accountable to the local citizens.
2. Another problem is that of sub-delegation, which means that the law making authority is handed down another level. This causes comments that much of our law is made by civil servants and merely 'rubber stamped' by the Minister of that department.
3. The large volume of delegated legislation also gives rise to criticism, since it makes it difficult to discover what the present law is. This problem is aggravated by a lack of publicity, as much delegated legislation is made in private,

in contrast to the public debates of Parliament.
4. Finally, delegated legislation shares with Acts of Parliament the same problem of obscure wording that can lead to difficulty in understanding the law. This difficulty of how to understand or interpret the law is dealt with next.

Examination questions

(a) Statutory instruments are one form of delegated legislation. Explain, using examples, what is meant by statutory instruments.   (10 marks)

(b) Explain either parliamentary or judicial controls on delegated legislation.   (10 marks)

(c) Discuss the disadvantages of delegated legislation as a form of law making.   (10 marks)

Examiner's tip

Where the question states 'using examples' (see part (a) above), make sure that you include at least two examples.

Chapter 4

Statutory Interpretation

As seen in Chapter 2, many Acts of Parliament are passed by Parliament each year. The meaning of the law in these statutes should be clear and explicit but this is not always achieved. In order to help with the understanding of a statute Parliament sometimes includes sections defining certain words used in that statute. Such sections are called interpretation sections. In the Theft Act 1968, for example, the definition of theft is given in s 1, and then ss 2 to 6 define the key words in that definition. To help the judges with general words Parliament has also passed the Interpretation Act 1978 which makes it clear that, unless the contrary appears, he includes she, and singular includes plural.

4.1 The need for statutory interpretation

Despite the aids mentioned above, many cases come before the courts because there is a dispute over the meaning of an Act of Parliament. In such cases the court's task is to decide the exact meaning of a particular word or phrase. There are many reasons why meaning may be unclear:

- **A broad term**
  There may be words designed to cover several possibilities; this can lead to problems as to how wide this should go. In the Dangerous Dogs Act 1991 there is a phrase 'any dog of the type known as the pit bull terrier'. This seems a simple phrase but has led to problems. What is meant by type? Does it mean the same as 'breed'? In *Brock v DPP* (1993) this was the key point in dispute and the Queen's Bench Divisional Court decided that 'type' had a wider meaning than 'breed'. It could cover dogs which were not pedigree pit bull terriers, but had a substantial number of the characteristics of such a dog.

- **Ambiguity**
  This is where a word has two or more meanings; it may not be clear which meaning should be used.
- **A drafting error**
  The Parliamentary Counsel who drafted the original Bill may have made an error which has not been noticed by Parliament; this is particularly likely to occur where the Bill is amended several times while going through Parliament.
- **New developments**
  New technology may mean that an old Act of Parliament does not apparently cover present day situations. This is seen in the case of *Royal College of Nursing v DHSS* (1981) where medical science and methods had changed since the passing of the Abortion Act in 1967. This case is discussed more fully at section 4.6.1.
- **Changes in the use of language**
  The meaning of words can change over the years. This was one of the problems in the case of *Cheeseman v DPP* (1990). The Times law report of this case is set out opposite in the activity section.

4.2 Literal approach versus purposive approach

The case of *Cheeseman* in the activity opposite illustrates several of the problems of statutory interpretation. It is an example of the courts taking the words literally.

However, it can be argued that the defendant was 'wilfully and indecently exposing his person in a street' and that he was caught doing that. Is it important whether the police officers were 'passengers'? After all they were there because of previous complaints about this type of behaviour and presumably the defendant thought they were ordinary members of the public. Some people would argue that the whole purpose of the act was to prevent this type of behaviour; this is the purposive approach to statutory interpretation.

Instead of looking at the precise meaning of each word a broader approach is taken.

This conflict between the literal approach and the purposive approach is one of the major issues in statutory interpretation. Should judges examine each word and take the words literally or should it be accepted that an Act of Parliament cannot cover every situation and that meanings of words cannot always be exact.

In European law the purposive approach is taken. This is important since as European laws are issued in several languages, it would be difficult, if not impossible, to take the meanings of words literally. It is not always possible to have an exact translation from one language to another.

4.3 The three rules

In English law the judges have not been able to agree on which approach should be used, but instead, over the years they have developed three different rules of (or approaches to) interpretation. These are:

- the Literal Rule;
- the Golden Rule;
- the Mischief Rule.

These rules take different approaches to interpretation and some judges prefer to use one rule, while other judges prefer another rule. This means that the interpretation of a statute may differ according to which judge is hearing the case. However, once an interpretation has been laid down, it may then form a precedent for future cases under the normal rules of judicial precedent. Since the three rules can result in very different decisions, it is important to understand them.

4.4 The Literal Rule

Under this rule courts will give words their plain, ordinary or literal meaning, even if the result is not very sensible. This idea was expressed by Lord

Activity

Read the following law report and answer the questions below.

Lurking policeman not 'passengers'

Cheeseman v Director of Public Prosecutions

Police officers who witnessed a man masturbating in a public lavatory were not 'passengers' within the meaning of section 28 of the Town Police Clauses Act 1847 when they had been stationed in the lavatory following complaints.

The Queen's Bench Divisional Court so held in allowing an appeal by way of case stated by Ashley Frederick Cheeseman against his conviction of an offence of wilfully and indecently exposing his person in a street to the annoyance of passengers.

Section 81 of the Public Health Acts Amendment Act 1907 extended the meaning of the word 'street' in section 28 to include, *inter alia*, any place of public resort under the control of the local authority.

LORD JUSTICE BINGHAM, concurring with Mr Justice Waterhouse, said that *The Oxford English Dictionary* showed that in 1847 when the Act was passed 'passenger' had a meaning, now unusual except in the expression 'foot-passenger' of 'a passer by or through; a traveller (usually on foot); a wayfarer'.

Before the meaning of 'street' was enlarged in 1907 that dictionary definition of passenger was not hard to apply: it clearly covered anyone using the street for ordinary purposes of passage or travel.

The dictionary definition could not be so aptly applied to a place of public resort such as a public lavatory, but on a commonsense reading when applied in context 'passenger' had to mean anyone resorting in the ordinary way to a place for one of the purposes for which people would normally resort to it.

If that was the correct approach, the two police officers were not 'passengers'. They were stationed in the public lavatory in order to apprehend persons committing acts which had given rise to earlier complaints. They were not resorting to that place of public resort in the ordinary way but for a special purpose and thus were not passengers.

Questions

1. In this case the meaning of the word 'street' was important. Why did the court decide the word 'street' in the Act included a public lavatory?

2. The meaning of the word 'passenger' was also important. How did the court discover what this word meant in 1847?

3. The court decided that 'passenger' meant 'a passer by or through; a traveller (usually on foot); a wayfarer'. Why did that definition **not** apply to the police officers who arrested the defendant?

4. The defendant was found not guilty because of the way the court interpreted 'passenger'. Do you think this was a correct decision? Give reasons for your answer.

Esher in *R v Judge of the City of London Court* (1892) when he said:

> If the words of an act are clear then you must follow them even though they lead to a manifest absurdity. The court has nothing to do with the question whether the legislature has committed an absurdity.

The rule developed in the early nineteenth century and was the main rule used for the first part of the twentieth century. It is still used as the starting point for interpreting any legislation.

4.4.1 Cases using the literal rule

The rule was used in *Whiteley v Chappell* (1868) where the defendant was charged under a section which made it an offence to impersonate 'any person entitled to vote'. The defendant had pretended to be a person whose name was on the voters' list, but who had died. The court held that the defendant was not guilty since a dead person is not, in the literal meaning of the words, 'entitled to vote'. Using the literal rule in this case made the law absurd.

The rule can also lead to what are considered harsh decisions. This occurred in *London & North Eastern Railway Co v Berriman* (1946) where a railway worker was killed while doing maintenance work, oiling points along a railway line. His widow tried to claim compensation because there had not been a look-out man provided by the railway company in accordance with a regulation under the Fatal Accidents Act which stated that a look-out should be provided for men working on or near the railway line 'for the purposes of relaying or repairing' it. The court took the words 'relaying' and 'repairing' in their literal meaning and said that oiling points was maintaining the line and not relaying or repairing so that Mrs Berriman's claim failed.

4.4.2 Advantages of the literal rule

The rule follows the words that Parliament has used. Parliament is our law-making body and it is right that judges should apply the law exactly as it is written. Using the literal rule to interpret Acts of Parliament prevents unelected judges from making law.

Using the literal rule should make the law more certain, as the law will be interpreted exactly as it is written. This makes it easier for people to know what the law is and how judges will apply it.

4.4.3 Disadvantages of the literal rule

The literal rule assumes every Act will be perfectly drafted. In fact it is not always possible to word an Act so that it covers every situation Parliament meant it to. This was seen in the case of *Whiteley v Chappell* (1868) where the defendant was not guilty of voting under another person's name (see section 4.4.1 above).

Words may have more than one meaning, so that the Act is unclear. Often in dictionaries words are defined with several different meanings. At section 4.1 we have already seen that there was difficulty in interpreting the word 'type' in the Dangerous Dogs Act 1991.

Following the words exactly can lead to unfair or unjust decisions. This was seen in *London & North Eastern Railway Co. v Berriman* (1946) (see section 4.4.1 above).

With decisions such as *Whiteley v Chappell* and the *Berriman* case, it is not surprising that Professor Michael Zander has denounced the literal rule as being mechanical and divorced from the realities of the use of language.

4.5 The Golden Rule

This rule is a modification of the literal rule. The golden rule starts by looking at the literal meaning but the court is then allowed to avoid an interpretation which would lead to an absurd result. There are two views on how far the golden rule should be used. The first is very narrow and is shown by Lord Reid's comments in *Jones v DPP* (1962) when he said:

> It is a cardinal principle applicable to all kinds of statutes that you may not for any reason attach to a statutory provision a meaning which the words of that provision cannot reasonably bear. If they are capable of more than one meaning, then you can choose between those meanings, but beyond this you cannot go.

So under the narrow application of the golden rule the court may only choose between the possible meanings of a word or phrase. If there is only one meaning then that must be taken.

The second and wider application of the golden rule is where the words have only one clear meaning, but that meaning would lead to a repugnant situation. This is a situation which the court feels that using the clear meaning would produce a result which should not be allowed. In such a case the court will use the golden rule to modify the words of the statute in order to avoid this problem.

4.5.1 Cases using the golden rule

The narrow view of the golden rule can be seen in practice in *R v Allen* (1872). In this case s 57 of the Offences Against the Person Act 1861 made it an offence to 'marry' whilst one's original spouse was still alive (and there had been no divorce). The word 'marry' can mean to become legally married to the other person or in a more general way it can mean that the person takes part or 'goes through' a ceremony of marriage.

The court decided that in the Offences Against the Person Act 1861 the word had this second meaning of go through a ceremony of marriage. This was because a person who is still married to another person cannot legally marry anyone else, so if the first meaning of being legally married was applied then there would be the absurd

situation that no-one could ever be guilty of bigamy.

A very clear example of the use of the wider application of the golden rule was the case of *Re Sigsworth* (1935). In this case the son had murdered his mother. The mother had not made a will, so normally her estate would have been inherited by her next of kin according to the rules set out in the Administration of Justice Act 1925. This meant that the murderer son would have inherited as her 'issue'.

There was no ambiguity in the words of the Act, but the court was not prepared to let a murderer benefit from his crime, so it was held that the literal rule should not apply, the golden rule would be used to prevent the repugnant situation of the son inheriting. Effectively the court was writing into the Act that the 'issue' would not be entitled to inherit where they had killed the person they would be inheriting from.

4.5.2 Advantages of the golden rule

It respects the exact words of Parliament except in limited situations. Where there is a problem with using the literal rule, the golden rule provides an 'escape route'.

It allows the judge to choose the most sensible meaning where there is more than one meaning to the words in the Act. It can also provide sensible decisions in cases where the literal rule would lead to a repugnant situation. It would clearly have been unjust to allow the son in *Re Sigsworth* to benefit from his crime.

This shows how it can avoid the worst problems of the literal rule.

4.5.3 Disadvantages of the golden rule

It is very limited in its use, so it is only used on rare occasions. Another problem is that it is not always possible to predict when courts will use the golden rule.

Michael Zander has described it as a 'feeble parachute'. In other words, it is an escape route but it cannot do very much.

4.6 The Mischief Rule

This rule gives a judge more discretion than the other two rules. The definition of the rule comes from *Heydon's case* (1584), where it was said that there were four points the court should consider. These, in the original language of that old case, were:

1. 'What was the common law before the making of the Act?
2. What was the mischief and defect for which the common law did not provide?
3. What was the remedy the Parliament hath resolved and appointed to cure the disease of the commonwealth?
4. The true reason of the remedy.
    Then the office of all the judges is always to make such construction as shall suppress the mischief and advance the remedy.'

So, under this rule, the court should look to see what the law was before the Act was passed in order to discover what gap or 'mischief' the Act was intended to cover. The court should then interpret the Act in such a way that the gap is covered. This is clearly a quite different approach to the literal rule.

4.6.1 Cases using the mischief rule

The mischief rule was used in *Smith v Hughes* (1960) to interpret section 1(1) of the Street Offences Act 1959 which said 'it shall be an offence for a common prostitute to loiter or solicit in a street or public place for the purpose of prostitution'.

The court considered appeals against the conviction under this section of six different women. In each case the women had not been 'in a street'. One had been on a balcony and the others had been at the windows of ground floor rooms, with the window either half open or closed. In each case the women were attracting the attention of men by calling to them or tapping on the window, but they argued that they were not guilty under this section since they were not literally 'in a street or public place'. The court decided that they were guilty, with Lord Parker saying:

> For my part I approach the matter by considering what is the mischief aimed at by this Act. Everybody knows that this was an Act to clean up the streets, to enable people to walk along the streets without being molested or solicited by common prostitutes. Viewed in this way it can matter little whether the prostitute is soliciting while in the street or is standing in the doorway or on a balcony, or at a window, or whether the window is shut or open or half open.

A similar point arose in *Eastbourne Borough Council v Stirling* (2000) where a taxi driver was charged with 'plying for hire in any street' without a licence to do so. His vehicle was parked on a taxi rank on the station forecourt, not on a street.

He was found guilty as, although the taxi was on private land, he was likely to get customers from the street. The court referred to *Smith v Hughes* and said that it was the same point.

Another case in which the House of Lords used the mischief rule was the *Royal College of Nursing v DHSS* (1981). In this case the wording of the Abortion Act 1967, which provided that a pregnancy should be 'terminated by a registered medical practitioner', was in issue.

When the Act was passed in 1967 the procedure to carry out an abortion was such that only a doctor (a registered medical practitioner) could do it. From 1972 onwards improvements in medical technique meant that the normal method of terminating a pregnancy was to induce premature labour with drugs. The first part of the procedure was carried out by a doctor, but the second part was performed by nurses without a doctor present. The court had to decide if this procedure was lawful under the Abortion Act. The case went to the House of Lords where the majority (3) of the judges held that it was lawful, whilst the other two said that it was not lawful.

The three judges in the majority based their decision on the mischief rule. They pointed out that the mischief Parliament was trying to remedy was the unsatisfactory state of the law before 1967 and the number of illegal abortions which put the lives of women at risk. They also said that the policy of the Act was to broaden the grounds for abortion and ensure that they were carried out with proper skill in hospital. The other two judges took the literal view and said that the words of the Act were clear and that terminations could only be carried out by a registered medical practitioner. They said that the other judges were not interpreting the Act but 'redrafting it with a vengeance'.

4.6.2 Advantages of the mischief rule

The mischief rule promotes the purpose of the law as it allows judges to look back at the gap in the law which the Act was designed to cover.

The emphasis is on making sure that the gap on the law is filled. This is more likely to produce a 'just' result. It also means that judges try to interpret the law in the way that Parliament meant it to work.

The Law Commission prefers the mischief rule and, as long ago as 1969, recommended that it should be the only rule used in statutory interpretation.

Activity

Read the facts of the case set out below then apply the different rules of interpretation.

CASE: *Fisher v Bell* [1960] 1 QB 394

The Restriction of Offensive Weapons Act 1959, s 1(1):

'Any person who manufactures, sells or hires or offers for sale or hire or lends or gives to any other person – (a) any knife which has a blade which opens automatically by hand pressure applied to a button, spring or other device in or attached to the handle of the knife, sometimes known as a 'flick knife' . . . shall be guilty of an offence'.

FACTS: The defendant was a shop keeper, who had displayed a flick knife marked with a price in his shop window; he had not actually sold any. He was charged under s 1(1) and the court had to decide whether he was guilty of offering the knife for sale. There is a technical legal meaning of 'offers for sale', under which putting an article in a shop window is **not** an offer to sell (students of contract law will learn this rule).

Consider the phrase 'offers for sale' and explain how you think the case would have been decided using:

(a) the literal rule;
(b) the golden rule;
(c) the mischief rule.

Note: the court's decision on the case is given on page 266.

Key facts

Literal rule	Golden rule	Mischief rule
Words in their ordinary grammatical meaning	Can choose best interpretation of ambiguous words OR avoid an absurd/repugnant result	Looks at the gap in the law prior to the Act and interprets words to 'suppress the mischief'
Case: *LNER v Berriman* Not 'relaying or repairing' track, but was oiling points (maintenance) Literal approach – held maintenance was not within the literal meaning of the words 'relaying or repairing' Could not claim compensation	Case: *R v Allen* 'Marry' meant go through a ceremony of marriage Case: *Re Sigsworth* Son not allowed to inherit money from mother because he murdered her	Case: *Smith v Hughes* Prostitutes calling from a house to men in the street were 'soliciting in a street' This was the mischief that the Act was intended to prevent
Advantages of literal rule ● leaves law-making to Parliament ● makes law more certain	Advantages of golden rule ● respects the words of Parliament as only used in limited situations ● avoids the worst problems of the literal rule	Advantages of mischief rule ● fills in the gaps in the law ● promotes the purpose of the Act ● produces 'just' results
Disadvantages of literal rule ● assumes that every Act is perfectly drafted ● words have more than one meaning ● can lead to absurd results ● can lead to unjust decisions	Disadvantages of golden rule ● can only be used in limited situations ● a 'feeble parachute' – Zander	Disadvantages of mischief rule ● risk of judicial law-making ● not as wide as the purposive approach ● limited to looking back to the law prior to the Act ● can make law uncertain

Figure 4.1 Key facts chart on the three 'rules' of statutory interpretation

4.6.3 Disadvantages of the mischief rule

There is the risk of judicial law-making. Judges are trying to fill the gaps in the law with their own views on how the law should remedy the gap. The case of *Royal College of Nursing v DHSS* (see section 4.6.1) shows that judges do not always agree on the use of the mischief rule.

Use of the mischief rule may lead to uncertainty in the law. It is impossible to know when judges will use the rule and also what result it might lead to. This makes it difficult for lawyers to advise clients on the law.

The mischief rule is not as wide as the purposive approach (see section 4.6) as it is limited to looking back at the gap in the old law. It cannot be used for a more general consideration of the purpose of the law.

It is clear that the three rules (literal, golden and mischief) can lead to different decisions on the meanings of words and phrases. See page 51 for an activity based on a real case in which the different rules could result in different decisions.

4.7 The purposive approach

This goes beyond the mischief rule in that the court is not just looking to see what the gap was in the old law. The judges are deciding what they believe Parliament meant to achieve.

4.7.1 Cases using the purposive approach

The purposive approach was used in *R v Registrar-General, ex parte Smith* (1990). The court had to consider s 51 of the Adoption Act 1976 which stated:

> (1) 'Subject to subsections (4) and (6), the Registrar-General shall on an application made in the prescribed manner by an adopted person a record of whose birth is kept by the Registrar-General and who has attained the age of 18 years supply to that person. . . such information as is necessary to enable that person to obtain a certified copy of the record of his birth'.

Subsection 4 said that before supplying that information the Registrar-General had to inform the applicant about counselling services available. Subsection 6 stated that if the adoption was before 1975 the Registrar-General could not give the information unless the applicant had attended an interview with a counsellor.

The case involved the application by Charles Smith for information to enable him to obtain his birth certificate. Mr Smith had made his application in the correct manner and was prepared to see a counsellor. On a literal view of the Act the Registrar-General had to supply him with the information, since the Act uses the phrase 'shall . . . supply'.

The problem was that Mr Smith had been convicted of two murders and was detained in Broadmoor as he suffered from recurring bouts of psychotic illness. A psychiatrist thought that it was possible he might be hostile towards his natural mother.

This posed a difficulty for the court; should they apply the clear meaning of the words in this situation? The judges in the Court of Appeal decided that the case called for the purposive approach. They said that, despite the plain language of the Act, Parliament could not have intended to promote serious crime. So, in view of the risk to the applicant's natural mother if he discovered her identity, they ruled that the Registrar-General did not have to supply any information.

Another case in which the purposive approach was used was R *(Quintavalle) v Secretary of State* (2003). In this case the House of Lords had to decide whether organisms created by cell nuclear replacement (CNR) came within the definition of 'embryo' in the Human Fertilisation and Embryology Act 1990. Section 1(1)(a) of this Act states that 'embryo means a live human embryo where fertilisation is complete'.

The problem was that when the Act was passed in 1990 there was only one way of creating an embryo outside the human body. This was by taking an egg from a woman and sperm from a man and fertilising the egg with the sperm. The fertilised egg could then be placed in a woman's uterus and, if it established itself, she would be pregnant. This is the normal method of helping those unable to conceive naturally to have children.

However, by 2003 another method of producing an embryo had become possible. This was through cell nuclear replacement (CNR). Fertilisation is not used in CNR. Instead, the nucleus from one cell of an unfertilised egg is removed. It is then replaced with the nucleus from an adult cell and, if the cell now divides, it is possible to produce an embryo. This technique is known as cloning.

Using the purposive approach, the House of Lords decided that embryos produced through CNR were covered by the 1990 Act. In his judgment in the case Lord Bingham said:

> [T]he court's task, within permissible bounds of interpretation is to give effect to Parliament's purpose ... Parliament could not have intended to distinguish between embryos produced by, or without, fertilisation since it was unaware of the latter possibility.

4.7.2 Advantages of the purposive approach

The purposive approach leads to justice in individual cases. It is a broad approach which allows the law to cover more situations than applying words literally.

The purposive approach is particularly useful where there is new technology which was unknown when the law was enacted. This is demonstrated by *R (Quintavalle) v Secretary of State*, the embryo case explained in section 4.6.1. If the literal rule/approach had been used in that case, it would have been necessary for Parliament to make a new law to deal with the situation.

It also gives judges more discretion than using the literal meanings of words. This allows judges to avoid the literal meaning where it would create an absurd situation. If the purposive approach had been used in *Whiteley v Chappell* (see section 4.4.1) then it is probable that the judges would have decided that Parliament's intention was to prevent people voting in another person's name and found the defendant guilty.

4.7.3 Disadvantages of the purposive approach

The problems with the purposive approach are that it means the judges refuse to follow the clear words of Parliament. How do the judges know what Parliament's intentions were? Opponents of the purposive approach say that it is impossible to discover Parliament's intentions; only the words of the statute can show what Parliament wanted. So using the purposive approach allows unelected judges to 'make' law as they are deciding what they think the law should be rather than using the words that Parliament enacted.

Another problem with the purposive approach is that it is difficult to discover the intention of Parliament. There are reports of debates in Parliament in Hansard (see section 4.8.2), but these give every detail of debates including those MPs who did not agree with the law that was under discussion. The final version of what Parliament agreed is the actual words used in the Act.

Literal approach Words taken in their ordinary grammatical meaning	Purposive approach Looks for the purpose of Parliament and interprets the law to ensure that purpose
Case: *LNER v Berriman* Not 'relaying or repairing' track, but was oiling points (maintenance) Literal approach – held maintenance was not within the literal meaning of the words 'relaying or repairing' Could not claim compensation	**Case: *R (Quintavalle) v Sec of State for Health*** Act stated embryo meant 'a live human embryo where fertilisation is complete' Embryos were created by cell nuclear replacement, so there was no fertilisation Purposive approach – Parliament could not have intended to distinguish between embryos, so the Act applied
Advantages of literal approach ● leaves law-making to Parliament ● makes law more certain	**Advantages of purposive approach** ● leads to justice in individual cases ● broad approach covering more situations ● allows for new technology
Disadvantages of literal approach ● assumes that every Act is perfectly drafted ● words have more than one meaning ● can lead to absurd results ● can lead to unjust decisions	**Disadvantages of purposive approach** ● leads to judicial law-making ● can make law uncertain ● difficult to discover the intention of Parliament

Figure 4.2 Comparing the literal approach and the purposive approach

Test Yourself

1. Explain two reasons why it may be necessary to interpret an Act.
2. Define the literal rule and give a case in which it was used.
3. Give one advantage and one disadvantage of using the literal rule.
4. Define the golden rule and give a case in which it was used.
5. Give one advantage and one disadvantage of using the golden rule.
6. Define the mischief rule and give a case in which it was used.
7. Give one advantage and one disadvantage of using the mischief rule.
8. Define the purposive approach and give a case in which it was used.
9. Give one advantage and one disadvantage of using the purposive approach.
10. Compare the literal and the purposive approaches.

It also leads to uncertainty in the law. It is impossible to know when judges will use this approach or what result it might lead to. This makes it difficult for lawyers to advise clients on the law.

4.8 Finding Parliament's intention

There are certain ways in which the courts can try to discover the intention of Parliament and certain matters which they can look at in order to help with the interpretation of a statute.

4.8.1 Internal aids

These are matters within the statute itself that may help to make its meaning clearer. The court can consider the long title, the short title and the preamble, if any. Older statutes usually have a preamble which sets out Parliament's purpose in enacting that statute. Modern statutes either do not have a preamble or contain a very brief one, for example the Theft Act 1968 states that it is an Act to modernise the law of theft. The long title may also explain briefly Parliament's intentions.

The other useful internal aids are any headings before a group of sections, and any schedules attached to the Act. There are often also marginal notes explaining different sections but these are not generally regarded as giving Parliament's intention as they will have been inserted after the Parliamentary debates and are only helpful comments put in by the printer.

4.8.2 External aids

These are matters which are outside the Act and it has always been accepted that some external sources can help explain the meaning of an Act. These undisputed sources are:

- previous Acts of Parliament on the same topic;
- the historical setting;
- earlier case law;
- dictionaries of the time.

As far as other external aids are concerned attitudes have changed. Originally the courts had very strict rules that other extrinsic aids should not be considered. However, for the following three aids the courts' attitude has changed. These three main external aids are:

- Hansard – that is the official report of what was said in Parliament when the Act was debated;
- Reports of law reform bodies such as the Law Commission which led to the passing of the Act;
- International conventions, regulations or directives which have been implemented by English legislation.

The use of Hansard

Until 1992 there was a firm rule that the courts could not look at what was said in the debates in Parliament. Some years earlier Lord Denning had tried to attack this ban on Hansard in *Davis v Johnson* (1979), which involved the interpretation of the Domestic Violence and Matrimonial Proceedings Act 1976. He admitted that he had indeed read Hansard before making his decision saying:

> Some may say . . . that judges should not pay any attention to what is said in Parliament. They should grope about in the dark for the meaning of an Act without switching on the light. I do not accede to this view.

The House of Lords disapproved of this and Lord Scarman explained their reasons by saying:

> Such material is an unreliable guide to the meaning of what is enacted. It promotes confusion, not clarity. The cut and thrust of debate and the pressures of executive responsibility . . . are not always conducive to a clear and unbiased explanation of the meaning of statutory language.

However, in *Pepper v Hart* (1993) the House of Lords relaxed the rule and accepted that Hansard could be used in a limited way. This case was unusual in that seven judges heard the appeal, rather than the normal panel of five. Those seven judges included the Lord Chancellor, who was the only judge to disagree with the use of Hansard. The majority ruled that Hansard could be consulted. Lord Browne-Wilkinson said in his judgment that:

> the exclusionary rule should be relaxed so as to permit reference to parliamentary materials where; (a) legislation is ambiguous or obscure, or leads to an absurdity; (b) the material relied on consists of one or more statements by a minister or other promoter of the Bill together if necessary with such other parliamentary material as is necessary to understand such statements and their effect; (c) the statements relied on are clear. Further than this I would not at present go.

So Hansard may be considered but only where the words of the Act are ambiguous or obscure or lead to an absurdity. Even then Hansard should only be used if there was a clear statement by the Minister introducing the legislation, which would resolve the ambiguity or absurdity. The Lord Chancellor opposed the use of Hansard on practical grounds, pointing out the time and cost it would take to research Hansard in every case.

The only time that a wider use of Hansard is permitted is where the court is considering an Act that introduced an international convention or European Directive into English law. This was pointed out by the Queen's Bench Divisional Court in *Three Rivers District Council and others v Bank of England (No 2)* (1996). In such a situation it is important to interpret the statute purposively and consistently with any European materials and the court can look at Ministerial statements, even if the statute does not appear to be ambiguous or obscure.

Since 1992, Hansard has been referred to in a number of cases. The Lord Chancellor's predictions on cost have been confirmed by some solicitors, with one estimating that it had added 25 per cent to the bill. On other occasions it is clear that Hansard has not been helpful or that the court would have reached the same conclusion in any event.

Law reform reports

As with Hansard, the courts used to hold that reports by law reform agencies such as the Law Reform Agency should not be considered by the courts. However this rule was relaxed in the *Black Clawson* case in 1975, when it was accepted that such a report should be looked at to discover the mischief or gap in the law which the legislation based on the report was designed to deal with. (See section 2.2.1 for detail on the Law Commission.)

Other aids

As well the above internal and external aids there are other matters which can help a court with interpretation. These are rules of language (see 4.11) and presumptions (see 4.12).

4.9 The effect of EU law

The purposive approach is the one preferred by most European countries when interpreting their own legislation. It is also the approach which has been adopted by the European Court of Justice in interpreting European law.

Since the United Kingdom became a member of the European Union in 1973 the influence of the European preference for the purposive approach has affected the English courts in two ways. Firstly they have had to accept that, at least for law which has been passed as a result of having to conform to a European law, the purposive approach is the correct one to use. Secondly the fact that judges are having to use the purposive approach for European law is making them more accustomed to it and, therefore, more likely to apply it to English law.

4.9.1 Interpreting EU Law

Where the law to be interpreted is based on European law, the English courts must interpret it in the light of the wording and purpose of the European law. This is because the Treaty of Rome, which sets out the duties of European member states, says that all member states are required to:

 take all appropriate measures … to ensure fulfilment of the obligations.

The European Court of Justice in the *Marleasing* case (1992) ruled that this included interpreting national law in the light and the aim of the European law.

4.10 The effect of the Human Rights Act 1998

Section 3 of the Human Rights Act says that, so far as it is possible to do so, legislation must be read and given effect in a way which is compatible with the rights in the European Convention on Human Rights. This applies to any case where one of the rights is concerned, but it does not apply where there is no involvement of human rights.

An example of the effect of the Human Rights Act on interpretation is *Mendoza v Ghaidan* (2002). In this case the Court of Appeal ignored a House of Lords' judgment about the Rent Act 1977 which had been made prior to the implementation of the Human Rights Act.

The Rent Act applied where a person who had the tenancy of a house or flat died. If the tenant had been living in the property with their spouse, then the spouse had the right to take over the tenancy. The Rent Act also allowed unmarried partners to succeed to the tenancy as it stated that 'a person who was living with the original tenant as his or her wife or husband shall be treated as the spouse of the original tenant'.

In *Mendoza v Ghaidan* the question was whether same sex partners had the right to take over the tenancy. A House of Lords' decision, made before the Human Rights Act came into effect, had ruled that same sex partners did not have the right under the Rent Act to take over the tenancy.

The Court of Appeal held that the Rent Act had to be interpreted to conform to the European Convention on Human Rights which forbids discrimination on the ground of gender. In order to make the Act compatible with human rights, the Court of Appeal read the words 'living with the original tenant as his or her wife or husband' to mean 'as *if they were* his or her wife or husband'. This allowed same sex partners to have the same rights as unmarried opposite sex couples.

The Court of Appeal pointed out the importance of conforming to the Convention rights when they said:

> In order to remedy this breach of the Convention the court must, if it can, read the Schedule so that its provisions are rendered compatible with the Convention rights of the survivors of same-sex partnerships.

In 2004 the House of Lords confirmed the Court of Appeal's decision in this case.

4.11 Rules of language

Even the literal rule does not take words in complete isolation. It is common sense that the other words in the Act must be looked at to see if they affect the word or phrase which is in dispute. In looking at the other words in the Act the courts have developed a number of minor rules which can help to make the meaning of words and phrases clear where a particular sentence construction has been used. These rules, which have Latin names, are:

- *ejusdem generis* rule;
- *expressio unius exclusio alterius* (the mention of one thing excludes others;
- *noscitur a sociis* (a word is known by the company it keeps).

4.11.1 The *ejusdem generis* rule (of the same kind)

This states that where there is a list of words which is followed by general words, then the general words are limited to the same kind of items as the specific words. This is easier to understand by looking at cases. In *Powell v Kempton Park Racecourse* (1899) the defendant was charged with keeping a 'house, office, room or other place for betting'. He had been operating betting at what is known as Tattersall's ring, which is outdoors. The court decided that the general words 'other place' had to refer to indoor

places since all the words in the list were indoor places and so the defendant was not guilty.

There must be at least two specific words in a list before the general word or phrase for this rule to operate. In *Allen v Emmerson* (1944) the court had to interpret the phrase 'theatres and other places of amusement' and decide if it applied to a funfair. As there was only one specific word 'theatres', it was decided that a funfair did come under the general term 'other places of amusement' even though it was not of the same kind as theatres.

4.11.2 *Expressio unius exclusio alterius* (the mention of one thing excludes others)

Where there is a list of words which is not followed by general words, then the Act applies only to the items in the list. In *Tempest v Kilner* (1846) the court had to consider whether the Statute of Frauds 1677, which required a contract for the sale of 'goods, wares and merchandise' of more than £10 to be evidenced in writing, applied to a contract for the sale of stocks and shares. The list 'goods, wares and merchandise' was not followed by any general words, so the court held that only contracts for those three types of things were affected by the statute; because stocks and shares were not mentioned they were not caught by the statute.

4.11.3 *Noscitur a sociis* (a word is known by the company it keeps)

This means that the words must be looked at in context and interpreted accordingly. It involves looking at other words in the same section or at other sections in the Act. Words in the same section were important in *Inland Revenue Commissioners v Frere* (1965), where the section set out rules for 'interest, annuities or other annual interest'. The first use of the word 'interest' on its own could have meant any interest paid, whether daily, monthly or annually. Because of the words 'other annual interest' in the section,

Key facts

	BRIEF DEFINITION	CASE EXAMPLES
Literal approach	Approaching problems of statutory interpretation by taking the words at their face value	*Fisher v Bell*
Purposive approach	Looking at the reasons why a law was passed and interpreting the words accordingly	*R v Registrar-General, ex parte Smith*
The 'three rules' Literal rule Golden rule Mischief rule	Words given ordinary, plain, grammatical meaning Avoids absurd or repugnant situations Looks at the gap in the previous law and interprets the words 'to advance the remedy'	*Whiteley v Chappell* *R v Allen* *Smith v Hughes*
Aids to finding Parliament's intention	Internal – within the Act, e.g. interpretation section External – outside the Act, e.g. Hansard Law Commission Reports	*Pepper v Hart* *Black Clawson*
Rules of language *Ejusdem generis* *Expressio unius* *Noscitur a sociis*	General words which follow a list are limited to the same kind The express mention of one thing excludes others A word is known by the company it keeps	*Powell v Kempton Park* *Tempest v Kilner* *IRC v Frere*
Presumptions	No change to common law Crown not bound *Mens rea* required No retrospective effect	*R v Leach* *Sweet v Parsley*

Figure 4.3 Key facts chart for statutory interpretation

the court decided that 'interest' only meant annual interest.

Other sections of the Act were considered by the House of Lords in *Bromley London Borough Council v Greater London Council* (1982). The issue in this case was whether the GLC could operate a cheap fare scheme on their transport systems, where the amounts being charged meant that the transport system would run at a loss. The decision in the case revolved around the meaning of the word 'economic'. The House of Lords looked at the whole Act and, in particular, at another section which imposed a duty to make up any deficit as far as possible. As a result they decided that 'economic' meant being run on business lines and ruled that the cheap fares policy was not legal since it involved deliberately running the transport system at a loss and this was not running it on business lines.

4.12 Presumptions

The courts will also make certain presumptions or assumptions about the law, but these are only a starting point. If the statute clearly states the opposite then the presumption will not apply and it is said that the presumption is rebutted. The most important presumptions are:

1. **A presumption against a change in the common law.**
   In other words it is assumed that the common law will apply unless Parliament has made it plain in the Act that the common law has

Test Yourself

1. Explain what is meant by an internal aid to statutory interpretation.
2. What is Hansard?
3. Which case allowed Hansard to be used for statutory interpretation?
4. What are the limitations on the use of Hansard in statutory interpretation?
5. Give two other aids to interpretation.
6. What approach does European law use in statutory interpretation?
7. How does the Human Rights Act 1998 affect interpretation in cases which involve human rights?
8. Explain the *ejusdem generis* (of the same kind) rule.
9. Explain one other rule of language.
10. Give two presumptions that are made when interpreting an Act.

---

been altered. An example of this occurred in *Leach v R* (1912), where the question was whether a wife could be made to give evidence against her husband under the Criminal Evidence Act 1898. Since the Act did not expressly say that this should happen it was held that the common law rule that a wife could not be compelled to give evidence still applied. If there had been explicit words saying that a wife was compellable then the old common law would not apply. This is now the position under s 80 of the Police and Criminal Evidence Act 1984, which expressly states that in a crime of violence one spouse can be made to give evidence against the other spouse.

2. **A presumption that *mens rea* is required in criminal cases.**
   The basic common law rule is that no-one can be convicted of a crime unless it is shown that they had the required intention to commit it. In *Sweet v Parsley* (1970) the defendant was charged with being concerned with the management of premises which were used for the purposes of smoking cannabis. The facts were that the defendant was the owner of premises which she had leased out and the tenants had smoked cannabis there without her knowledge. She was clearly 'concerned in the management' of the premises and cannabis had been smoked there, but because she had no knowledge of the events she had no *mens rea*. The key issue was whether *mens rea* was required; the Act did not say there was any need for knowledge of the events. The House of Lords held that she was not guilty as the presumption that *mens rea* was required had not been rebutted.

3. **A presumption that the Crown is not bound** by any statute unless the statute expressly says so.

4. **A presumption that legislation does not apply retrospectively.** This means that no Act of Parliament will apply to past happenings; each Act will normally only apply from the date it comes into effect.

Examination questions

When interpreting an Act of Parliament, judges can use a range of rules (approaches) and can also rely on internal and external aids to interpretation.

(a) Briefly describe the literal rule and the internal aids used by judges when interpreting Acts of Parliament.   (10 marks)

(b) Briefly describe the golden rule and the external aids used by judges when interpreting Acts of Parliament.   (10 marks)

(c) Discuss the disadvantages of any two of the rules of (approaches to) statutory interpretation.   (10 marks)

Examiner's tip

When a question allows you to choose which point you will write about, make sure that you choose one you know enough about.

Look at part (c) of the question above. This asks for the disadvantages of any two of the rules/approaches to statutory interpretation. Make sure you choose rules/approaches that you can write about a range of disadvantages and support these disadvantages with case examples.

Chapter 5

Judicial Precedent

Judicial precedent refers to the source of law where past decisions of the judges create law for future judges to follow. This source of law is also known as case law. It is a major source of law, both historically and today.

5.1 The doctrine of precedent

The English system of precedent is based on the Latin maxim *stare decisis et non quieta movere* (usually shortened to *stare decisis*). This means stand by what has been decided and do not unsettle the established. This supports the idea of fairness and provides certainty in the law.

5.1.1 Judgments

Precedent can only operate if the legal reasons for past decisions are known, so at the end of a case there will be a judgment. This is a speech made by the judge (or judges) hearing the case giving the decision and explaining the reasons for the decision. In a judgment the judge usually gives a summary of the facts of the case, reviews the arguments put to him by the advocates in the case, and then explains the principles of law he is using to come to the decision.

These principles are the important part of the judgment and are known as the *ratio decidendi* which means the reason for deciding (and is pronounced ray-she-o dess-id-end-i). This is what creates a precedent for judges to follow in future cases. The rest of the judgment is known as *obiter dicta* (other things said).

It is also worth realising that there can be more than one speech at the end of a case depending on the number of judges hearing the case. In courts of first instance there will be only one judge and therefore one judgment. However, in the Divisional Courts and the Court of Appeal cases are heard by at least two judges and usually three. In the Supreme Court, the panel of judges must consist of an uneven number, so it could be three, five, seven or even nine. This means that there can be more than one judgment.

The fact that there are two or more judges does not mean that there will always be several judgments as it is quite common for one judge to give the judgment and the other judge/judges simply to say 'I agree'! However, in cases where there is a particularly important or complicated point of law, more than one judge may want to explain his legal reasoning on the point. This can cause problems in later cases as each judge may have had a different reason for his decision, so there will be more than one *ratio decidendi*.

5.1.2 *Ratio decidendi*

As already stated, this is the only part of the judgment which forms a precedent. A major problem when looking at a past judgment is to divide the *ratio decidendi* from the *obiter dicta*, as older judgments are usually in a continuous form, without any headings specifiying what is meant to be part of the *ratio* and what is not. This means that the person reading the judgment (especially a judge in a later case) will have to decide what the *ratio* is. Sir Rupert Cross defined the *ratio decidendi* as 'any rule expressly or impliedly treated by the judge as a necessary step in reaching his conclusion'. Michael Zander says that it is 'a proposition of law which decides the case, in the light or in the context of the material facts.

It depends on the level of the court making the decision as to whether the ratio has to be followed by a later court (a binding precedent) or whether it merely has to be considered by that court.

5.1.3 *Obiter dicta*

The remainder of the judgment is called *obiter dicta* (other things said) and judges in future cases do not have to follow it. Sometimes a judge will speculate on what his decision would have been if the facts of the case had been different. This hypothetical situation is part of the *obiter dicta* and the legal reasoning put forward in it may be considered in future cases, although as with all *obiter* statements it is not binding precedent.

As well as learning the Latin phrases *ratio decidendi, obiter dicta* and *stare decisis* there are some English phrases which are important for understanding the concept of judicial precedent.

These are original precedent, binding precedent and persuasive precedent.

5.1.4 Original precedent

If the point of law in a case has never been decided before, then whatever the judge decides will form a new precedent for future cases to follow. It is an original precedent. As there are no past cases for the judge to base his decision on he is likely to look at cases which are the closest in principle and he may decide to use similar rules. This way of arriving at a judgment is called reasoning by analogy.

5.1.5 Binding precedent

This is a precedent from an earlier case which must be followed even if the judge in the later case does not agree with the legal principle. A binding precedent is only created when the facts of the second case are sufficiently similar to the original case and the decision was made by a court which is senior to (or in some cases the same level as) the court hearing the later case.

5.1.6 Persuasive precedent

This is a precedent that is not binding on the court but the judge may consider it and decide that it is a correct principle so he is persuaded that he should follow it. Persuasive precedent comes from a number of sources as explained below:

1. **Courts lower in the hierarchy**
   Such an example can be seen in *R v R* (1991) where the House of Lords agreed with and followed the same reasoning as the Court of Appeal in deciding that a man could be guilty of raping his wife.
2. **Decisions of the Judicial Committee of the Privy Council**
   This court is not part of the court hierarchy in England and Wales and so its decisions are not binding. However, as many of its judges are also members of the Supreme Court (formerly the House of Lords), the judgments of the

Privy Council are treated with respect and may often be followed. An example of this can be seen in the law on remoteness of damage in the law of tort and the decision made by the Privy Council in the case of *The Wagon Mound (No 1)* (1961).

More recently, in *A-G for Jersey v Holley* (2005) the Privy Council ruled that in the defence of provocation a defendant is to be judged by the standard of a person having ordinary powers of self-control. This was contrary to an earlier judgment by the House of Lords. In cases in 2005 and 2006 the Court of Appeal followed the Privy Council decision rather than the decision of the House of Lords.

3. **Statements made *obiter dicta***

   This is clearly seen in the law on duress as a defence to a criminal charge. The House of Lords in *R v Howe* (1987) ruled that duress could not be a defence to a charge of murder. In the judgment the Lords also commented, as an obiter statement, that duress would not be available as a defence to someone charged with attempted murder. When, later, in *R v Gotts* (1992) a defendant charged with attempted murder tried to argue that he could use the defence of duress, the obiter statement from *Howe* was followed as persuasive precedent by the Court of Appeal.

4. **A dissenting judgment**

   When a case has been decided by a majority of judges (for example 2-1 in the Court of Appeal), the judge who disagreed will have explained his reasons. This is a dissenting judgment. If that case goes on appeal to the Supreme Court, or if there is a later case on the same point which goes to the Supreme Court, it is possible that the Supreme Court may prefer the dissenting judgment and decide the case in the same way. The dissenting judgment has persuaded them to follow it.

5. **Decisions of courts in other countries**

   This is especially so where the other country uses the same ideas of common law as in our system. This applies to Commonwealth countries such as Canada, Australia and New Zealand.

5.2 The hierarchy of the courts

In England and Wales our courts operate a very rigid doctrine of judicial precedent which has the effect that:

- every court is bound to follow any decision made by a court above it in the hierarchy; and
- in general, appellate courts are bound by their own past decisions.

So the hierarchy of the courts is the next important point to get clear. Which courts come where in the hierarchy? Figure 5.1 shows this in the form of a cascade model and Figure 5.2 gives each court and its position in respect of the other courts. The position of each court is considered in this section. Extra detail on the use of precedent in the House of Lords and the new Supreme Court and Court of Appeal is given in sections 5.3 and 5.4.

Note that the most senior court in the legal system of this country used to be the House of

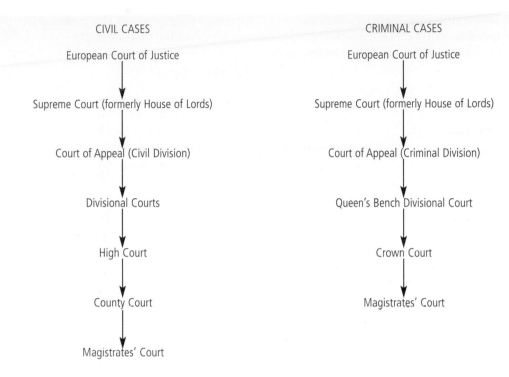

CIVIL CASES

European Court of Justice

↓

Supreme Court (formerly House of Lords)

↓

Court of Appeal (Civil Division)

↓

Divisional Courts

↓

High Court

↓

County Court

↓

Magistrates' Court

CRIMINAL CASES

European Court of Justice

↓

Supreme Court (formerly House of Lords)

↓

Court of Appeal (Criminal Division)

↓

Queen's Bench Divisional Court

↓

Crown Court

↓

Magistrates' Court

Figure 5.1 Cascade model of judicial precedent operating in the hierarchy of the courts

Lords. This court was abolished in October 2009 and replaced by the Supreme Court.

5.2.1 Appellate courts

Appellate courts are those that hear appeals.

The European Court of Justice

Since 1973 the highest court affecting our legal system is the European Court of Justice. Points of EU law can be referred to it by courts in England and Wales. The European Court of Justice only decides the point of law; the case then comes back to the court in this country to apply that law to the case.

All decisions made by the European Court of Justice are binding on all courts in England and Wales for points of EU law. It does not affect other areas of law.

An important feature of the European Court of Justice is that it is prepared to overrule its own past decisions if it feels it is necessary. This

flexible approach to past precedents is seen in other legal systems in Europe, and it is a contrast to the more rigid approach of our national courts.

Supreme Court

The most senior national court is the Supreme Court and its decisions bind all other courts in the English legal system. The Supreme Court is not bound by its own past decisions, although it generally will follow them. This point is discussed in detail at 5.3.

Court of Appeal

At the next level down in the hierarchy is the Court of Appeal; this has two divisions, Civil and Criminal. Both divisions of the Court of Appeal are bound to follow decisions of the European Court of Justice and the Supreme Court. In addition they must usually follow past decisions of their own, although there are some limited exceptions to this rule. The Court of Appeal

(Criminal Division) is more flexible where the point involves the liberty of the subject. The position of the two divisions is discussed in detail in 5.4.

Divisional courts

The three divisional courts (Queen's Bench, Chancery and Family) are bound by decisions of the European Court of Justice, the Supreme Court and the Court of Appeal. In addition the divisional courts are bound by their own past decisions, although they operate similar exceptions to those operated by the Court of Appeal (see 5.4.2). This was decided in *Police Authority for Huddersfield v Watson* (1947). It is also probably correct to say that the divisional courts have the same flexibility as the Criminal Division of the Court of Appeal where the case involves a person's liberty (see 5.4.3). Certainly this was the attitude taken in *R v Greater Manchester Coroner, ex parte Tal* (1984), and more recently in *Shaw v DPP* (1992).

5.2.2 Courts of first instance

The term 'courts of first instance' refers to any court where the original trial of a case is held. The appellate courts considered in the previous section do not hear any original trials. They only deal with appeals from decisions of other courts. Quite often an appeal will be about a point of law. This allows the appellate courts to decide the law. This is why appellate courts are much more important than courts of first instance when it comes to creating precedent.

The High Court

This is bound by decisions of all the courts above and in turn it binds the lower courts. High Court judges do not have to follow each others' decisions but will usually do so. In *Colchester Estates (Cardiff) v Carlton Industries plc* (1984) it was held that where there were two earlier decisions which conflicted, then, provided the first decision had been fully considered in the later case, that later decision should be followed.

Inferior courts

These are the Crown Court, the county court and the magistrates' court. They are bound to follow decision by all higher courts and it is unlikely that a decision by an inferior court can create precedent. The one exception is that a ruling on a point of law by a judge in the Crown Court technically creates precedent for the magistrates' court. However, since such rulings are rarely recorded in the law reports, this is of little practical effect.

5.3 The House of Lords (now the Supreme Court)

The main debate about the former House of Lords and precedent was the extent to which it should follow its own past decisions and the

Test Yourself

1. What part of a judgment forms a precedent for future cases?
2. What is the rest of the judgment known as?
3. What is meant by 'original precedent'?
4. What is meant by 'binding precedent'?
5. What effect do decisions of the Judicial Committee of the Privy Council have on future cases?
6. What is meant by a dissenting judgment?
7. Give two other types of persuasive precedent.
8. What is the highest court in the legal system in England and Wales?
9. Where a point of European law is involved, the decisions of which court must be followed?
10. Which courts do not create precedents?

Court	Courts bound by it	Courts it must follow
European Court	All courts	None
Supreme Court	All other courts in the English legal system	European Court
Court of Appeal	Itself (with some exceptions) Divisional Courts All other lower courts	European Court Supreme Court
Divisional Courts	Itself (with some exceptions) High Court All other lower courts	European Court Supreme Court Court of Appeal
High Court	County Court Magistrates' Court	European Court Supreme Court Court of Appeal Divisional Courts
Crown Court	possibly Magistrates' Court	All higher courts

County Court and Magistrates' Court do not create precedent and are bound by all higher courts

Figure 5.2 The courts and precedent

ideas on this have changed over the years.

Originally the view was that the House of Lords had the right to overrule past decisions, but gradually during the nineteenth century this more flexible approach disappeared. By the end of that century, in *London Street Tramways v London County Council* (1898), the House of Lords held that certainty in the law was more important than the possibility of individual hardship being caused through having to follow a past decision.

So from 1898 to 1966 the House of Lords regarded itself as being completely bound by its own past decisions unless the decision had been made *per incuriam*, that is 'in error'. However, this idea of error referred only to situations where a decision had been made without considering the effect of a relevant statute.

This was not felt to be satisfactory. The law could not change to meet changing social conditions and opinions, nor could any possible 'wrong' decisions be changed by the courts. If there was an unsatisfactory decision by the House

of Lords, then the only way it could be changed was by Parliament passing a new Act of Parliament.

This happened in the law on intention as an element of a criminal offence. The House of Lords in *DPP v Smith* (1961) had ruled that an accused could be guilty of murder if a reasonable person would have foreseen that death or very serious injury might result from the accused's actions. This decision was criticised as it meant that the defendant could be guilty even if he had not intended to cause death or serious injury, nor even realised that his actions might have that effect. Eventually Parliament changed the law by passing the Criminal Justice Act 1967.

5.3.1 The Practice Statement

It was realised that the House of Lords should have more flexibility, so in 1966 the Lord Chancellor issued a Practice Statement announcing a change to the rule in *London Street*

Tramways v London County Council. The Practice Statement said:

> Their Lordships regard the use of precedent as an indispensable foundation upon which to decide what is the law and its application to individual cases. It provides at least some degree of certainty upon which individuals can rely in the conduct of their affairs, as well as a basis for orderly development of legal rules.
>
> Their Lordships nevertheless recognise that the rigid adherence to precedent may lead to injustice in a particular case and also unduly restrict the proper development of the law. They, therefore, propose to modify their present practice and while treating former decisions of this House as normally binding, to depart from a previous decision when it appears right to do so.
>
> In this connection they will bear in mind the danger of disturbing retrospectively the basis on which contracts, settlement of property and fiscal arrangements have been entered into and also the especial need for certainty as to the criminal law.
>
> This announcement is not intended to affect the use of precedent elsewhere than in this House.

Activity

Read the following passage which comes from an extra explanatory note given to the press when the Practice Statement was issued and answer the questions below.

'The statement is one of great importance, although it should not be supposed that there will frequently be cases in which the House thinks it right not to follow their own precedent. An example of a case in which the House might think it right to depart from a precedent is where they consider that the earlier decision was influenced by the existence of conditions which no longer prevail, and that in modern conditions the law ought to be different.

One consequence of this change is of major importance. The relaxation of the rule of judicial precedent will enable the House of Lords to pay greater attention to judicial decisions reached in the superior courts of the Commonwealth, where they differ from earlier decisions of the House of Lords. That could be of great help in the development of our own law. The superior courts of many other countries are not rigidly bound by their own decisions and the change in the practice of the House of Lords will bring us more into line with them.'

Questions

1. Why was the Practice Statement of great importance?

2. Did the note suggest that the Practice Statement was likely to be used often?

3. Do you agree that 'in modern conditions' (see the passage above) the law ought to be different from earlier law decided when social or other conditions in this country were different? Give reasons and examples to support your answer.

4. Why should the House of Lords (now the Supreme Court) want to consider decisions from Commonwealth countries? What authority do such decisions have in the English legal system?

Key facts

1898	House of Lords decides in the case of *London Street Tramways* that it is bound to follow its own previous decisions
1966	Issue of the Practice Statement House of Lords will depart from previous decisions when 'it is right to do so'
1968	First use of Practice Statement in *Conway v Rimmer* Only involves technical law on discovery of documents
1972	First major use of Practice Statement in *Herrington v British Railways Board* on the duty of care owed to child trespassers
1980s and 1990s	House of Lords shows an increasing willingness to use Practice Statement to overrule previous decisions eg *R v Shivpuri* (criminal attempts) *Pepper v Hart* (use of Hansard in statutory interpretation)
2003	Practice Statement used to overrule the decision in *Caldwell* on recklessness in the criminal law

Figure 5.3 Key facts chart for the operation of judicial precedent in the House of Lords

5.3.2 Use of the Practice Statement

From 1966, this Practice Statement allowed the House of Lords to change the law if they believe that an earlier case was wrongly decided. They had the flexibility to refuse to follow an earlier case when 'it appears right to do so'. This phrase is, of course, very vague and gave little guidance as to when the House of Lords might overrule a previous decision. In fact the House of Lords was reluctant to use this power, especially in the first few years after 1966. The first case in which the Practice Statement was used was *Conway v Rimmer* (1968), but this only involved a technical point on discovery of documents.

The first major use did not occur until 1972 in *Herrington v British Railways Board* (1972), which involved the law on the duty of care owed to a child trespasser. The earlier case of *Addie v Dumbreck* (1929) had decided that an occupier of land would only owe a duty of care for injuries to a child trespasser if those injuries had been caused deliberately or recklessly. In *Herrington* the Lords held that social and physical conditions had changed since 1929, and the law should also change.

There was still great reluctance in the House of Lords to use the Practice Statement, as can be seen by the case of *Jones v Secretary of State for Social Services* (1972). This case involved the interpretation of the National Insurance (Industrial Injuries) Act 1946 and four out of the seven judges hearing the case regarded the earlier decision in *Re Dowling* (1967) as being wrong. Despite this the Lords refused to overrule that earlier case, preferring to keep to the idea that certainty was the most important feature of precedent. The same attitude was shown in *Knuller v DPP* (1973) when Lord Reid said:

> Our change of practice in no longer regarding previous decisions of this House as absolutely binding does not mean that whenever we think a previous precedent was wrong we should reverse it. In the general interest of certainty in the law we must be sure that there is some very good reason before we so act.

From the mid 1970s onwards the House of Lords showed a little more willingness to make use of the Practice Statement. For example in *Miliangos v George Frank (Textiles) Ltd* (1976) the House of Lords used the Practice Statement to overrule a previous judgment that damages could only be awarded in sterling. Another major case was *Pepper v Hart* (1993) where the previous ban on the use of Hansard in statutory interpretation was overruled.

5.3.3 The Practice Statement in criminal law

The Practice Statement stressed that criminal law needs to be certain, so it was not surprising that the House of Lords did not rush to overrule any judgments in criminal cases. The first use in a criminal case was in *R v Shivpuri* (1986) which overruled the decision in *Anderton v Ryan* (1985) on attempts to do the impossible. The interesting point was that the decision in *Anderton* had been made less than a year before, but it had been severely criticised by academic lawyers. In *Shivpuri* Lord Bridge said:

> I am undeterred by the consideration that the decision in *Anderton v Ryan* was so recent. The Practice Statement is an effective abandonment of our pretention to infallibility. If a serious error embodied in a decision of this House has distorted the law, the sooner it is corrected the better.

In other words, the House of Lords recognised that they might sometimes make errors and the most important thing then was to put the law right. Where the Practice Statement is used to overrule a previous decision, that past case is then effectively ignored. The law is now that set out in the new case.

A more recent major case on the use of the Practice Statement by the House of Lords in criminal law is *R v G and R* (2003). The House of Lords overruled their previous decision in the case of *Metropolitan Police Commissioner v Caldwell*

(1982) on the law of criminal damage.

In *Caldwell* the House of Lords had ruled that recklessness included the situation where the defendant had not realised the risk of his action causing damage, but an ordinary careful adult would have realised there was a risk. In *R v G and R* it was held that this was the wrong test to use. The Law Lord overruled *Caldwell* and held that a defendant is only reckless if he realised there is risk and goes ahead and takes that risk.

5.3.4 The Supreme Court

With the changeover from the House of Lords to the Supreme Court in October 2009, the Practice Statement does not, strictly speaking, apply to the Supreme Court. However, the Practice Rules of the Supreme Court state that 'If an application for permission to appeal asks the Supreme Court to depart from one of its own decisions or from one of the House of Lords' this should be stated clearly in the application and full details must be given.

This suggests that the Supreme Court will operate a similar system as that under the Practice Statement.

5.4 The Court of Appeal

As already stated there are two divisions of this court, the Civil Division and the Criminal Division, and the rules for precedent are not quite the same in these two divisions.

5.4.1 Decisions of courts above the Court of Appeal

Both divisions of the Court of Appeal are bound by decisions of the European Court of Justice and the House of Lords (now the Supreme Court). This is true even though there were attempts in the past, mainly by Lord Denning, to argue that the Court of Appeal should not be bound by the House of Lords. In *Broome v Cassell & Co. Ltd* (1971) Lord Denning refused to follow an earlier decision of the House of Lords in *Rookes v Barnard* (1964) on the circumstances in which exemplary damages could be awarded.

Key facts

General rules	Comment
Bound by European Court of Justice	Since 1972 all courts in England and Wales are bound by the European Court of Justice.
Bound by Supreme Court/ House of Lords	This is because the House of Lords (now the Supreme Court) is above the Court of Appeal in the court hierarchy. Also necessary for certainty in the law. Court of Appeal tried to challenge this rule in *Broome v Cassell* (1971) and also in *Miliangos* (1976). The House of Lords rejected this challenge. The Court of Appeal must follow decisions of the Supreme Court/House of Lords.
Bound by its own past decisions	Decided by the Court of Appeal in *Young's* case (1944), though there are minor exceptions (see below). In *Davis v Johnson* (1979) the Court of Appeal tried to challenge this rule but the House of Lords confirmed that the Court of Appeal had to follow its own previous decisions.
Exceptions	**Comment**
Exceptions in *Young's* case	Court of Appeal need not follow its own previous decisions where: <ul><li>there are conflicting past decisions</li><li>there is a House of Lords'/Supreme Court decision which effectively overrules the Court of Appeal decision</li><li>the decision was made *per incuriam* (in error)</li></ul>
Limitation of *per incuriam*	Only used in 'rare and exceptional cases'.
Special exception for the	If the law has been 'misapplied or misunderstood' (*R v Gould* (1968)).

Figure 5.4 Key facts chart for the Court of Appeal and the doctrine of precedent

Again in the cases of *Schorsch Meier GmbH v Henning* (1975) and *Miliangos v George Frank (Textiles) Ltd* (1976) the Court of Appeal under Lord Denning's leadership refused to follow a decision of the House of Lords in *Havana Railways* (1961) which said that damages could only be awarded in sterling (English money). Lord Denning's argument for refusing to follow the House of Lords' decision was that the economic climate of the world had changed, and sterling was no longer a stable currency; there were some situations in which justice could only be done by awarding damages in another currency. The case of *Schorsch Meier GmbH v Henning* did not get appealed to the House of Lords, but *Miliangos v George Frank (Textiles) Ltd*

did go on appeal to the Lords where it was pointed out that the Court of Appeal had no right to ignore or overrule decisions of the House of Lords. The more unusual feature of *Miliangos* was that the House of Lords then used the Practice Statement to overrule their own decision in *Havana Railways*.

5.4.2 The Court of Appeal and its own decisions

The first rule is that decisions by one division of the Court of Appeal will not bind the other division. However, within each division, decisions are normally binding, especially for the Civil Division. This rule comes from the case of *Young v*

Activity

Read the following comments by Lord Scarman in his judgment in *Tiverton Estates Ltd v Wearwell Ltd* (1975) and answer the questions below.

'The Court of Appeal occupies a central, but intermediate position in our legal system. To a large extent, the consistency and certainty of the law depend upon it . . . If, therefore, one division of the court should refuse to follow another because it believed the other's decision to be wrong, there would be a risk of confusion and doubt arising where there should be consistency and certainty.

The appropriate forum for the correction of the Court of Appeal's errors is the House of Lords, where the decision will at least have the merit of being final and binding, subject only to the House's power to review its own decisions. The House of Lords as the court of last resort needs this power of review; it does not follow that an intermediate court needs it.'

Questions

1. Why did Lord Scarman describe the Court of Appeal as occupying 'a central but intermediate position'?

2. Do you agree with his view that there would be a 'risk of confusion and doubt' if the Court of Appeal was not obliged to follow its own past decisions?

3. Describe the situations in which the Court of Appeal may refuse to follow its own past decisions.

4. Why does the House of Lords (now the Supreme Court) need the power of review?

Bristol Aeroplane Co. Ltd (1944) and the only exceptions allowed by that case are:

- where there are conflicting decisions in past Court of Appeal cases, the court can choose which one it will follow and which it will reject;
- where there is a decision of the Supreme Court/House of Lords which effectively overrules a Court of Appeal decision the Court of Appeal must follow the decision of the Supreme Court/House of Lords;
- where the decision was made *per incuriam*, that is carelessly or by mistake because a relevant Act of Parliament or other regulation has not been considered by the court.

The rule in *Young's case* was confirmed in *Davis v Johnson* (1979). In this case the Court of Appeal refused to follow a decision made only days earlier regarding the interpretation of the Domestic Violence and Matrimonial Proceedings Act 1976. The case went to the House of Lords on appeal, where the Law Lords, despite agreeing with the actual interpretation of the law, ruled that the Court of Appeal had to follow its own previous decisions and said that they 'expressly, unequivocally and unanimously reaffirmed the rule in *Young v Bristol Aeroplane*'.

Since this case the Court of Appeal has not challenged the rule in *Young's case,* though it has made some use of the *per incuriam* exception allowed by *Young's case*. For example in *Williams v Fawcett* (1986) the Court refused to follow previous decisions because these had been based on a misunderstanding of the County Court rules dealing with procedure for committing to prison those who break court undertakings.

In *Rickards v Rickards* (1989) Lord Donaldson said that it would only be in 'rare and exceptional cases' that the Court of Appeal would be justified in refusing to follow a previous decision. *Rickards v Rickards* was considered a 'rare and exceptional

case' because the mistake was over the critical point of whether the court had the power to hear that particular type of case. Also it was very unlikely that the case would be appealed to the House of Lords.

5.4.3 The Court of Appeal (Criminal Division)

The Criminal Division, as well as using the exceptions from *Young's case*, can also refuse to follow a past decision of its own if the law has been 'misapplied or misunderstood'. This extra exception arises because in criminal cases people's liberty is involved. This idea was recognised in *R v Taylor* (1950). The same point was made in *R v Gould* (1968).

Also in *R v Spencer* (1985) the judges said that there should not in general be any difference in the way that precedent was followed in the Criminal Division and in the Civil Division, 'save that we must remember that we may be dealing with the liberty of the subject and if a departure from authority is necessary in the interests of justice to an appellant, then this court should not shrink from so acting'.

5.5 Distinguishing, overruling, disapproving and reversing

5.5.1 Distinguishing

This is a method which can be used by a judge to avoid following a past decision which he would otherwise have to follow. It means that the judge finds that the material facts of the case he is deciding are sufficiently different for him to draw a distinction between the present case and the previous precedent. He is not then bound by the previous case.

Two cases demonstrating this process are *Balfour v Balfour* (1919) and *Merritt v Merritt* (1971). Both cases involved a wife making a claim against her husband for breach of contract. In *Balfour* it was decided that the claim could not

Comment

The main argument in favour of the Court of Appeal being able to ignore House of Lords' (now the Supreme Court) decisions is that very few cases reach the Supreme Court, so that if there is an error in the law it may take years before a suitable case is appealed all the way to the Supreme Court.

The cases of *Schorsch Meier* and *Miliangos* illustrate the potential for injustice if there is no appeal to the Supreme Court. What would have happened if the Court of Appeal in *Schorsch Meier* had decided that it had to follow the House of Lords' decision in *Havana Railways*? It is quite possible that the later case of *Miliangos* would not have even been appealed to the Court of Appeal. After all, why waste money on an appeal when there have been previous cases in both the Court of Appeal and the House of Lords ruling on that point of law. The law would have been regarded as fixed and it might never have been changed.

On the other hand, if the Court of Appeal could overrule the Supreme Court, the system of precedent would break down and the law would become uncertain. There would be two conflicting precedents for lower courts to choose from. This would make it difficult for the judge in the lower court. It would also make the law so uncertain that it would be difficult for lawyers to advise clients on the law. However, since the case of *Miliangos*, there has been no further challenge by the Court of Appeal to this basic idea in our system of judicial precedent that lower courts must follow decisions of courts above them in the hierarchy.

succeed because there was no intention to create legal relations; there was merely a domestic arrangement between a husband and wife and so there was no legally binding contract. The second case was successful because the court held that the facts of the two cases were sufficiently different in that, although the parties were husband and wife, the agreement was made after they had separated. Furthermore the agreement was made in writing. This distinguished the case from *Balfour*; the agreement in *Merritt* was not just a domestic arrangement but meant as a legally enforceable contract.

5.5.2 Overruling

This is where a court in a later case states that the legal rule decided in an earlier case is wrong.

Overruling may occur when a higher court overrules a decision made in an earlier case by a lower court, for example the Supreme Court overruling a decision of the Court of Appeal. It can also occur where the European Court of Justice overrules a past decision it has made; or when the Supreme Court uses its power under the Practice Statement to overrule a past decision of its own.

5.5.3 Disapproving

This is where a judge states in his judgment that he believes the decision in an earlier case is wrong. This may occur where the present case is on a related point of law, but the point of law is not sufficiently similar for the earlier decision to be overruled. It can also occur where the judge is

	Key facts		
Concept	**Definition**		**Comment**
stare decisis	Stand by what has been decided		Follow the law decided in previous cases for certainty and fairness
ratio decidendi	Reason for deciding		The part of the judgment which creates the law
obiter dicta	Other things said		The other parts of the judgment – these do not create law
binding precedent	A previous decision which has to be followed		Decisions of higher courts bind lower courts
persuasive precedent	A previous decision which does not have to be followed		The court may be 'persuaded' that the same legal decision should be made
original precedent	A decision in a case where there is no previous legal decision or law for the judge to use		This leads to judges 'making' law
Distinguishing	A method of avoiding a previous decision because facts in the present case are different		e.g. *Balfour v Balfour* not followed in *Merritt v Merritt*
Overruling	A decision which states that a legal rule in an earlier case is wrong		e.g. in *Pepper v Hart* the House of Lords overruled *Davis v Johnson* on the use of *Hansard*
Reversing	Where a higher court in the same case overturns the decision of the lower court		This can only happen if there is an appeal in the case

Figure 5.5 Key facts chart for the basic concepts of judicial precedent

in a court lower in the hierarchy than the court which made the original decision. In this situation the lower cannot overrule the higher court, but they can disapprove of the decision by expressing their view that it was wrong.

An example where the court disapproved of an earlier case occurred in *R v Hasan* (2005). This case was about the availability of the defence of duress by threats to a criminal offence. The main point of the case was on whether a defendant could use the defence of duress if he ought to have realised that he was putting himself in a position where he might be pressurised into committing an offence.

However, the House of Lords also commented on whether the threats had to be immediate or whether the fact that they could be carried out in the future was enough. When discussing this they disapproved of the earlier case of *R v Hudson and Taylor* (1971). In *R v Hudson and Taylor* two girls committed perjury (lied when giving evidence in court) because they had been threatened that they would be 'cut up' if they gave evidence against a particular man. While they were giving evidence the man who had threatened them was watching in the public gallery. Obviously he could not carry out his threat at that moment. The Court of Appeal held that the defence of duress was available even though the threats were not 'immediate'. The disapproval of the House of Lords does not change the precedent set by *R v Hudson and Taylor*. However, it is possible that if the same point has to be decided again in the future, the disapproving judgment by the House of Lords in *R v Hasan* might lead to the precedent in *R v Hudson and Taylor* being overruled.

5.5.4 Reversing

This is where a court higher up in the hierarchy overturns the decision of a lower court on appeal in the same case. For example, the Court of Appeal may disagree with the legal ruling of the High Court and come to a different view of the law; in this situation they reverse the decision made by the High Court.

5.6 Precedent and Acts of Parliament

Precedent is subordinate to statute law, delegated legislation and European regulations. This means that if, for example, an Act of Parliament is passed, and that Act contains a provision which contradicts a previously decided case, that case decision will cease to have effect; the Act of Parliament is now the law on that point. This happened when Parliament passed the Law Reform (Year and a Day Rule) Act in 1996. Up to then judicial decisions meant that a person could only be charged with murder or manslaughter if the victim died within a year and a day of receiving his injuries. The Act enacted that there was no time limit, and a person could be guilty even if the victim died several years later, so cases after 1996 follow the Act and not the old judicial decisions.

5.7 Advantages of precedent

As can be seen from the previous sections there are both advantages and disadvantages to the way in which judicial precedent operates in England and Wales. In fact it could be said that every advantage has a corresponding disadvantage. The main advantages are:

1. **Certainty**
   Because the courts follow past decisions people know what the law is and how it is likely to be applied in their case; it allows lawyers to advise clients on the likely outcome of cases; it also allows people to operate their businesses knowing that financial and other arrangements they make are recognised by law. The House of Lords Practice Statement points out how important certainty is.
2. **Consistency and fairness in the law**
   It is seen as just and fair that similar cases should be decided in a similar way, just as in any sport it is seen as fair that the rules of the game apply equally to each side. The law must be consistent if it is to be credible.

3. **Precision**

As the principles of law are set out in actual cases the law becomes very precise; it is well illustrated and gradually builds up through the different variations of facts in the cases that come before the courts.

4. **Flexibility**

There is room for the law to change as the House of Lords/Supreme Court can use the Practice Statement to overrule cases. The use of distinguishing also gives all courts some freedom to avoid decisions and develop the law.

5. **Time-saving**

Precedent can be considered a useful time-saving device. Where a principle has been established, cases with similar facts are unlikely to go through the lengthy process of litigation.

5.8 Disadvantages of precedent

1. **Rigidity**

The fact that lower courts have to follow decisions of higher courts together with the fact that the Court of Appeal has to follow its own past decisions can make the law too inflexible so that bad decisions made in the past may be perpetuated. There is the added problem that so few cases go to the Supreme Court. Change in the law will only take place if parties have the courage, the persistence and the money to appeal their case.

2. **Complexity**

Since there are nearly half a million reported cases it is not easy to find all the relevant case law even with computerised databases. Another problem is in the judgments themselves, which are often very long with no clear distinction between comments and the reasons for the decision. This makes it difficult in some cases to extract the *ratio decidendi*; indeed in *Dodd's Case* (1973) the judges in the Court of Appeal said they were unable to find the *ratio* in a decision of the House of Lords.

3. **Illogical distinctions**

The use of distinguishing to avoid past decisions can lead to 'hair-splitting' so that some areas of the law have become very complex. The differences between some cases may be very small and appear illogical.

4. **Slowness of growth**

Judges are well aware that some areas of the law are unclear or in need of reform, however they cannot make a decision unless there is a case before the courts to be decided. This is one of the criticisms of the need for the Court of Appeal to follow its own previous decisions, as only about 50 cases go to the Supreme Court each year. There may be a long wait for a suitable case to be appealed as far as the Supreme Court.

Test Yourself

1. When was the Practice Statement issued?
2. To which court did the Practice Statement apply?
3. Why was the Practice Statement made?
4. The Court of Appeal has to follow decisions of court(s) above it in the hierarchy. Which court(s) are these?
5. Why has the Court of Appeal in the past thought that it should be able to ignore precedents of courts above it?
6. What rules did *Young's* case set out for the Court of Appeal in relation to past decisions of its own?
7. What is meant by 'distinguishing'?
8. What is meant by 'overruling'?
9. Give three advantages of using judicial precedent.
10. Give three disadvantages of using judicial precedent.

5.9 Law reporting

In order to follow past decisions there must be an accurate record of what those decisions were. Written reports have existed in England and Wales since the thirteenth century, but many of the early reports were very brief and, it is thought, not always accurate. The earliest reports from about 1275 to 1535 were called Year Books, and contained short reports of cases, usually written in French. From 1535 to 1865 cases were reported by individuals who made a business out of selling the reports to lawyers. The detail and accuracy of these reports varied enormously. However, some are still occasionally used today.

In 1865 the Incorporated Council of Law Reporting was set up. This was controlled by the courts. Reports became accurate, with the judgment usually noted down word for word. This accuracy of reports was one of the factors in the development of the strict doctrine of precedent. These reports still exist and are published according to the court that the case took place in. For example, case references abbreviated to Ch stand for Chancery and the case will have been decided in the Chancery Division; while QB stands for Queen's Bench Division.

There are also other well established reports today, notably the All England series (abbreviated to All ER) and the Weekly Law Reports (WLR). Newspapers and journals also publish law reports, but these are often abbreviated versions in which the law reporter has tried to pick out the essential parts of the judgment.

Internet reports

All High Court, Court of Appeal, Supreme Court (and House of Lords for 1996–2009) cases are now reported on the Internet. Some websites give the full report free; others give summaries or an index of cases. There are also subscription sites which contain virtually all the cases. The main ones of these are LexisNexis and Westlaw.

@ Internet Research

Search at least one website and find a recent law report. If your school or college does not have access to subscription sites try the following free sites:

www.lawreports.co.uk – the Daily Notes section of this site gives summaries of recent important cases

www.supremecourt.gov.uk – this has reports of Supreme Court judgments

www.parliament.uk – this has reports of the House of Lords judgments for 1996 to 2009

www.bailii.org – this has cases for the High Court and the Court of Appeal.

Examination questions

(a) Outline the key features of the doctrine of judicial precedent. (10 marks)

(b) Describe any two ways in which judges can avoid following an earlier precedent (10 marks)

(c) Discuss the disadvantages of the doctrine of judicial precedent. (10 marks)

AQA LAW01 January 2009

Examiner's tip

Judicial precedent is a topic where it is essential to use real case examples in order to reach the top mark bands. The whole of precedent is based on real cases.

Chapter 6

Civil Courts

As already stressed in Chapter 1 it is important to understand the differences between civil cases and criminal cases. Since civil cases cover a wide range there cannot be a very specific definition which will cover all of them, but a basic definition for civil claims is to say that these arise when an individual or a business believes that their rights have been infringed in some way. Some of the main areas of civil law are contract law, law of tort, family law, employment law and company law.

As well as dealing with different areas of law, the types of dispute that can arise within these areas are equally varied. A company may be claiming that money is owed to them (contract law); this type of claim may be for a few pounds or for several million. An individual may be claiming compensation for injuries suffered in an accident (the tort of negligence), while in another tort case the claim might not be for money but for another remedy such as an injunction to prevent someone from building on disputed land. Other types of court orders include the winding up of a company which cannot pay its debts or a decree of divorce for a marriage that has failed. The list is almost endless.

The two courts in which civil cases are tried are:

- the County Court;
- the High Court.

The types of cases they deal with are explained below. There is also material on civil courts and the procedure in civil cases in the section of this book that covers Unit 2. This is at section 18.4 in the chapter on tort and section 19.7 in the chapter on contract.

The Royal Courts of Justice

6.1 County Court

There are about 230 County Courts, so that most major towns will have a court. The County Court can try nearly all civil cases. The main areas of jurisdiction are:

- small claims, that is a claim for less than £5,000;
- fast-track cases between £5,000 and £25,000;
- multi-track cases for over £25,000 can also be dealt with;
- all contract and tort claims;
- all cases for the recovery of land;
- disputes over partnerships, trusts and inheritance up to a value of £30,000.

Cases in the County Court are heard by a circuit judge or a district judge. On very rare occasions it is possible for the judge to sit with a jury of eight. This will only happen for defamation cases or the torts of malicious prosecution or false imprisonment.

6.2 High Court

The High Court is based in London but also has judges sitting at 26 towns and cities throughout England and Wales. It has the power to hear any civil case and has three divisions, each of which specialises in hearing certain types of case. These divisions are the Queen's Bench Division, the Chancery Division and the Family Division.

6.2.1 Queen's Bench Division

There are nearly 70 High Court judges sitting in this division. It deals with contract and tort cases usually where the amount claimed is over £50,000. However, it is possible for a claimant to start an action for any amount over £25,000.

Cases are normally tried by a single judge, but there is a right to jury trial for fraud, libel, slander, malicious prosecution and false imprisonment cases. When a jury is used there will be 12 members.

6.2.2 Chancery Division

There are about 18 High Court judges sitting to hear cases in this division. The main business of this division involves disputes concerned with such matters as:

- insolvency, both for companies and individuals;

- the enforcement of mortgages;
- disputes relating to trust property;
- copyright and patents;
- intellectual property matters;
- contested probate actions.

There is also a special Companies Court in the division which deals mainly with winding up companies.

Cases are heard by a single judge. Juries are never used in the Chancery Division.

6.2.3 Family Division

There are 18 High Court judges sitting to hear cases in this division. It has jurisdiction to hear wardship cases and all cases relating to children under the Children Act 1989. It also deals with other matters regarding the family such as declarations for nullity of marriage. It also grants probate in non-disputed probate cases.

Cases are heard by a single judge and, although juries were once used to decide defended divorce cases, juries are not now used in this division.

6.3 Appeal routes in civil cases

Once a decision has been made in either the County Court or the High Court, there is always the possibility of appealing against that decision. There are different appeal routes from the County Court and the High Court. In addition, the value of the claim and the level of judge who heard the case affect which appeal route should be used.

6.3.1 Appeals from the County Court

For all claims of under £25,000 (this includes both small claims cases and what are known as fast track cases) the appeal route depends on the level of judge hearing the case. This means that:

- if the case was heard by a district judge, then the appeal is to a circuit judge in the same County Court
- if the case was heard by a circuit judge, then the appeal is to a High Court judge.

Second appeals

There is the possibility of a second or further appeal. This appeal will always be to the Court of Appeal (Civil Division). However, such further appeals are only allowed in exceptional cases as set out in s 55 of the Access to Justice Act 1999 which states:

> no appeal may be made to the Court of Appeal … unless the Court of Appeal considers that—
>
> (a) the appeal would raise an important point of principle or practice, or
>
> (b) there is some other compelling reason for the Court of Appeal to hear it.

For claims over £25,000 which have been dealt with as multi-track cases the appeal route is always to the Court of Appeal (Civil Division) with a further appeal to the Supreme Court.

These appeal routes are shown in Figure 6.1.

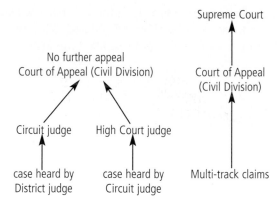

Figure 6.1 Appeal routes from the County Court

6.3.2 Appeals from the High Court

From a decision in the High Court the appeal usually goes to the Court of Appeal (Civil Division).

In rare cases there may be a 'leap-frog' appeal direct to the Supreme Court under the Administration of Justice Act 1969. Such an appeal must involve a point of law of general public importance which is either concerned with the interpretation of a statute or where there is a binding precedent of the Court of Appeal or the Supreme Court or of a previous decision of the House of Lords which the trial judge must follow. In addition the Supreme Court has to give permission to appeal.

Further appeals

From a decision of the Court of Appeal there is a further appeal to the Supreme Court but only if the Supreme Court or Court of Appeal give permission to appeal.

These appeal routes are shown in Figure 6.2.

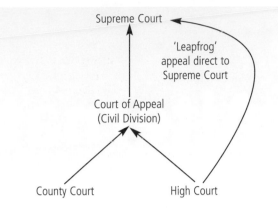

Figure 6.2 Appeal routes from the High Court

Also note that if a point of European law is involved the case may be referred to the European Court of Justice under Article 267 of the Treaty of Rome. Such a referral can be made by any English court.

Test Yourself

1. Name two types of case that the County Court can hear.
2. What types of judges sit in the County Court?
3. What are the three divisions of the High Court?
4. In which division of the High Court is it possible for a jury to try certain types of cases?
5. Where are appeals from decisions in the County Court dealt with?
6. After the first appeal, there is the possibility of a second appeal in exceptional cases. Which court would hear this second appeal?
7. Where are appeals from decisions in the High Court dealt with?
8. After the first appeal, there is the possibility of a second appeal. To which court is this made?
9. What is a leap frog appeal?
10. When may a case be referred to the European Court of Justice?

Chapter 7

Alternative Methods of Dispute Resolution

In Chapter 6 we looked at courts which hear civil cases. Using the courts to resolve disputes can be costly, in terms of both money and time. It can also be traumatic for the individuals involved and may not lead to the most satisfactory outcome for the case. An additional problem is that court proceedings are usually open to the public and the press, so there is nothing to stop the details of the case being published in local or national newspapers. It is not surprising, therefore, that more and more people and businesses are seeking other methods of resolving their disputes. Alternative methods are referred to as 'ADR', which stands for 'Alternative Dispute Resolution', and includes any method of resolving a dispute without resorting to using the courts. There are many different methods which can be used, ranging from very informal negotiations between the parties, to a comparatively formal commercial arbitration hearing.

7.1 Negotiation

Anyone who has a dispute with another person can always try to resolve it by negotiating directly with them. This has the advantage of being completely private, and is also the quickest and cheapest method of settling a dispute. If the parties cannot come to an agreement, they may decide to take the step of instructing solicitors, and those solicitors will usually try to negotiate a settlement.

In fact, even when court proceedings have been commenced, the lawyers for the parties will often continue to negotiate on behalf of their clients, and this is reflected in the high number of cases which are settled out of court. Once lawyers are involved, there will be a cost element – clearly, the longer negotiations go on, the higher the costs will be. One of the worrying aspects is the number of cases that drag on for years, only to end in an agreed settlement literally 'at the door of the court' on the morning that the trial is due to start. It is this situation that other alternative dispute resolution methods and, in particular, the Woolf reforms try to avoid.

ARE YOU SURE THIS IS A FORM OF ALTERNATIVE DISPUTE RESOLUTION?

7.2 Mediation

This is where a neutral mediator helps the parties to reach a compromise solution. The role of a mediator is to consult with each party and see how much common ground there is between them. He/she will explore the position with each party, looking at their needs and carrying offers to and fro, while keeping confidentiality. A mediator will not usually tell the parties his/her own views of the merits of the dispute; it is part of the job to act as a 'facilitator', so that an agreement is reached by the parties. However, a mediator can be asked for an opinion of the merits, and in this case the mediation becomes more of an evaluation exercise, which again aims at ending the dispute.

Mediation is only suitable if there is some hope that the parties can co-operate. Companies who are used to negotiating contracts with each other are most likely to benefit from this approach. Mediation can also take different forms, and the parties will choose the exact method they want. The important point in mediation is that the parties are in control: they make the decisions.

7.2.1 Formalised settlement conference

This is a more formal method of approaching mediation. It involves a 'mini-trial' where each side presents its case to a panel composed of a decision-making executive from each party, and a neutral party. Once all the submissions have been made, the executives, with the help of the neutral adviser, will evaluate the two sides' positions and try to come to an agreement. If the executives cannot agree the neutral adviser will act as a mediator between them. Even if the whole matter is not resolved, this type of procedure may be able to narrow down the issues so that if the case does go to court, it will not take so long.

An advantage of mediation and mini-trials is that the decision need not be a strictly legal one sticking to the letter of the law. It is more likely to be based on commercial commonsense and compromise. The method will also make it easier for companies to continue to do business with each other in the future, and it may include agreements about the conduct of future business between the parties. This is something that cannot happen if the court gives judgment, as the court is only concerned with the present dispute. It avoids the adversarial conflict of the court room and the winner/loser result of court proceedings – it has been said that with mediation, everyone wins.

7.2.2 Mediation services

There are a growing number of commercial mediation services. One of the main ones is the Centre for Dispute Resolution which was set up in London in 1991. It has many important companies as members including almost all of the big London law firms. Businesses say that using the Centre to resolve disputes has saved several thousands of pounds in court costs. The typical cost of a mediator is about £1,000 to £1,500 a day. This compares with potential litigation costs which are frequently over £100,000 and sometimes may even come to more than one million pounds, especially in major commercial cases.

The main disadvantage of using mediation services is that there is no guarantee the matter will be resolved, and it will then be necessary to go to court after the failed attempt at mediation. In such situations there is additional cost and delay through trying mediation. However the evidence is that a high number of cases will be resolved; the Centre for Dispute Resolution claims that over 80 per cent of cases in which it is asked to act are settled. There is also the possibility that the issues may at least have been clarified, and so any court hearing will be shorter than if mediation had not been attempted.

There are also mediation services aimed at resolving smaller disputes, for example, those between neighbours. An example of such a service is the West Kent Independent Mediation Service. This offers a free service that will try to help resolve disagreements between neighbours arising from such matters as noise, car-parking, dogs or boundary fence disputes. The Service is run by trained volunteers who will not take sides or make judgements on the rights and wrongs of an issue. They will usually visit the party who has made the complaint to hear their side of the matter, then, if that party agrees, ask to visit the other person and get their point of view. Finally, if both parties are willing, the mediator arranges a meeting between them in a neutral place. The parties are in control and can withdraw from the mediation process at any time.

The latest idea is Online Dispute Resolution. There are an increasing number of websites offering this, e.g. www.theclaimroom.com and www.mediate.com/odr.

7.3 Conciliation

This has similarities to mediation in that a neutral third party helps to resolve the dispute, but the main difference is that the conciliator will usually

Negotiation	Parties themselves
Mediation	Parties with help of neutral third party
Conciliation	Parties with help of neutral third party who plays an active role in suggesting a solution
Arbitration	Parties agree to let third party make a binding decision
Litigation	Parties go to court and a judge decides the case

Figure 7.1 Methods of dispute resolution

Arbitration

24. If any difference shall arise between the PROPRIETOR and the PUBLISHERS touching the meaning of this Agreement or the rights and liabilities of the parties hereto, the same shall in the first instance be referred to the informal Disputes Settlement Scheme of the Publishers' Association, and failing agreed submission by both parties to such Scheme shall be referred to the arbitration of two persons (one to be named by each party) or their mutually agreed umpire in accordance with the provisions of the Arbitration Act 1996, or any amending or substituted statute for the time being in force.

Figure 7.2 Arbitration clause from author's contract

play a more active role. He will be expected to suggest grounds for compromise, and the possible basis for a settlement. In industrial disputes ACAS can give an impartial opinion on the legal position. As with mediation, conciliation does not necessarily lead to a resolution and it may be necessary to continue with a court action.

7.4 Arbitration

The word 'arbitration' is used to cover two quite different processes. The first is where the courts use a more informal procedure to hear cases; this is the way proceedings in the Commercial Court of the Queen's Bench Division are described. The second meaning of the word 'arbitration' is where the parties agree to submit their claims to private arbitration; this is the type of arbitration that is relevant to alternative dispute resolution, as it is another way of resolving a dispute without the need for a court case.

Private arbitration is now governed by the Arbitration Act 1996 and section 1 of that Act sets out the principles behind it. This says that:

" (a) the object of arbitration is to obtain the fair resolution of disputes by an impartial tribunal without unnecessary delay or expense;

(b) the parties should be free to agree how their disputes are resolved, subject only to such safeguards as are necessary in the public interest. **"**

So arbitration is the voluntary submission by the parties, of their dispute, to the judgment of some person other than a judge. Such an agreement will usually be in writing, and indeed the Arbitration Act 1996 applies only to written arbitration agreements. The precise way in which the arbitration is carried out is left almost entirely to the parties' agreement.

7.4.1 The agreement to arbitrate

The agreement to go to arbitration can be made by the parties at any time. It can be before a dispute arises or when the dispute becomes apparent. Many commercial contracts include what is called a *Scott v Avery* clause, which is a clause where the parties in their original contract agree that in the event of a dispute arising between them, they will have that dispute settled by arbitration. Figure 7.2 shows a *Scott v Avery* clause in the author's contract for writing this book.

Where there is an arbitration agreement in a contract, the Arbitration Act 1996 states that the court will normally refuse to deal with any dispute; the matter must go to arbitration as agreed by the parties. The rules, however, are different for consumer claims where the dispute is for an amount which can be dealt with in the small claims track. In such circumstances the consumer may choose whether to abide by the agreement to go to private arbitration, or whether to insist that the case be heard in the small claims track.

An agreement to go to arbitration can also be made after the dispute arises. Arbitration is becoming increasingly popular in commercial cases.

7.4.2 The arbitrator

Section 15 of the Arbitration Act 1996 states that the parties are free to agree on the number of arbitrators, so that a panel of two or three may be used or there may be a sole arbitrator. If the parties cannot agree on a number then the Act provides that only one arbitrator should be appointed. The Act also says that the parties are free to agree on the procedure for appointing an arbitrator.

In fact most agreements to go to arbitration will either name an arbitrator or provide a method of choosing one. In commercial contracts it is often provided that the president of the appropriate trade organisation will appoint the arbitrator.

There is also the Institute of Arbitrators which provides trained arbitrators for major disputes. In many cases the arbitrator will be someone who has expertise in the particular field involved in the dispute, but if the dispute involves a point of law the parties may decide to appoint a lawyer. If there is no agreement on who or how to appoint, then, as a last resort, the court can be asked to appoint an appropriate arbitrator.

7.4.3 The arbitration hearing

The actual procedure is left to the agreement of the parties in each case, so that there are many forms of hearing. In some cases the parties may opt for a 'paper' arbitration, where the two sides put all the points they wish to raise into writing and submit this, together with any relevant documents, to the arbitrator. He will then read all the documents, and make his decision.

Alternatively, the parties may send all these documents to the arbitrator, but before he makes his decision both parties will attend a hearing at which they make oral submissions to the arbitrator to support their case. Where necessary

witnesses can be called to give evidence. If witnesses are asked to give evidence orally then this will not normally be given on oath, i.e. the person will not have to swear to tell the truth. However, if the parties wish, then the witness can be asked to give evidence on oath and the whole procedure will be very formal. If witnesses are called to give evidence, the Arbitration Act 1996 allows for the use of court procedures to ensure the attendance of those witnesses.

The date, time and place of the arbitration hearing are all matters for the parties to decide in consultation with the arbitrator. This gives a great degree of flexibility to the proceedings; the parties can choose what is most convenient for all the people concerned.

7.4.4 The award

The decision made by the arbitrator is called an award and is binding on the parties. It can even be enforced through the courts if necessary. The decision is usually final, though it can be challenged in the courts on the grounds of serious irregularity in the proceedings or on a point of law (s 68 Arbitration Act 1996).

7.4.5 Advantages of arbitration

There are several advantages which largely arise from the fact that the parties have the freedom to make their own arbitration agreement, and decide exactly how formal or informal they wish it to be. The main advantages are:

- The parties may choose their own arbitrator, and can therefore decide whether the matter is best dealt with by a technical expert or by a lawyer or by a professional arbitrator;
- If there is a question of quality this can be decided by an expert in the particular field, saving the expense of calling expert witnesses and the time that would be used in explaining all the technicalities to a judge;
- The hearing time and place can be arranged to suit the parties;
- The actual procedure used is flexible and the parties can choose that which is most suited

to the situation; this will usually result in a more informal and relaxed hearing than in court;

- The matter is dealt with in private and there will be no publicity;
- The dispute will be resolved more quickly than through a court hearing;
- Arbitration proceedings are usually much cheaper than going to court;
- The award is normally final and can be enforced through the courts.

7.4.6 Disadvantages of arbitration

However, there are some disadvantages of arbitration, especially where the parties are not on an equal footing as regards their ability to present their case. This is because legal funding is not available for arbitration and this may disadvantage an individual in a case against a business; if the case had gone to court, a person on a low income would have qualified for legal funding and so had the benefit of a lawyer to present their case. The other main disadvantages are that:

- An unexpected legal point may arise in the case which is not suitable for decision by a non-lawyer arbitrator;
- If a professional arbitrator is used, his fees may be expensive;
- It will also be expensive if the parties opt for a formal hearing, with witnesses giving evidence and lawyers representing both sides;
- The rights of appeal are limited;
- The delays for commercial and international arbitration may be nearly as great as those in the courts if a professional arbitrator and lawyers are used.

This problem of delay and expense has meant that arbitration has, to some extent, lost its popularity with companies as a method of dispute resolution. More and more businesses are turning to the alternatives offered by centres such as the Centre for Dispute Resolution or, in the case of international disputes, are choosing to have the matter resolved in another country.

Arbitration in consumer disputes

Arbitration is also offered as an option in consumer disputes, such as those arising from package holidays (see Figure 7.3). This gives the possibility of resolving a dispute by arbitration, but not as a binding agreement to go to arbitration. This optional use of arbitration in consumer disputes is a welcome move away from the previous practice of including an arbitration clause in consumer contracts so that the consumer had no choice. In other words if the consumer wanted to go ahead with the main contract, such as booking a package holiday, then they had to accept that any dispute would be dealt with by arbitration, whether they really

Activity

Find an arbitration clause in a consumer contract, for example, for a package holiday or insurance or for a mobile phone.

D Complaints

3. Disputes arising out of, or in connection with, this contract which cannot be amicably settled may (if you so wish) be referred to arbitration under a special scheme devised by arrangement with the Association of British Travel Agents (ABTA) but administered independently by the Chartered Institute of Arbitrators. The scheme provides for a simple and inexpensive method of Arbitration on documents alone, with restricted liability on you in respect of costs. The scheme does not apply to claims greater than £1500 per person or £7500 per booking form or to claims which are solely or mainly in respect of physical injury or illness or the consequences of such injury or illness. If you elect to use the scheme, written notice requesting arbitration must be made within 9 months after the scheduled date of return from holiday.

Figure 7.3 Optional arbitration clause in a consumer contract

Method of dispute resolution	Who makes the decision	Advantages	Disadvantages
Negotiation	The parties themselves	Quick, no cost, parties in control	None
Mediation/Conciliation	The parties with the help of a mediator	Cheaper than courts Parties agree to outcome	Not binding May not lead to settlement
Arbitration	The arbitrator	Cheaper than courts but more expensive than mediation Binding	Can be formal Arbitrator's fee may be high Not suitable if dispute is on a point of law
Litigation in the courts	A judge	Decision is final and binding	Expensive Lengthy Formal Adversarial Public hearing

Figure 7.4 Comparing different methods of dispute resolution

wanted this or not. Of course, in most cases, the consumer would probably be unaware of the clause or its implications until they tried to take legal action against the company.

7.5 Comparing courts and ADR

Methods of ADR are usually much cheaper than going to court. For ADR it is unlikely that the parties will use a lawyer, so this also saves costs. The most expensive is arbitration where lawyers are sometimes used, but, even so, it is cheaper than a court case. All methods of ADR are also much quicker than going to court.

Another advantage of most forms of ADR is that the parties are in control. In negotiation, mediation and conciliation sessions, the parties can choose to stop at any time. An agreement will only be reached if both sides accept it. The fact that the parties come to an agreement has another

Test Yourself

1. Why is an alternative form of dispute resolution often preferred to going to court?
2. Explain what is meant by negotiation.
3. Name one advantage and one disadvantage of negotiation.
4. What is the role of a mediator?
5. Give an example of a mediation service.
6. Name one advantage and one disadvantage of mediation.
7. What is the role of a conciliator?
8. Name one advantage and one disadvantage of conciliation.
9. Who makes the decision in arbitration?
10. Name one advantage and one disadvantage of arbitration.

advantage; it means they will be able to go on doing business with each other. Court proceedings are more adversarial, and will end with one party winning and one party losing. This is likely to make the parties very bitter about the dispute.

The main points about ADR and going to court have been summarised in Figure 7.4.

7.6 Tribunals

Tribunals operate alongside the court system and have become an important part of the legal system. Many tribunals were created in the second half of the twentieth century, with the development of the welfare state. They were created in order to give people a method of enforcing their entitlement to certain social rights. However, unlike alternative dispute resolution where the parties decide not to use the courts, the parties in tribunal cases cannot go to court to resolve their dispute. The tribunal must be used instead of court proceedings.

7.6.1 Role of tribunals

Tribunals enforce rights which have been granted through social and welfare legislation. There are many different rights, such as:

- the right to a mobility allowance for those who are too disabled to walk more than a very short distance;
- the right to a payment if one is made redundant from work;
- the right not to be discriminated against because of one's sex, race, age or disability;
- the right of immigrants to have a claim for political asylum heard.

These are just a few of the types of rights that tribunals deal with.

7.6.2 Tribunals, Courts and Enforcement Act 2007

Tribunals were set up as the welfare state developed, so new developments resulted in the creation of a new tribunal. This led to more than 70 different types of tribunal. Each tribunal was

separate and the various tribunals used different procedures. This made the system confused and complicated.

The whole system was reformed by the Tribunals, Courts and Enforcement Act 2007. This created a unified structure for tribunals, with a First-tier Tribunal to hear cases at first instance and an Upper Tribunal to hear appeals.

First tier Tribunal

Since the First-tier Tribunal deals with about 300,000 cases each year and has nearly 200 judges and 3,600 lay members, it operates in seven Chambers (divisions). These are:

- Social Entitlement Chamber – this covers a wide range of matters such as Child Support, Criminal Injuries Compensation and Gender Recognition;
- Health, Education and Social Care Chamber – this includes the former Mental Health Review Tribunal which dealt with appeals against the continued detention of those in mental hospitals – this Chamber also deals with Special Educational Needs issues;
- War Pensions and Armed Forces Compensation Chamber;
- General Regulatory Chamber;
- Taxation Chamber;
- Land, Property and Housing Chamber;
- Asylum and Immigration Chamber.

As well as these, there is one tribunal which still operates separately from the First-tier Tribunal. This is the Employment Tribunal. However, it is likely that this will eventually become part of the First-tier Tribunal.

Upper Tribunal

The Upper Tribunal is divided into four Chambers (divisions). These are:

- Administrative Appeals Chamber which hears appeals from Social Entitlement Chamber, Health, Education and Social Care Chamber and War Pensions and Armed Forces Compensation Chamber;

- Tax and Chancery Chamber;
- Lands Chamber;
- Asylum and Immigration Chamber.

From the Upper Tribunal there is a further possible appeal route to the Court of Appeal and from here a final appeal to the Supreme Court.

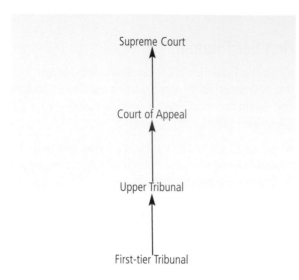

Figure 7.5 Appeal route in tribunal cases

7.6.3 Composition

Cases in the First-tier Tribunal are heard by a tribunal judge. Also, for some types of case, two lay members will sit with the judge to make the decision. These lay members will have expertise in the particular field of the tribunal. For example, the lay members in a hearing about a claim to mobility allowance would be medically qualified, while there would be surveyors sitting on the Lands Tribunal. In Employment Tribunals there are also two lay members. These will usually be one person from an employers' organisation and one from an employees' organisation. This gives them a very clear understanding of employment issues.

7.6.4 Procedure

Both sides must be given an opportunity to put their case. In some tribunals, especially employment and asylum tribunals, this will be done in a formal way with witnesses giving evidence on oath and being cross-examined. Other tribunals will operate in a less formal way.

Funding for representation is only available in a few tribunals, so most applicants will not have a lawyer, but will present their own case. Where an applicant is putting his own case, then the tribunal judge must try to make sure that the applicant puts the case fully.

The decision of the tribunal is binding.

7.6.5 The Administrative Justice and Tribunals Council

This was set up under the Tribunals, Courts and Enforcement Act 2007. It replaced the previous Council on Tribunals which had operated since 1957. Its duties include:

- keeping the working of tribunals under review;
- reporting on the constitution and working of tribunals;
- considering and reporting on any other matter relating to tribunals.

A member of the Council may attend (as observer) any proceedings of a tribunal.

7.6.6 Advantages of tribunals

Tribunals were set up to prevent the overloading of the courts with the extra cases that social and welfare rights claims generate.

For the applicant in tribunal cases, the advantages are that such cases are dealt with:

- more cheaply;
- more quickly;
- more informally;
- by experts in the area.

Cheapness

As applicants are encouraged to represent themselves and not use lawyers, tribunal hearings do not normally involve the costs associated with court hearings. It is also rare for an order for costs to be made by a tribunal, so that an applicant need not fear a large bill if they lose the case.

Key facts

First-tier Tribunal	• operates in seven Chambers (divisions) • deals with about 300,000 cases a year NB Employment Tribunal Operates separately
Upper Tribunal	• operates in four Chambers (divisions) • hears appeals from the First-tier Tribunal • there is a further appeal to the Court of Appeal
Panel	• cases may be heard by a Tribunal Judge OR • by a Tribunal judge sitting with two experts
Legal aid availability	• only for certain types of case, e.g. asylum rights or the right of a mental patient not to be detained
Administrative Justice and Tribunals Council	• keeps the work of tribunals under review • reports on the work of tribunals

Figure 7.6 Key facts chart on tribunals

Quick hearings

Most tribunal hearings are very short and can be dealt with in one day.

Informality

The hearing is more informal than in court. Parties are encouraged to present their own case. In addition, most cases are heard in private.

Expertise

In some tribunals two lay members sit to hear the case with the Tribunal judge. These lay members are experts in the type of case being heard. This gives them good knowledge and understanding of the issue in dispute.

7.6.7 Disadvantages of tribunals

Lack of funding

Public funding is not available for most tribunals, which may put an applicant at a disadvantage if the other side (often an employer or government department) uses a lawyer. Legal aid is available for cases where fundamental human rights are involved, such as in cases about whether an asylum seeker has the right to remain in the

Test Yourself

1. What is the main difference between tribunals and alternative forms of dispute resolution?
2. Give two examples of types of case which may be heard by a tribunal.
3. Which Act simplified the system of tribunals?
4. Who hears the case in a tribunal hearing?
5. After a decision by the First-tier Tribunal, to where can an appeal be made?
6. Which Council reviews the working of the tribunal system?
7. Explain one advantage of using a tribunal.
8. Explain one disadvantage of using a tribunal.

United Kingdom or whether a patient should remain in a secure mental hospital.

More formal than ADR

A tribunal hearing is more formal than using ADR. The place is unfamiliar and the procedure can be confusing for individuals presenting their own cases. Where applicants are not represented the judge is expected to take an inquisitorial role and help to establish the points that the applicant wishes to make. But this ideal is not always achieved.

Delay

Although the intention is that cases are dealt with quickly, the number of cases dealt with by tribunals means that there can be delays in getting a hearing. The use of lay members can add to this problem as they sit part-time, usually one day a fortnight. If a case is complex lasting several days this can lead to proceedings being spread over a number of weeks or even months.

Examination questions

There are various forms of dispute resolution, other than taking a case to the civil courts. They include Tribunals, Arbitration, Negotiation, Conciliation and Mediation.

(a) Including reference to the types of cases dealt with, describe dispute resolution by Tribunals.

(b) Including reference to the types of cases dealt with, describe the dispute resolution by two of the following:
   ● Mediation;
   ● Conciliation;
   ● Negotiation.

(c) Discuss the advantages of dispute resolution by means other than the civil courts.

AQA LAW 01 January 2009

Examiner's tip

In part (b) of the question above you are asked to deal with two matters. You must deal with two in your answer. If you do not then you cannot get to the top mark band.

Chapter 8

Criminal Courts

Unit 1 of the specification requires knowledge of the criminal courts, the types of cases they hear and also appeal routes in criminal cases. All these are dealt with in this chapter. Unit 2 also requires knowledge of criminal courts and some of the pre-trial procedure in cases. This is dealt with in Chapter 16.

8.1 Classification of offences

The type of offence will make a difference as to where the case will be tried and who will try it. For trial purposes criminal offences are divided into three categories. These are:

- summary offences;
- triable either way offences;
- indictable offences.

8.1.1 Summary offences

These are the least serious offences. They are always tried in the Magistrates' Court. They include nearly all driving offences. They also include common assault and criminal damage which has caused less than £5,000 damage.

8.1.2 Triable either way offences

These are the middle range of crimes. As the name implies, these cases can be tried in either the Magistrates' Court or the Crown Court. They include a wide range of offences such as theft and assault causing actual bodily harm.

In order to decide whether a triable either way offence will be tried in the Magistrates' Court or the Crown Court, the defendant is first asked whether he or she is pleading guilty or not guilty. If the defendant is pleading guilty the case is heard by the magistrates. Where the plea is not guilty the defendant then has the right to ask for the case to be tried at the Crown Court by a jury. The full procedure for this is explained in Chapter 17.

8.1.3 Indictable offences

These are the most serious crimes and include murder, manslaughter and rape. The first preliminary hearing for such an offence will be at the Magistrates' Court, but then the case is transferred to the Crown Court. All indictable offences must be tried at the Crown Court by a judge and jury.

Category of offence	Place of trial	Examples of offences
Summary	Magistrates' Court	Driving without insurance Common assault Criminal damage under £5,000
Triable either way	Magistrates' Court OR Crown Court	Theft Assault causing actual bodily harm
Indictable	Crown Court	Murder Manslaughter Rape Robbery

Figure 8.1 The three categories of offence

8.2 Magistrates' Courts

There are over 400 Magistrates' Courts in England and Wales. They are local courts so there will be a Magistrates' Court in almost every town, while big cities will have several courts. Each court deals with cases that have a connection with its geographical area and they have jurisdiction over a variety of matters involving criminal cases.

Cases are heard by magistrates, who are either qualified district judges or unqualified lay justices (see Chapter 9 for further details on magistrates). There is also a legally qualified clerk attached to each court to assist the magistrates.

8.2.1 Jurisdiction of the Magistrates' Courts

In criminal cases the Magistrates Courts deal with a variety of matters. They have a very large workload as they do the following:

1. Try all summary cases.
2. Try any triable either way offences in which the magistrates are prepared to accept jurisdiction and where the defendant agrees to summary trial by the magistrates.

These two categories account for about 97 per cent of all criminal cases and about 2 million cases take place each year in Magistrates' Courts. As well as these the magistrates also:

1. Deal with the preliminary hearings of any triable either way offence which is going to be tried in the Crown Court.
2. Deal with the first preliminary hearing of all indictable offences.
3. Deal with all the side matters connected to criminal cases, such as issuing warrants for arrest and deciding bail applications.
4. Try cases in the youth court where the defendants are aged 10-17 inclusive.

8.3 Appeals from the Magistrates' Court

There are two different routes of appeal from the Magistrates' Court. The route used will depend on whether the appeal is only on a point of law or whether it is for other reasons. The two appeal routes are to the Crown Court or to the Queen's Bench Divisional Court.

Giving evidence to a Magistrates' Court

8.3.1 Appeals to the Crown Court

This is the normal route of appeal from the Magistrates' Court. It is only available to the defence. If the defendant pleaded guilty at the Magistrates' Court, then he can only appeal against sentence. If the defendant pleaded not guilty and was convicted then the appeal can be against conviction and/or sentence. In both cases the defendant has an automatic right to appeal and does not need to get leave (permission) to appeal.

At the Crown Court the case is completely reheard by a judge and two magistrates. They can come to the same decision as the magistrates and confirm the conviction or they can decide that the case is not proved and reverse the decision. In some cases it is possible for them to vary the decision and find the defendant guilty of a lesser offence.

Where the appeal is against sentence, the Crown Court can confirm the sentence or they can increase or decrease it. However, any increase can only be up to the magistrates' maximum powers for the case.

If it becomes apparent that there is a point of law to be decided, then the Crown Court can decide that point of law, but there is the possibility of a further appeal by way of case stated being made to the Queen's Bench Divisional Court (see below).

8.3.2 Case stated appeals

A case stated appeal is an appeal on a point of law that goes to the Queen's Bench Divisional Court. Both the prosecution and the defence can use this appeal route. The appeal can be made direct from the Magistrates' Court or following an appeal to the Crown Court as above.

This route is only used by the defendant against a conviction or by the prosecution against an acquittal in situations where they claim the magistrates came to the wrong decision because they made a mistake about the law.

The magistrates (or the Crown Court) are asked to state the case by setting out their findings of fact and their decision. The appeal is then argued on the basis of what the law is on those facts; no witnesses are called. The appeal is heard by a panel of two or three High Court judges from the Queen's Bench Division.

The Divisional Court may confirm, vary or reverse the decision or remit (send back) the case to the Magistrates' Court for the magistrates to implement the decision on the law.

8.3.3 Further appeal to the Supreme Court

From the decision of the Queen's Bench Divisional Court there is a possibility of a further appeal to the Supreme Court. Such an appeal can only be made if:

(a) The Divisional Court certifies that a point of law of general public importance is involved; and

(b) The Divisional Court or the Supreme Court gives permission to appeal because the point is one which ought to be considered by the Supreme Court.

An example of a case which followed this appeal route was *C v DPP* (1994). This case concerned the legal point about the presumption of criminal responsibility of children from the age of ten up to their fourteenth birthday. Until this case it had been accepted that a child of this age could only be convicted if the prosecution proved that the child knew he was doing wrong. The Divisional Court held that times had changed and that children were more mature and the rule was not needed. So they decided that children of this age were presumed to know the difference between right and wrong and that the prosecution did not need to prove 'mischievous discretion'.

The case was then appealed to the House of Lords (now the Supreme Court) who overruled the Divisional Court. The Law Lords held that the law was still that a child of this age was presumed not to know he was doing wrong and therefore not to have the necessary intention for any criminal offence. A child of this age could only be convicted if the prosecution disproved this presumption by bringing evidence to show that the child was aware that what he was doing was seriously wrong. The House of Lords ruling was

on the basis that it was for Parliament to make such a major change to the law, not the courts. The courts were bound by precedent.

In fact Parliament did later change the law on this point.

A diagram setting out the appeal routes from the Magistrates' Court is shown in Figure 8.3.

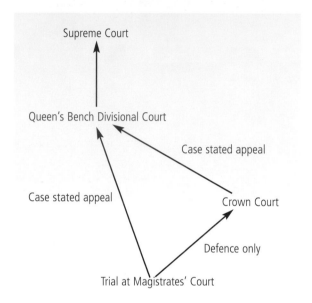

Figure 8.3 Diagram of appeal routes from the Magistrates' Court

8.4 The Crown Court

The Crown Court currently sits in 90 different centres throughout England and Wales. There are three kinds of centre:

1. **First tier**
   These exist in main centres throughout the country, for example there are first tier Crown Courts in Bristol, Birmingham, Leeds and Manchester. At each court there is a High Court and a Crown Court with separate judges for civil and criminal work. The Crown Court is permanently staffed by High Court judges as well as Circuit judges and Recorders and the court can deal with all categories of crime triable on indictment.

2. **Second tier**

   This is a Crown Court only, but High Court judges sit there on a regular basis to hear criminal cases, as well as Circuit judges and Recorders. All categories of crime triable on indictment can be tried here.

3. **Third tier**

   This is staffed only by Circuit judges and Recorders. The most serious cases, such as murder, manslaughter and rape are not usually tried here as there is no High Court judge to deal with them.

Each year the Crown Court deals with about 80,000 cases.

8.5 Appeals from the Crown Court

8.5.1 Appeals by the defendant

The defendant has the possibility of appealing against conviction and/or sentence to the Court of Appeal (Criminal Division). So, at the end of any trial in which a defendant has been found guilty, his lawyer should advise him on the possibility of an appeal.

Leave to appeal

In all cases the defendant must get leave to appeal from the Court of Appeal or a certificate that the case is fit for appeal from the trial judge. The idea is that cases which are without merit are filtered out and the court's time saved.

The application for leave to appeal is considered by a single judge of the Court of Appeal in private, although if he refuses it is possible to apply to a full Court of Appeal for leave.

Grounds for appeal

The Criminal Appeal Act 1995 simplified the grounds under which the court can allow an appeal. The Act states that the Court of Appeal:

> (a) shall allow an appeal against conviction if they think that the conviction is unsafe; and
>
> (b) shall dismiss such an appeal in any other case.

If the Court of Appeal decides that the conviction is unsafe, they can allow the defendant's appeal and quash the conviction. Alternatively they can vary the conviction to that of a lesser offence of which the jury could have convicted the defendant. If the appeal is against sentence, the court can decrease the sentence but cannot increase it on the defendant's appeal.

The Court of Appeal also has the power to order that there be a retrial of the case in front of a new jury. This power is only used in about 50 to 60 cases each year.

If the Court of Appeal decides that the conviction is safe, then they will dismiss the appeal.

8.5.2 Appeals by the prosecution

Originally the prosecution had no right to appeal against either the verdict or sentence passed in the Crown Court. Gradually, however, some limited rights of appeal have been given to them by Parliament.

Against a judge's ruling

If the trial judge gives a ruling on a point of law which effectively stops the case against the defendant, the prosecution now have the right to appeal against that ruling. This right was given by the Criminal Justice Act 2003. It makes sure that an error of law by the judge does not lead to an acquittal.

Against acquittal

There are only two limited situations in which the prosecution can appeal against an acquittal by a jury.

1. Where the acquittal was the result of the jury being 'nobbled'.

   This is where one or more jurors are bribed or threatened by associates of the defendant. In these circumstances, provided there has been an actual conviction for jury nobbling, the Criminal Procedure and Investigations Act 1996 allows the prosecution to appeal and the Court of Appeal can order a retrial.

   Once the acquittal is quashed, the prosecution could then start new proceedings for the same offence.

2. Where there is new and compelling evidence of the acquitted person's guilt and it is in the public interest for the defendant to be retried. This power is given by the Criminal Justice Act 2003 and it is only available for some 30 serious offences, including murder, manslaughter, rape and terrorism offences. It is known as double jeopardy, since the defendant is being tried twice for the same offence.

   The DPP has to consent to the reopening of investigations in the case. Once the evidence has been found, then the prosecution have to apply to the Court of Appeal for the original acquittal to be quashed.

   This power has been used in cases where new techniques of DNA testing now show that a defendant who is acquitted is in fact the offender. The first case in which this power was used is shown in the article opposite.

Referring a point of law

Where the judge may have made an error in explaining the law to the jury, the prosecution have the right to refer a point of law to the Court of Appeal if the defendant is acquitted. This right is under s 36 of the Criminal Justice Act 1972 which allows the Attorney-General to refer the point of law to the Court of Appeal in order to get a ruling on the law. The decision by the Court of Appeal on that point of law does not affect the acquittal but it creates a precedent for any future case involving the same point of law.

Example

Man admits murder in first UK double jeopardy case

Fifteen years after he was cleared of murder, the first person in Britain to face a retrial under new double jeopardy rules admitted today that he killed his victim.

Billy Dunlop, 43, pleaded guilty to murdering pizza delivery girl Julie Hogg, 22, in Billingham, Teeside, when he appeared at the Old Bailey today.

Dunlop stood trial twice in 1991 for her murder but each time a jury failed to reach a verdict. He was formally acquitted under the convention that the prosecution do not ask for a third trial in such circumstances.

But in April last year the double jeopardy rule – which prevented a defendant who had been acquitted from being tried again for the same offence – was changed under the Criminal Justice Act 2003.

The following November the Director of Public Prosecutions announced the legal process to retry Dunlop had begun. The case was sent to the Court of Appeal where his acquittal was quashed.

Taken from an article in the Daily Mail, *11 September 2006*

Against sentence

Under s 36 of the Criminal Justice Act 1988 the Attorney-General can apply for leave to refer an unduly lenient sentence to the Court of Appeal for re-sentencing. This power was initially available for indictable cases only, but was extended in 1994 to many triable either way offences, provided that the trial of the case took place at a Crown Court.

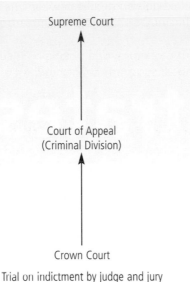

Supreme Court

↑

Court of Appeal
(Criminal Division)

↑

Crown Court

Trial on indictment by judge and jury

Figure 8.4 Appeal routes from the Crown Court

8.5.3 Further appeals to the Supreme Court

Both the prosecution and the defence may appeal from the Court of Appeal to the Supreme Court, but it is necessary to have the case certified as involving a point of law of general public importance and to get permission to appeal, either from the Supreme Court or from the Court of Appeal. There are very few criminal appeals heard by the Supreme Court.

Test Yourself

1. Where can a summary offence be tried?
2. Give an example of a summary offence.
3. Where can a triable either way offence be tried?
4. Give an example of a triable either way offence.
5. Where can an indictable offence be tried?
6. Give an example of an indictable offence.

7. To which court is an appeal normally made from the magistrates' courts?
8. What is a case stated appeal?
9. To which court is an appeal made after a trial in the Crown Court?
10. What rights do the prosecution have to make an appeal after an acquittal in the Crown Court?

Examination questions

(a) Identify the different criminal courts, including appeal courts, that can hear criminal cases involving adults. Outline the types of criminal offences that are dealt with by these courts. (10 marks)

AQA LAW01 June 2009

NB Parts (b) and (c) of this question can be found at the end of Chapter 10.

Examiner's tip

Questions on the courts need very accurate knowledge. If you know this topic, then the question is very straightforward and you can easily get into the top mark band. If you do not know the topic, then do not choose it as one of the ones to answer in the examination.

Chapter 9

Lay Magistrates

There is a tradition of using lay people, i.e. people who are not legally qualified, in the decision-making process in our courts. Today this applies particularly to the Magistrates' Courts and the Crown Court. However, in the past lay people were also frequently used to decide civil cases in the High Court and the County Court, and there are still some cases in which a jury can be used in the civil courts. There are also lay people with expertise in a particular field who sit as part of a panel as lay assessors. This occurs mainly in tribunals but lay assessors are also used in the Patents Court and the Admiralty Court in the High Court.

This chapter concentrates on lay magistrates and the next chapter looks at juries. It is possible for examination questions to be set on the use of lay people in the legal system in general. Remember that for such a question you will need to use material from both chapters.

9.1 Lay magistrates

There are about 29,000 lay magistrates sitting as part-time judges in the Magistrates' Courts; another name for lay magistrates is Justices of the Peace. They sit to hear cases as a bench of two or three magistrates. The size of panel has been limited to a maximum of three, whereas before 1996 there could be up to seven magistrates sitting together to hear a case. A single lay magistrate sitting on his or her own has very limited powers. They can, however, issue search warrants and warrants for arrest and conduct Early Administrative Hearings.

There are also District judges (Magistrates' Courts) who work in Magistrates' Courts. These are not lay people but are qualified lawyers who can sit on their own to hear any of the cases that come before the court. Under section 16(3) of the Justices of the Peace Act 1979 they have the same powers as a bench of lay magistrates. Since the duties of these District judges are the same as those of lay magistrates and since the history of the two is linked, details of District judges (formerly known as Stipendiary magistrates) are also included in this chapter.

9.2 History of the magistracy

The office of Justice of the Peace is very old, dating back to the twelfth century at least – in 1195 Richard I appointed 'keepers of the peace'. By the mid-thirteenth century the judicial side of their position had developed and by 1361 the title Justice of the Peace was being used. Over the years they were also given many administrative duties, for example, being responsible for the poor law, highways and bridges, and weights and measures. In the nineteenth century elected local authorities took over most of these duties, though some remnants remain, especially in the licensing powers of the Magistrates' Courts.

The poor quality of the local Justices of the Peace in London and the absence of an adequate police force became a matter of concern towards the end of the eighteenth century. This led to seven public offices with paid magistrates being set up in 1792 and until 1839 they were in charge of the police as well as hearing cases in court. Outside London the first appointment of a paid magistrate was in Manchester in 1813. In 1835 the Municipal Corporations Act gave a general power for boroughs to request the appointment of a paid magistrate. At the beginning a paid magistrate did not have to have any particular qualifications, but from 1839 they could only be appointed from barristers. Solicitors did not become eligible to be appointed until 1949.

9.2.1 Qualifications

Lay magistrates

Lay magistrates do not have to have any qualifications in law. There are, however, some requirements as to their character. In 1998, the Lord Chancellor set out six key qualities which candidates should have. These are:

- good character;
- understanding and communication;
- social awareness;
- maturity and sound temperament;
- sound judgment;
- commitment and reliability.

They must have certain 'judicial' qualities – it is particularly important that they are able to assimilate factual information and make a reasoned decision upon it. They must also be able to take account of the reasoning of others and work as a team.

There are also formal requirements as to age and residence: lay magistrates must be aged between 18 and 65 on appointment. Not many people under the age of 27 are appointed as it is felt they do not have enough experience. However, since the age for appointment was reduced to 18 in 2003, more young magistrates have been appointed. For example, in 2004 one aged 21 was appointed in Shropshire and another aged 23 in West Yorkshire. However, the statistics for 2009 show that only 4 per cent of magistrates were under the age of 40.

9.2.2 Area

Up to 2003 it was necessary for lay magistrates to live within 15 miles of the commission area for the court which they sat in. In 2003 the Courts Act abolished commission areas. Instead there is now one commission area for the whole of England and Wales. However the country is divided into local justice areas. These areas are specified by the Lord Chancellor and lay magistrates are expected to live or work within or near to the local justice area to which they are allocated.

9.2.3 Commitment

The other requirement is that lay magistrates are prepared to commit themselves to sitting at least 26 half days each year. It is thought that this level of commitment deters many people from becoming lay magistrates.

9.2.4 Restrictions on appointment

Some people are not eligible to be appointed. These include people with serious criminal convictions, though a conviction for a minor motoring offence will not automatically disqualify a candidate. Others who are disqualified include undischarged bankrupts, members of the forces and those whose work is incompatible with sitting as a magistrate, such as police officers and traffic wardens. Relatives of those working in the local criminal justice system are not likely to be appointed as it would not appear 'just' if, for example, the wife or husband of a local police officer were to sit to decide cases. In addition people whose hearing is impaired, or who by reason of infirmity cannot carry out all the duties of a justice of the peace cannot be appointed. Close relatives will not be appointed to the same bench.

Activity

1. Put the list of six key qualities in 9.2.1 into order with the one that you think is most important first and the least important last.
2. Compare your list with those of two other people.
3. Explain what other qualities you think magistrates need.

9.2.5 District judges (Magistrates' Courts)

These were previously known as stipendiary magistrates. They must have a seven-year general qualification, that is a right of audience as an advocate, and are usually chosen from practising barristers or solicitors, or from others with relevant experience such as court clerks. They are only appointed to courts in London or other places with busy courts. Before becoming a District judge they will usually be an acting judge sitting part time for two years to gain experience of sitting judicially, and to establish their suitability for full-time appointment.

9.3 Appointment

About 1,500 new lay magistrates are appointed each year. The appointments are made by the Lord Chancellor, on behalf of the Queen. In order to decide who to appoint the Lord Chancellor relies on recommendations made to him by the local advisory committees and this method of appointment is much criticised.

9.3.1 Local Advisory Committees

The membership of the committees used to be secret but since 1993 all names must be published. The members tend to be current or ex-Justices of the Peace. About half the members have to retire in rotation every three years. The committees should have a maximum of 12 members and these should include a mixture of magistrates and non-magistrates.

Anyone can apply to become a magistrate. The process is explained online at www.magistrates-association.org.uk or at www.direct.gov.uk.

Advertisements are used to try and encourage as wide a range of potential candidates as possible. Advertisements have been placed in local papers, or newspapers aimed at particular ethnic groups, and even on buses! Also, in Leeds, radio adverts have been used. People are also encouraged to go to open evenings at their local Magistrates' Court. All this is aimed at getting as wide a spectrum of potential candidates as possible. The intention is to create a panel that is representative of all aspects of society.

A balance of occupations is aimed at. The Lord Chancellor has set down 11 broad categories of occupations, and advisory committees are recommended that they should not have more than 15 per cent of the bench coming from any one category.

9.3.2 Interview panels

There is usually a two-stage interview process. At the first interview the panel tries to find out more about the candidate's personal attributes, in particular looking to see if they have the six key qualities required. The interview panel will also explore the candidate's attitudes on various criminal justice issues such as youth crime or drink driving. The second interview is aimed at testing candidates' potential judicial aptitude and this is done by a discussion of at least two case studies which are typical of those heard regularly in magistrates' courts. The discussion might, for example, focus on the type of sentence which should be imposed on specific case facts.

The advisory committees will then submit names of those they think are suitable to the Lord Chancellor, who will then appoint new magistrates from this list. Once appointed, magistrates may continue to sit until the age of 70.

9.4 Composition of the bench today

The traditional image of lay justices is that they are 'middle-class, middle-aged and middle-minded'. This image is to a certain extent true. A report, *The Judiciary in the Magistrates' Courts* (2000), found that lay magistrates:

- were drawn overwhelmingly from professional and managerial ranks; and
- 40 per cent of them were retired from full-time employment.

However, in other respects the bench is well balanced, with 50 per cent of magistrates women, as against 12 per cent of professional judges.

Also, ethnic minorities are reasonably well represented in the magistracy. Over 7 per cent of magistrates are from ethnic minorities. This compares very favourably to the professional judiciary where less than 2 per cent are from ethnic minority backgrounds.

The relatively high level of ethnic minority magistrates is largely a result of campaigns to attract a wider range of candidates. Adverts are placed in national newspapers and also in TV guides and women's magazines. In an effort to encourage those from ethnic minorities to apply, adverts have also appeared in such publications as the *Caribbean Times*, the *Asian Times* and *Muslim News*. This has led to an increase in the numbers of ethnic minority appointments.

Disabled people are encouraged to apply to become magistrates. This has included appointing blind persons as lay magistrates.

@ **Internet Research**

Look up the composition of the magistracy for your area at www.judiciary.gov.uk. Find out:

1. how many male and female magistrates are there in your area?
2. how many magistrates from an ethnic minority are there in your area?

9.5 Magistrates' duties

Magistrates have a very wide workload which is mainly connected to criminal cases, although they also deal with some civil matters, especially family cases. They try 97 per cent of all criminal cases and deal with preliminary hearings in the remaining 3 per cent of criminal cases. This will involve Early Administrative Hearings, remand hearings, bail applications and transfer proceedings where serious criminal cases are sent to the Crown Court for trial.

Magistrates also deal with civil matters which include the enforcing of debts owed to the utilities (gas, electric and water), non-payment of the council tax and non-payment of television licences. In addition they hear appeals against the refusal of the local authority to grant licences for the sale of alcohol and licences for betting and gaming establishments.

9.5.1 Youth court

Specially nominated and trained justices from the Youth Court panel hear criminal charges against young offenders aged 10 to 17 years old. These magistrates must be under 65 and a panel must usually include at least one man and one woman. There is also a special panel for the Family Court to hear family cases including orders for protection against violence, affiliation cases, adoption orders and proceedings under the Children Act 1989.

9.5.2 Appeals

Lay magistrates also sit at the Crown Court to hear appeals from the Magistrates' Court. In these cases the lay justices form a panel with a qualified judge.

9.6 Training of lay magistrates

The training of lay magistrates is supervised by the Magistrates' Committee of the Judicial Studies Board. This Committee has drawn up a syllabus of the topics which lay magistrates should cover in their training. However, because of the large numbers of lay magistrates, the actual training is carried out in local areas, sometimes through the clerk of the court, sometimes through weekend courses organised by universities with magistrates from the region attending.

Since 1998 magistrates' training has been monitored more closely. There were criticisms prior to then that, although magistrates were required to attend a certain number of hours training, there was no assessment of how much they had understood. In 1998 the Magistrates New Training Initiative was introduced (MNTI 1). In 2004 this was refined by the Magistrates National Training Initiative (MNTI 2).

The framework of training is divided into four areas of competence, the first three of which are relevant to all lay magistrates. The fourth competence is for chairmen of the bench. The four areas of competence are:

1. Managing yourself – this focuses on some of the basic aspects of self-management in relation to preparing for court, conduct in court and ongoing learning.
2. Working as a member of a team – this focuses on the team aspect of decision-making in the Magistrates' Court.
3. Making judicial decisions – this focuses on impartial and structured decision-making.
4. Managing judicial decision-making – this is for the chairman's role and focuses on working with the legal adviser, managing the court and ensuring effective, impartial decision-making.

For delivering training there are Bench Training and Developmental Committees (BTDCs) and s 19(3) of the Courts Act 2003 sets out a statutory obligation on the Lord Chancellor to provide training and training materials.

9.6.1 Training for new magistrates

There is a syllabus for new magistrates which is divided into three parts:

1. Initial introductory training – this covers such matters as understanding the organisation of the bench and the administration of the court and the roles and responsibilities of those involved in the Magistrates' Court.
2. Core training – this provides the new magistrate with the opportunity to acquire and develop the key skills, knowledge and understanding required of a competent magistrate.
3. Activities – these will involve observations of court sittings and visits to establishments such as a prison or a probation office.

9.6.2 Training sessions

These are organised and carried out at local level within the 42 court areas. Much of the training is delivered by Justices' Clerks. The Judicial Studies Board intends that most training should still be delivered locally, however, they take into account the need to collaborate regionally and nationally where appropriate. In particular, the training of Youth and Family Panel Chairmen will be delivered nationally for areas which do not have enough such chairmen needing training to run an effective course locally.

9.6.3 Wingers

After doing the core training and observing cases, a new magistrate will sit as a 'winger' to hear cases. This means that they will be one of a panel of three. The chairman (who sits in the middle) is a very experienced magistrate and the magistrates who sit on either side of the chairman are known as 'wingers'.

9.6.4 Appraisal

During the first two years of the new magistrate sitting in court, between 8 and 11 of the sessions will be mentored. In the same period the magistrate is also expected to attend about seven training sessions. After two years, or whenever it is felt that the magistrate is ready, an appraisal will take place to check if they have acquired the competencies.

Any magistrate who cannot show that they have achieved the competencies will be given extra training. If they still cannot achieve the competencies, then the matter is referred to the local Advisory Committee, who may recommend to the Lord Chancellor that the magistrate is removed from sitting.

This new scheme involves practical training 'on the job'. It also answers the criticisms of the old system where there was no check made on whether the magistrate had actually benefited from the training session they attended.

Those magistrates who chair the bench are also appraised for this role, so that the quality of the chairing in court should also improve. The training programme for new magistrates should normally follow the pattern set out in Figure 9.1.

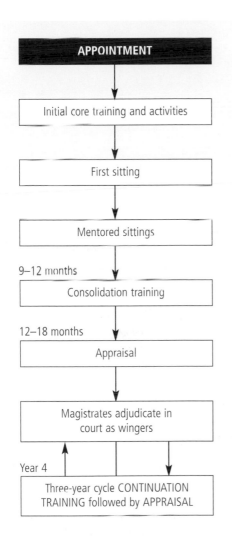

Figure 9.1 New magistrates' training and appraisal pathway

Source: MNTI2 Handbook issued by the Judicial Studies Board

9.7 Retirement and removal

9.7.1 Retirement

The retirement age is 70, but when magistrates become 70 they do not officially retire – instead their names are placed on the Supplemental List. This means that they can no longer sit in the Magistrates' Court. However, they can continue to carry out some administrative functions mainly connected with signing documents. Lay magistrates who move from the area for which they were appointed cannot continue as magistrates in that area. If they wish to continue as magistrates their names will be placed on the Supplemental List until there is a vacancy in their new area. Lay magistrates may, of course, resign from office at any time and many will resign before reaching 70.

9.7.2 Removal

Section 11 of the Courts Act 2003 gives the Lord Chancellor powers to remove a lay justice for the following reasons:

- on the ground of incapacity or misbehaviour;
- on the ground of a persistent failure to meet such standards of competence as are prescribed by a direction given by the Lord Chancellor; or
- if the Lord Chancellor is satisfied that the lay justice is declining or neglecting to take a proper part in the exercise of his functions as a justice of the peace.

Qualifications	Live or work near court in which they sit Need common sense, integrity Disqualified for serious criminal record, bankruptcy or work that is incompatible
Appointment	By Lord Chancellor on the recommendation of local advisory committees
Training	Four basic competencies: Personal Development Log of progress Mentors and mentored sessions Attend training sessions Appraisal
Composition of bench	29,000 lay magistrates, 50% men 50% women Good representation of ethnic minorities Tend to be older (40% retired from work) and from the professional classes
Work	Summary trials Sending cases to Crown Court for trial Bail applications Youth court Family court Licensing appeals Sit in Crown Court in appeals from the Magistrates' Court

Figure 9.2 Key facts chart on law magisatrates

Removal for misbehaviour usually occurs when a magistrate is convicted of a criminal offence. There about 10 such removals each year. However, on occasions in the past there have been removals for such matters as taking part in a CND march or transvestite behaviour. There was considerable criticism of the Lord Chancellor's use of his power of removal in such circumstances and it is unlikely that such behaviour today would lead to removal from the bench.

9.8 The magistrates' clerk

Every bench is assisted by a clerk, also known as a legal adviser. The senior clerk in each court has to be qualified as a barrister or solicitor for at least five years. The clerk's duty is to guide the magistrates on questions of law, practice and procedure. This is set out in s 28(3) of the Justices of the Peace Act 1979 which says:

> " It is hereby declared that the functions of a justices' clerk include the giving to the justices . . . of advice about law, practice or procedure on questions arising in connection with the discharge of their functions. "

The clerk is not meant to assist in the decision-making and should not normally retire with the magistrates when they go to make their decision. In *R v Eccles Justices, ex parte Farrelly* (1992) the Queen's Bench Divisional Court quashed convictions because the clerk had apparently participated in the decision-making process.

Clerks deal with routine administrative matters. They can also issue warrants for arrest, extend police bail, adjourn criminal proceedings and deal with Early Administrative Hearings.

9.9 Advantages of lay magistrates

9.9.1 Cross-section of society

The system involves members of the community and provides a wider cross-section on the bench than would be possible with the use of professional judges. This is particularly true of women, with 50 per cent of magistrates being women. Also, there is considerable involvement of ethnic minorities.

9.9.2 Local knowledge

Since lay magistrates have to live or work near the court, it is intended that they should have local knowledge of particular problems in the area. However, as most magistrates come from the professional and managerial classes, it is unlikely that they live in, or have any real knowledge of, the problems in the poorer areas. Their main value is that they will have more awareness of local events, local patterns of crime and local opinions than a professional judge from another area.

9.9.3 Cost

The use of unpaid lay magistrates is cheap. The cost of replacing them with paid judges has been estimated at £100 million a year (there would also be the problem of recruiting sufficient qualified lawyers). The cost of a trial in the Magistrates' Court is also much cheaper than in the Crown Court.

9.9.4 Training

Improved training means that lay magistrates are not complete 'amateurs'. The majority of decisions require common sense rather than professional training.

9.9.5 Legal adviser

Since 1999 all newly appointed magistrates' clerks have to be legally qualified. In addition, existing clerks under the age of 40 in 1999 have to qualify within 10 years. This brings a higher level of legal skill to the Magistrates' Court. The availability of a legal adviser gives the magistrates access to any necessary legal advice on points that may arise in any case. This overcomes any criticism of the fact that lay magistrates are not themselves legally qualified.

9.9.6 Few appeals

Comparatively few defendants appeal against the magistrates' decisions, and many of the appeals that are made are against sentence, not against the finding of guilt. From a total workload of nearly 2 million cases there are only a small number of appeals. In most years there are between 5,000 and 6,000 appeals against conviction. Less than half of these appeals are successful. There are also about 6,000 appeals each year against the sentence imposed by the magistrates. Again, less than half of these are successful.

There are also very few instances where an error of law is made. This is shown by the fact that in 2008 there were only 72 appeals by way of case stated to the Queen's Bench Divisional Court. Of these appeals 30 were allowed. From this it can be argued that, despite the amateur status of lay magistrates, they do a remarkably good job.

9.10 Disadvantages of lay magistrates

9.10.1 Middle aged, middle class

Lay magistrates are often perceived as being middle aged and middle class. The report *The Judiciary in the Magistrates' Courts* (2000) showed that this was largely true. They found that 40 per cent of lay magistrates were retired and also that they were overwhelmingly from a professional or managerial background. However, lay magistrates are from a much wider range of backgrounds than professional judges.

OF COURSE, WE UNDERSTAND YOUR PROBLEMS

However, this has to be seen in context. Only 4 per cent of offenders dealt with by magistrates receive a prison sentence, so that the problem may not be as severe as thought. Also, since these figures were compiled there has been a new edition of the Magistrates' Association's Sentencing Guidelines. It is thought that these guidelines are helping to promote common standards.

However, the 2004 statistics did not show any improvement. Magistrates in Sunderland discharged 36.4 per cent of all defendants, whereas only 9.2 per cent of defendants in Birmingham were discharged. In Newcastle, magistrates sentenced only 7.2 per cent of defendants to an immediate custodial sentence. In Hillingdon in West London, the magistrates sentenced 32 per cent of defendants to an immediate custodial sentence.

9.10.2 Inconsistency in sentencing

Magistrates in different areas often pass very different sentences for what appear to be similar offences. The government's White Paper, *Justice for All*, set out differences found in the Criminal Statistics for 2001 when it gave these following examples:

- for burglary of dwellings, 20 per cent of offenders are sentenced to immediate custody in Teesside, compared with 41 per cent of offenders in Birmingham; 38 per cent of burglars at Cardiff magistrates' courts receive community sentences, compared with 66 per cent in Leicester;
- for driving while disqualified, the percentage of offenders sentenced to custody ranged from 21 per cent in Neath Port Talbot (South Wales) to 77 per cent in mid-north Essex;
- for receiving stolen goods, 3.5 per cent of offenders sentenced at Reading Magistrates' Court received custodial sentences compared with 48 per cent in Greenwich and Woolwich (south London) and 39 per cent at Camberwell Green (south London).

9.10.3 Reliance on the clerk

The lack of legal knowledge of the lay justices should be offset by the fact that a legally qualified clerk is available to give advice. However, this will not prevent inconsistencies in sentencing since the clerk is not allowed to help the magistrates decide on a sentence. In some courts it is felt that the magistrates rely too heavily on their clerk.

9.10.4 Prosecution bias

It is often said that lay magistrates tend to be prosecution-biased, believing the police too readily. However, part of the training is aimed at eliminating this type of bias. It is also true that at courts outside London they will see the same Crown Prosecution Service prosecutor frequently and this could affect their judgment. There is a low acquittal rate in Magistrates' Courts with only 20 per cent of defendants being acquitted. By comparison 60 per cent of defendants pleading not guilty at the Crown Court were acquitted.

Key facts

Advantages	Disadvantages
Cross-section of local people	Not a true cross-section
Good gender balance	40% are retired people
Improving ethnic balance	Majority are from professional or managerial background
Much better cross-section than District judges	Older than District judges
Live (or work) locally and so know the area and its problems	Unlikely to live in the poorer areas and so do not truly know the area's problems
Cheaper than using professional judges as they are only paid expenses	–
Cheaper than sending cases to the Crown Court	–
Improved training through MNTI2 and the increased role of Judicial Studies Board	There are inconsistencies in sentencing and decisions on bail
Have legal adviser for points of law	Not legally qualified
Very few appeals	–

Figure 9.3 Key facts chart on advantages and disadvantages of using lay magistrates in the legal system

9.10.5 Training

There are the criticisms that the training is variable in quality and inadequate for the workload. This poor training may be the cause of marked variations in sentencing and granting of bail between different benches.

Test Yourself

1. What two types of 'judge' sit to hear cases in the magistrates' courts?
2. What qualifications (age, character) must lay magistrates have?
3. How are potential lay magistrates selected and by whom?
4. Who appoints lay magistrates?
5. What types of cases do magistrates deal with in the magistrates' courts?
6. What does the Youth Court deal with?
7. How are lay magistrates trained?
8. At what age must lay magistrates retire?
9. Give three advantages of using lay magistrates.
10. Give three disadvantages of using lay magistrates.

Examination questions

(a) Alicia is charged with theft (an either-way offence). Her case could be tried either by magistrates or by a jury in the Crown Court.
Explain the work of lay magistrates in criminal courts.

AQA Unit 1 Specimen Paper Part question

Examiner's tip

Read the question carefully. In this question you are only asked for the work of lay magistrates in CRIMINAL cases. So make sure you concentrate on criminal cases. Do not mention any of their civil work as it will not gain any marks.

Chapter 10

Juries

10.1 History of the jury system

Juries have been used in the legal system for over 1,000 years. There is evidence that they were used even before the Norman Conquest. However, in 1215 when trial by ordeal was condemned by the Church and (in the same year) the Magna Carta included the recognition of a person's right to trial by 'the lawful judgment of his peers', juries became the usual method of trying criminal cases. Originally they were used for providing local knowledge and information, and acted more as witnesses than decision-makers. By the middle of the fifteenth century juries had become independent assessors and assumed their modern role as deciders of fact.

10.1.1 The independence of the jury

The independence of the jury became even more firmly established following *Bushell's Case* (1670). In that case several jurors refused to convict Quaker activists of unlawful assembly. The trial judge would not accept the not guilty verdict, and ordered the jurors to resume their deliberations without food or drink. When the jurors persisted in their refusal to convict, the court fined them and committed them to prison until the fines were paid. On appeal, the Court of Common Pleas ordered the release of the jurors, holding that jurors could not be punished for their verdict. This established that the jury were the sole arbiters of fact and the judge could not challenge their decision.

A modern-day example, demonstrating that judges must respect the independence of the jury, is *R v McKenna* (1960). In that case the judge at the trial had threatened the jury that if they did not return a verdict within another 10 minutes they would be locked up all night. The jury then returned a verdict of guilty, but the defendant's conviction was quashed on appeal because of the judge's interference.

10.2 Modern-day use of the jury

Only a small percentage of cases is tried by jury today. However, juries are used in the following courts:

- Crown Court for criminal trials on indictment;
- High Court, Queen's Bench Division (but only for certain types of cases);
- County Court (for the same types of cases as in the Queen's Bench Division);
- Coroners' Courts (in some cases).

10.2.1 Juries in criminal cases

The most important use of juries today is in the Crown Court where they decide whether the defendant is guilty or not guilty. Jury trials, however, account for less than 1 per cent of all criminal trials. This is because 97 per cent of cases are dealt with in the Magistrates' Court and of the cases that go to the Crown Court, about two out of every three defendants will plead guilty. Also

Key facts

Court	Type of case	Role	Number on jury
Crown Court	Serious criminal cases, e.g. murder, manslaughter, rape	Decide verdict Guilty or Not guilty	12
High Court	Defamation False imprisonment Malicious prosecution Any case alleging fraud	Decide liability If finding for the claimant also decides amount of damages	12
County Court	Defamation False imprisonment Malicious prosecution Any case alleging fraud	Decide liability If finding for the claimant also decides amount of damages	8
Coroners' Court	Deaths: ● in custody; ● resulting from an act of a police officer; ● caused by a notifiable accident, poisoning or disease; ● where Senior Coroner thinks necessary	Decide cause of death	7–11

Figure 10.1 Key facts chart on the use of juries

some of the cases at the Crown Court, in which the defendant has entered a not guilty plea, will not go before a jury as the case will be discharged by judge without any trial. This occurs where the Crown Prosecution Service withdraws the charges, possibly because a witness refuses to give evidence. A jury in the Crown Court has 12 members.

10.2.2 Juries in civil cases

Juries in civil cases are now only used in very limited circumstances, but where they are used they have a dual role. They decide whether the claimant has proved his case or not, then, if they decide that the claimant has won the case, the jury also go on to decide the amount of damages that the defendant should pay to the claimant.

Up to 1854 all common law actions were tried by jury, but from 1854 the parties could agree not to use a jury and gradually their use declined. Then in 1933 the Administration of Justice Act limited the right to use a jury, so that juries could not be used in disputes over breach of contract.

The present rules for when juries may be used in civil cases are set out in s 69 of the Supreme Court Act 1981 for High Court cases, and s 66 of the County Courts Act 1984 for cases in that court. These Acts state that parties have the right to jury trial only in the following types of case:

● defamation, i.e. cases of libel and slander (this is the most frequent use of juries);
● false imprisonment;
● malicious prosecution;
● fraud.

All these cases involve character or reputation and it is for this reason that jury trial has been retained. Even for these cases a jury trial can be refused by the judge if the case involves complicated documents or accounts or scientific evidence and is therefore thought to be unsuitable for jury trial.

There are now very few civil cases in which a jury is used. Some years there are none in the County Court and less than 10 in the High Court. Where a jury is used in the High Court there will be 12 members; in the County Court a jury consists of eight.

Use of juries in personal injury cases

In other civil cases in the Queen's Bench Division of the High Court the parties can apply to a judge for trial by jury, but it is very rare for such a request to be granted. This follows the case of *Ward v James* (1966) where the claimant was claiming for injuries caused in a road crash. In this case the Court of Appeal laid down guidelines for personal injury cases. These were:

- Personal injury cases should normally be tried by a judge sitting alone, because such cases involve assessing compensatory damages which have to have regard to the conventional scales of damages.
- There have to be exceptional circumstances before the court will allow a jury to be used in such a case.

The decision in *Ward v James* effectively stopped the use of juries for personal injury cases. The following cases show how the courts have proved very reluctant to let juries be used. In *Singh v London Underground* (1990) a request for a jury to try a personal injury case arising from the King's Cross underground fire was refused. It was held that the case was unsuitable for jury trial because it involved such wide issues and technical points.

The case of *H v Ministry of Defence* (1991) further reinforced the rule in *Ward v James*; the claimant was a soldier who had received negligent medical treatment necessitating the amputation of part of his penis. He applied for jury trial, but it was held that jury trial for a personal injury claim would only be allowed in very exceptional circumstances and this case was

not such a one. The court said that an example of when jury trial might be appropriate was where the injuries resulted from someone deliberately abusing their authority and there might well be a claim for exemplary damages.

10.2.3 Coroners' courts

In these courts a jury of between 7 and 11 members may be used to enquire into deaths.

The Coroners and Justice Act 2009 changed the use of juries in Coroners' Courts. Under this a jury must be used if there is reason to suspect that the deceased died while in custody and that either:

(a) (i) the death was a violent or unnatural one, or
    (ii) the cause of death is unknown;
(b) that the death resulted from an act or omission of a police officer.

A jury must also be used where the death was caused by a notifiable accident, poisoning or disease.

A jury will also be used if the senior coroner thinks that there is sufficient reason for it.

A coroner is no longer obliged to summon a jury to decide cases involving road accidents or suspected homicide. He has a discretion as to whether a jury should be used in such cases. A jury was used to inquire into the death of Princess Diana.

10.3 Jury qualifications

10.3.1 Basic qualifications

History

The qualifications for jury service were revised in 1972 following the Morris Committee Report on jury service. Before this date there was a property qualification – in order to be a juror it was necessary to be the owner or tenant of a dwelling. This restriction meant that women and young people who were less likely to own or rent property were prevented from serving on a jury.

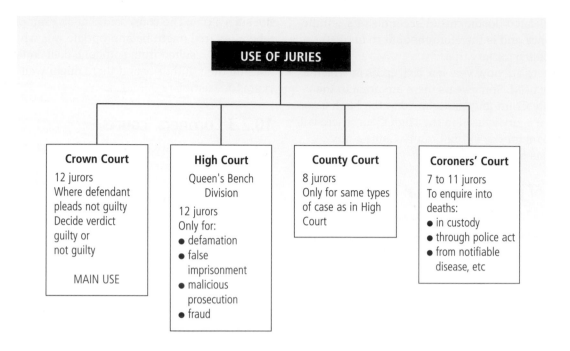

Figure 10.2 Use of juries

The Morris Committee thought that being a juror should be part of the responsibilities of being a citizen. As a result, the qualifications for jury service were widened in the Criminal Justice Act 1972 and based on the right to vote.

Present qualifications

The present qualifications are set out in the Juries Act 1974 (as amended) so that to qualify for jury service a person must be:

- aged between 18 and 70;
- registered as a parliamentary or local government elector;
- ordinarily resident in the United Kingdom, the Channel Islands or the Isle of Man for at least five years since their thirteenth birthday.

However, certain people are not permitted to sit on a jury even though they are within these basic qualifications; these are people who are disqualified or mentally disordered.

10.3.2 Disqualification

Disqualified permanently from jury service are those who at any time have been sentenced to:

- imprisonment for life, detention for life or custody for life;
- detention during Her Majesty's pleasure or during the pleasure of the Secretary of State;
- imprisonment for public protection or detention for public protection;
- an extended sentence;
- a term of imprisonment of five years or more or a term of detention of five years or more.

Those in the following categories are disqualified for 10 years:

- at any time in the last 10 years served a sentence of imprisonment;
- at any time in the last 10 years had a suspended sentence passed on them;
- at any time in the last 10 years had a community order or other community sentence passed on them.

In addition anyone who is currently on bail in criminal proceedings is disqualified from sitting as a juror.

If a disqualified person fails to disclose that fact and turns up for jury service, they may be fined up to £5,000.

10.3.3 Mentally disordered persons

A mentally disordered person is defined in the Criminal Justice Act 2003 as:

> **1.** A person who suffers or has suffered from mental illness, psychopathic disorder, mental handicap or severe mental handicap and on account of that condition either:
>
> (a) is resident in a hospital or similar institution, or
>
> (b) regularly attends for treatment by a medical practitioner.
>
> **2.** A person for the time being under guardianship under section 7 of the Mental Health Act 1983.
>
> **3.** A person who, under Part 7 of that Act, has been determined by a judge to be incapable of administering his property and affairs.

10.3.4 The right to be excused jury service

Prior to April 2004 people in certain essential occupations, such as doctors and pharmacists, had a right to be excused jury service if they did not want to do it. The Criminal Justice Act 2003 abolished this category. This means that doctors and other medical staff are no longer able to refuse to do jury service, though they can apply for a discretionary excusal.

Members of the forces

Full-time serving members of the forces will be excused from jury service if their commanding officer certifies their absence from duty (because of jury service) would be prejudicial to the efficiency of the service.

10.3.5 Discretionary excusals

Anyone who has problems which make it very difficult for them to do their jury service may ask to be excused or for their period of service to be put back to a later date. The court has a discretion to grant such an excusal but will only do so if there is a sufficiently good reason. Such reasons include being too ill to attend court or suffering from a disability that makes it impossible for the person to sit as a juror, or being a mother with a small baby. Other reasons could include business appointments that cannot be undertaken by anyone else, examinations or holidays that have been booked.

In these situations the court is most likely to defer jury service to a more convenient date, rather than excuse the person completely. This is stated in the current guidance for summoning officers which is aimed at preventing the high number of discretionary excusals shown in the statistics in the Activity on page 120. The guidance states that:

> The normal expectation is that everyone summoned for jury service will serve at the time for which they are summoned. It is recognised that there will be occasions where it is not reasonable for a person summoned to serve at the time for which they are summoned. In such circumstances the summoning officer should use his/her discretion to defer the individual to a time more appropriate. Only in extreme circumstances, should a person be excused from jury service.

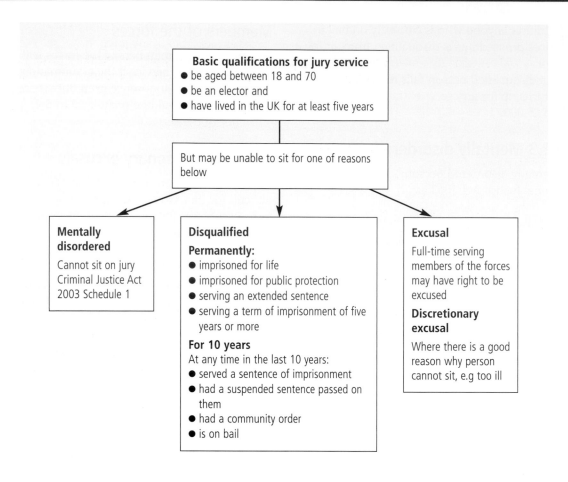

Figure 10.3 Qualifications of jurors

If a person is not excused from jury service they must attend on the date set or they may be fined up to £1,000 for non-attendance.

10.3.6 Lawyers and police officers

There used to be a category of people who were ineligible for jury service. This included judges and others who had been involved in the administration of justice within the previous 10 years. This category was abolished by the Criminal Justice Act 2003. This means that judges, lawyers, police, etc are now eligible to serve on juries. Many people feel that this could lead to bias or to a legally well-qualified juror influencing

the rest of the jury.

In *R v Abdroikof, R v Green and R v Williamson* (2007) the House of Lords considered appeals where a police officer or prosecutor had been one of the jury members.

They held that the fact that one of the members of jury was a police officer did not of itself make a trial unfair. However, a majority of three of the five judges held that in the situation where a police officer on the jury had worked in the same station as a police officer giving evidence for the prosecution in the trial, then there was the risk of bias. The test to be applied in such cases was:

whether the fair-minded and informed observer, having considered the facts, would conclude that there was a real possibility that the tribunal was biased.

The House of Lords also quoted from the decision in *R v Sussex Justices, ex parte McCarthy* (1924) where the judge stated that justice must not only be done, but must be seen to be done.

The same three judges in a majority decision also held that the presence of a juror who was a local Crown Prosecutor in the Crown Prosecutor Service meant that justice was clearly not being seen to be done. Lord Bingham stated:

 It is, in my opinion, clear that justice is not seen to be done if one discharging the very important neutral role of juror is a full-time, salaried, long-serving employee of the prosecutor.

Judges on jury service

In June 2004 (just two months after the rules on jury service changed) a judge from the Court of Appeal, Lord Justice Dyson, was summoned to attend as a juror. This prompted the Lord Chief Justice, Lord Woolf, to issue observations to judges who are called for jury service. These point out that

- a judge serves on a jury as part of his duty as a private citizen;
- excusal from jury service will only be granted in extreme circumstances;
- deferral of jury service to a later date should be sought where a judge has judicial commitments which make it particularly inconvenient for him to do jury service at the time he was called to do so;
- at court if a judge knows the presiding judge or other person in the case, he should raise this with the jury bailiff or a member of the court staff if he considers it could interfere with his responsibilities as a juror;
- it is a matter of discretion for an individual judge sitting as a juror as to whether he

discloses the fact of his judicial office to the other members of the jury;
- judges must follow the directions given to the jury by the trial judge on the law and should avoid the temptation to correct guidance which they believe to be inaccurate as this is outside their role as a juror.

Activity

Discuss whether you think the following people should sit on a jury:

1. A woman who was fined for shoplifting a month ago.
2. A man who was fined and disqualified from driving for taking cars without the consent of the owner.
3. A doctor who works in general practice.
4. A doctor who works in an accident and emergency unit of a busy city hospital.
5. A circuit judge who frequently tries cases in the Crown Court.

The point about letting the court know when someone involved in the case is personally known to the juror is also relevant to practising lawyers who are called for jury service. It was noticeable that when a Queen's Counsel was summoned for jury service at the Central Criminal Court (the Old Bailey) in the summer of 2004, he was prevented from sitting in each case that he was called for, on the grounds that he knew one or more people involved in each trial.

10.3.7 Lack of capacity

A judge at the court may discharge a person from being a juror for lack of capacity to cope with the trial. This could be because the person does not understand English adequately or because of some disability which makes them unsuitable as a juror. This includes anyone who is blind, and who would be unable to see plans and photographs produced in evidence. Section 9B(2) of the Juries

Test Yourself

1. In which criminal court is a jury used?
2. In which civil courts may a jury be used?
3. What age limits are there for jury service?
4. What two other basic qualifications are there for jury service?
5. Give two situations in which a person is disqualified from jury service.
6. What special rule is there about jury service for serving members of the armed forces?
7. What is meant by a 'discretionary excusal' from jury service?
8. What is the name of the case in which the House of Lords considered the effect of a police officer or prosecutor sitting as a jury member?
9. What test does the Supreme Court state should be used in cases where a jury member was a police officer or prosecutor?
10. Why was it ruled that a deaf person could not sit on a jury?

Act 1974 (which was added into the Act by the Criminal Justice and Public Order Act 1994, s 41) makes it clear that the mere fact of a disability does not prevent someone from acting as a juror. The judge can only discharge the juror if he is satisfied that the disability means that that juror is not capable of acting effectively as a juror.

Deaf jurors

In June 1995 a deaf man was prevented from sitting on a jury at the Old Bailey despite wishing to serve and bringing with him a sign language interpreter. The judge pointed out that that would mean an extra person in the jury room and this was not allowed by law. He also said that the way in which witnesses gave evidence and the tone of their voice was important: 'a deaf juror may not be able to pick up these nuances and to properly judge their credibility'.

In November 1999 another deaf man challenged the ban on him sitting as a juror. The judge in this case felt that there was no practical reason why he should not sit, but the law only allowed the 12 jury members to be present in the jury room. It did not allow a thirteenth person – a sign-language interpreter – to be present. This made it impossible for the deaf man to be a juror.

10.4 Selecting a jury

At each Crown Court there is an official who is responsible for summonsing enough jurors to try the cases that will be heard in each two-week period. This official will arrange for names to be selected at random from the electoral registers, for the area which the court covers. This is done through a computer selection at a central office. It is necessary to summons more than 12 jurors as most courts have more than one courtroom and it will not be known how many of those summonsed are disqualified or may be excused. In fact, at the bigger courts up to 150 summonses may be sent out each fortnight.

Those summonsed must notify the court if there is any reason why they should not or cannot attend. All others are expected to attend for two weeks' jury service, though, of course, if the case they are trying goes on for more than two weeks they will have to stay until the trial is completed. Where it is known that a trial may be exceptionally long, such as a complicated fraud trial, potential jurors are asked if they will be able to serve for such a long period.

10.4.1 Vetting

Once the list of potential jurors is known, both the prosecution and the defence have the right to see that list. In some cases it may be decided that this pool of potential jurors should be 'vetted', i.e. checked for suitability. There are two types of vetting:

- police checks, and
- wider background check.

Police checks

Routine police checks are made on prospective jurors to eliminate those disqualified. In *R v Crown Court at Sheffield, ex parte Brownlow* (1980) the defendant was a police officer and the defence sought permission to vet the jury panel for convictions. The judge gave permission but the Court of Appeal, while holding that they had no power to interfere, said that vetting was 'unconstitutional' and a 'serious invasion of privacy' and not sanctioned by the Juries Act 1974.

However, in *R v Mason* (1980) where it was revealed that the Chief Constable for Northamptonshire had been allowing widespread use of unauthorised vetting of criminal records, the Court of Appeal approved of this type of vetting. Lawton LJ pointed out that, since it is a criminal offence to serve on a jury while disqualified, the police were only doing their normal duty of preventing crime by checking for criminal records. Furthermore, the court said that,

Key facts

Court	Crown Court
Qualifications	18–70 age Registered to vote Resident in UK for at least five years since age 13
Disqualified	Sentenced to five years' or more imprisonment – disqualified for life Served a prison sentence OR suspended sentence OR a community service order – disqualified for 10 years Community order – disqualified for 10 years On bail – disqualified while on bail
Discretionary excusals	Ill, business commitments, or other 'good reason', but expectation is that nearly everyone will serve
Selection	A central office selects names from the lists of electors Summons sent to these people Must attend unless disqualified, ineligible or excused
Vetting	May be checked for criminal record – *R v Mason* (1980) In cases of national security may be subject to a wider check on background subject to Attorney-General's guidelines
Challenges	Individual juror may be challenged for cause, e.g. knows defendant Whole panel may be challenged for biased selection – but no right to a multi-racial jury (*R v Ford* (1989)) Prosecution may 'stand by' any juror
Function	Decide verdict – Guilty or Not guilty Sole arbiters of fact but judge directs them on law
Verdict	Must try for a unanimous verdict BUT if cannot reach a unanimous verdict then a majority verdict of 10:2 or 11:1 can be accepted

Figure 10.4 Key facts chart on the use of juries in criminal cases

Activity

Read the following extract from *Diversity and Fairness in the Jury System* (2007) and answer the questions below.

The Criminal Justice Act 2003 removed ineligibility and the right of excusal from jury service for a number of groups (those aged 65 to 69, MPs, clergy, medical professionals and those in the administration of justice). But summoned jurors may still be disqualified or excused from jury service (due to age, residency, mental disability, criminal charges, language, medical or other reasons).

- The study found that the most significant factors predicating whether a summoned juror will serve or not are income and employment status, not ethnicity. Summoned jurors in the lower income brackets and those who are economically inactive are far less likely to serve than those in medium to high income brackets and those who are employed.

- In 2005, of all those who replied to their summonses, 64 per cent of jurors served, 9 per cent were disqualified or ineligible, 27 per cent were excused. Of those excused, most were for medical reasons that prevented serving (34%) or child care (15%) and work

reasons (12%). Fifteen per cent of all the summonses in the survey were either returned as undeliverable or not responded to, which occurred most often in areas of high residential mobility.

- The report established that most current thinking about who does and does not do jury service is based on myth, not reality.

Myth: Ethnic minorities are under-represented among those doing jury service.

Reality: Analysis showed that, in almost all courts (81 of the 84 surveyed), there was no significant difference between the proportion of black and ethnic minority jurors serving and the black and ethnic minority population levels in the local juror catchment area for each court.

Myth: Women and young people are under-represented among serving jurors, and the self-employed are virtually exempt from jury service.

Reality: The study establishes that jury pools at individual courts closely reflected the local population in terms of gender and age, and the self-employed are represented among serving jurors in direct proportion to their representation in the population.

Questions

1. What are the age limits for jury service?

2. What is the residency requirement to qualify for jury service?

3. What categories of people are disqualified from doing jury service?

4. What categories of people are less likely to serve on a jury?

5. What percentage failed to reply to their summons to do jury service?

6. For what types of reason were people excused from jury service?

7. What does the study show about the representative nature of juries?

if in the course of looking at criminal records convictions were revealed which did not disqualify, there was no reason why these should not be passed on to prosecuting counsel, so that this information could be used in deciding to stand by individual jurors (see 10.4.3 for information on the right of stand by).

Juror's background

A wider check is made on a juror's background and political affiliations. This practice was brought to light by the 'ABC' trial in 1978 where two journalists and a soldier were charged with collecting secret information. It was discovered that the jury had been vetted for their loyalty. The trial was stopped and a new trial ordered before a fresh jury. Following this, the Attorney-General published guidelines in 1980 on when political vetting of jurors should take place. These guidelines state that:

(a) vetting should only be used in exceptional cases involving:
  - national security where part of the evidence is likely to be given *in camera*
  - terrorist cases

(b) vetting can only be carried out with the Attorney-General's express permission.

10.4.2 Selection at court

The jurors are usually divided into groups of 15 and allocated to a court. At the start of a trial the court clerk will select 12 out of these 15 at random. If there are not enough jurors to hear all the cases scheduled for that day at the court, there is a special power to select anyone who is qualified to be a juror from people passing by in the streets or from local offices or businesses. This is called 'praying a talesman'. It is very unusual to use this power but it was used at Middlesex Crown Court in January 1992 when about half the jury panel failed to turn up after the New Year's holiday and there were not sufficient jurors to try the cases.

10.4.3 Challenging

Once the court clerk has selected the panel of 12 jurors, these jurors come into the jury box to be sworn in as jurors. At this point, before the jury is sworn in, both the prosecution and defence have certain rights to challenge one or more of the jurors. These are:

- to the array;
- for cause;
- prosecution right to stand by jurors.

To the array

This right to challenge is given by s 5 of the Juries Act 1974 and it is a challenge to the whole jury on the basis that it has been chosen in an unrepresentative or biased way. This challenge was used successfully against the 'Romford' jury at the Old Bailey in 1993 when, out of a panel of 12 jurors, nine came from Romford, with two of them living within 20 doors of each other in the same street. A challenge to the array was also used in *R v Fraser* (1987) where the defendant was of an ethnic minority background but all the jurors were white. The judge in that case agreed to empanel another jury. However, in *R v Ford* (1989) it was held that if the jury was chosen in a random manner then it could not be challenged simply because it was not multi-racial.

For cause

This involves challenging the right of an individual juror to sit on the jury. To be successful the challenge must point out a valid reason why that juror should not serve on the jury. An obvious reason is that the juror is disqualified, but a challenge for cause can also be made if the juror knows or is related to a witness or defendant. If such people are not removed from the jury there is a risk that any subsequent conviction could be quashed. This occurred in *R v Wilson* and *R v Sprason* (1995) where the wife of a prison officer was summonsed for jury service. She had asked to be excused attendance on that ground, but this request had not been granted. She served on the jury which convicted the two defendants of robbery. Both defendants had been on remand at Exeter prison where her husband worked. The Court of Appeal said that justice must not only be done, it must be seen to be done and the presence of Mrs Roberts on the jury prevented that, so that the convictions had to be quashed.

Prosecution right to stand by jurors

This is a right that only the prosecution can exercise. It allows the juror who has been stood by to be put to the end of the list of potential jurors, so that they will not be used on the jury unless there are not enough other jurors. The prosecution does not have to give a reason for 'standing by', but the Attorney-General's guidelines make it clear that this power should be used sparingly.

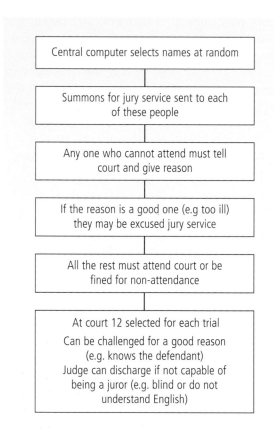

Figure 10.5 Selecting a jury

10.5 The jury's role in criminal cases

The jury is used only at the Crown Court for cases where the defendant pleads not guilty. This means that a jury is used in about 30,000 cases each year.

10.5.1 Split function

The trial is presided over by a judge and the functions split between the judge and jury. The judge decides points of law and the jury decides the facts. At the end of the prosecution case, the judge has the power to direct the jury to acquit the defendant if he decides that, in law, the prosecution's evidence has not made out a case against the defendant. This is called a directed acquittal and occurs in about 10 per cent of cases.

Where the trial continues, the judge will sum up the case at the end, to the jury and direct them on any law involved. The jury retire to a private room and make the decision on the guilt or innocence of the accused in secret. Initially the jury must try to come to a unanimous verdict, i.e. one on which they are all agreed. The judge must accept the jury verdict, even if he or she does not agree with it. This long established principle goes back to *Bushell's case* (1670). The jury do not give any reasons for their decision.

10.5.2 Majority verdicts

If, after at least two hours (longer where there are several defendants), the jury have not reached a verdict, the judge can call them back into the courtroom and direct them that he can now accept a majority verdict. Majority verdicts have been allowed since 1967. Where there is a full jury of 12, the verdict can be 10:2 or 11:1 either for guilty or for not guilty. If the jury has fallen below 12 for any reason (such as the death or illness of a juror during the trial) then only one can disagree with the verdict. That is, if there are 11 jurors, the verdict can be 10:1; if there are 10 jurors it can be 9:1. If there are only nine jurors the verdict must be unanimous. A jury cannot go below nine.

Majority verdicts were introduced because of the fear of jury 'nobbling', that is jurors being bribed or intimidated by associates of the defendant into voting for a not guilty verdict. When a jury had to be unanimous, only one member need be bribed to cause a 'stalemate' in which the jury were unable to reach a decision. It was also thought that the acquittal rates in jury trials were too high and majority decisions would result in more convictions.

Where the jury convict a defendant on a majority verdict, the foreman of the jury must announce the numbers both agreeing and disagreeing with the verdict in open court. This provision is contained in s 17(3) of the Juries Act 1974 and is aimed at making sure the jury have come to a legal majority, and not one, for example of eight to four, which is not allowed. About 20 per cent of convictions by juries each year are by majority verdict.

10.5.3 Secrecy

The jury discussion takes place in secret and there can be no inquiry into how the jury reached its verdict. This is because s 8 of the Contempt of Court Act 1981 makes disclosure of anything that happened in the jury room a contempt of court which is a criminal offence. It is a contempt 'to obtain, disclose or solicit any particulars of statements made, opinions expressed, arguments advanced or votes cast by members of a jury in the course of their deliberations in any legal proceedings'. The section was brought in because newspapers were paying jurors large sums of money for 'their story'. This is obviously not desirable, but the total ban on finding out what happens in the jury room means that it is difficult to discover whether jurors have understood the evidence in complex cases.

10.6 Advantages of jury trial

10.6.1 Public confidence

On the face of it, asking 12 strangers who have no legal knowledge and without any training to decide what may be complex and technical points is an absurd one. Yet the jury is considered one of the fundamentals of a democratic society. The right to be tried by one's peers is a bastion of liberty against the state and has been supported by eminent judges. For example, Lord Devlin said juries are 'the lamp that shows that freedom lives'. The tradition of trial by jury is very old and people seem to have confidence in the impartiality and fairness of a jury trial. This can be seen in the objection to withdrawing the right to jury trial from cases of 'minor' theft.

10.6.2 Jury equity

Since juries are not legal experts, they are not bound to follow the precedent of past cases or even Acts of Parliament, and do not have to give reasons for their verdict, it is possible for them to decide cases on their idea of 'fairness'. This is sometimes referred to as jury equity. Several cases have shown the importance of this, in particular *Ponting's case* (1984) in which a civil servant was charged under the old wide-ranging s 2 of the Official Secrets Act 1911. He had leaked information on the sinking of the ship, The *General Belgrano*, in the Falklands war to an MP. At his trial he pleaded not guilty, claiming that his actions had been in the public interest. The jury refused to convict him even though the judge ruled there was no defence. The case also prompted the government to reconsider the law and to amend s 2.

10.6.3 Open system of justice

The use of a jury is viewed as making the legal system more open. Justice is seen to be done as members of the public are involved in a key role and the whole process is public. It also helps to keep the law clearer as points have to be explained to the jury, enabling the defendant to understand the case more easily.

Against this is the fact that the jury deliberate in private and that no one can inquire into what happened in the jury room. In addition, the jury do not have to give any reason for their verdict. When a judge gives a judgment he explains his reasoning and, if he has made an error, it is known and can be appealed against.

10.6.4 Secrecy of the jury room

This can be seen as an advantage, since the jury are free from pressure in their discussion. Jurors are protected from outside influences when deciding on the verdict. This allows juries to bring in verdicts that may be unpopular with the public as well as allowing jurors the freedom to ignore the strict letter of the law. It has been suggested that people would be less willing to serve on a jury if they knew that their discussions could be made public.

10.6.5 Impartiality

A jury should be impartial as they are not connected to anyone in the case. The process of random selection should result in a cross-section of society and this should also lead to an impartial jury, as they will have different prejudices and so should cancel out each others' biases. No one individual person is responsible for the decision. A jury is also not case-hardened since they sit for only two weeks and are unlikely to try more than three or four cases in that time. After the end of the case the jury dissolves and, as Sir Sebag Shaw said, it is 'anonymous and amorphous'.

10.7 Disadvantages of jury trial

10.7.1 Perverse decisions

In section 10.6.2 we looked at the idea of jury equity. That is the fact that the jury can ignore an unjust law. However, in some circumstances this type of decision can be seen as a perverse decision and one which was not justified. Juries have refused to convict in other clear-cut cases such as *R v Randle and Pottle* (1991) where the defendants were charged with helping the spy George Blake to escape from prison. Their prosecution did not occur until 25 years after the

escape, when they wrote about what they had done and the jury acquitted them, possibly as a protest over the time lapse between the offence and the prosecution.

Another case where the evidence was clear, yet the jury acquitted the defendants was *R v Kronlid and others* (1996). In this case, the defendants admitted they had caused £1.5 million damage to a plane. They pleaded not guilty on the basis that they were preventing the plane from being sent to Indonesia where it would have been used in attacks against the people of East Timor. The jury acquitted them.

10.7.2 Secrecy

Earlier we considered how the secrecy of the jury protects jurors from pressure. However, the secrecy of the jury room is also a disadvantage because as no reasons have to be given for the verdict, there is no way of knowing if the jury understood the case and came to the decision for the right reasons.

In *R v Mirza* (2004) the House of Lords ruled that it could not inquire into discussions in a jury room. Two separate cases were considered in the appeal. These were *R v Mirza* and *R v Connor and Rollock*.

In *Mirza* the defendant was a Pakistani who settled in the UK in 1988. He had an interpreter to help him in the trial and during the trial the jury sent notes asking why he needed an interpreter. He was convicted on a 10:2 majority. Six days after the jury verdict, one juror wrote to the defendant's counsel alleging that from the start of the trial there had been a 'theory' that the use of an interpreter was a 'ploy'. The juror also said that she had been shouted down when she objected and reminded her fellow jurors of the judge's directions.

In *Connor and Rollock* a juror wrote to the Crown Court stating that while many jurors thought it was one or other of the defendants who had committed the stabbing, they should convict both to 'teach them a lesson'. This was five days after the verdict but before sentence was passed. As in *Mirza* there was a majority verdict

Key facts

Advantages	Disadvantages
Public confidence	High acquittal rates undermine confidence in the criminal justice system
Considered to be a fundamental part of a democratic society	
New qualifications for jury service mean that almost everyone can serve on a jury	Doing jury service is unpopular
Jury equity: *Ponting's case*	Perverse verdicts: *Randle and Pottle* *R v Kronlid*
Open system of justice	Media influence
Involves members of the public	Reporting may influence the decision: *Taylor and Taylor*
Secrecy of the jury room protects jurors from pressure	Secrecy means that: ● the reasons for the decision are not known ● the jury's understanding of the case cannot be checked Exception: *Young (Stephen)*
Impartiality	Bias
Having 12 members with no direct interest in the case should cancel out any bias	In some cases there has been racial bias *Sander v UK*

Figure 10.6 Key facts chart of advantages and disadvantages of jury trial

The judicial statistics show that in most years more than half of acquittals are ordered by the judge without a jury even being sworn in to try the case. This happens where the prosecution drop the case at the last minute and offer no evidence against the defendant. Usually about 10–15 per cent of acquittals are by a jury but on the direction of a judge. This occurs where the judge rules that there is no case against the defendant; it might be because of a legal point or because the prosecution evidence is not sufficient in law to prove the case. When these decisions are excluded from the statistics it is found that juries actually acquit in less than 40 per cent of cases.

10.7.8 Other disadvantages

The compulsory nature of jury service is unpopular, so that some jurors may be against the whole system, while others may rush their verdict in order to leave as quickly as possible. Jury service can be a strain, especially where jurors have to listen to horrific evidence. Jurors in the Rosemary West case were offered counselling after the trial to help them cope with the evidence they had seen and heard.

Jury 'nobbling' does occur and in some cases jurors have had to be provided with police protection. In order to try to combat this, the Criminal Procedure and Investigations Act 1996 allows for a retrial to be ordered if someone is subsequently proved to have interfered with the jury.

The use of juries makes trials slow and expensive. This is because each point has to be explained carefully to the jury and the whole procedure of the case takes longer.

10.8 Special problems of using juries in civil cases

10.8.1 Amount of damages

Juries in civil cases decide both the liability of the parties in the case and also the amount of damages that will be awarded. The awards vary greatly as each jury has its own ideas and does not follow past cases. The amount is, therefore, totally unpredictable which makes it difficult for lawyers to advise on settlements. Judges look back to past awards when deciding awards of damages in personal injury cases, and then apply an inflation factor so that there is consistency between similar cases. Juries in defamation cases cause particular problems with very large awards; one judge called it Mickey Mouse money.

Until 1990 the Court of Appeal had no power to correct awards which were thought to be far too high. But under s 8 of the Courts and Legal Services Act 1990 the Court of Appeal has special powers in such cases. The Court of Appeal can order a new trial or substitute such sum as appears proper to the court, if they feel the damages were excessive or inadequate. This power was first used in a case brought by the MP Teresa Gorman where the Court of Appeal reduced the damages awarded to her by the jury from £150,000 to £50,000. It was also used in *Rantzen v Mirror Group Newspapers* (1993) when the award to Esther Rantzen, the founder of 'Childline' (a charity set up to help abused children) over allegations that she had deliberately kept quiet about the activities of a suspected child abuser, was reduced from £250,000 to £110,000.

10.8.2 Unreasoned decision

The jury does not have to give a reason either for its decision or for the amount it awards. A judge always gives a judgment, which makes it easier to see if there are good grounds for an appeal.

10.8.3 Bias

The problems of bias in civil cases is different to that encountered in criminal cases. In some defamation cases the claimants and/or the defendants may be public figures so that jurors will know and possibly hold views about them. Alternatively there is the fact that the defendant in a defamation case is often a newspaper and jurors may be biased against the press or may feel that 'they can afford to pay'.

10.8.4 Cost

Civil cases are expensive and the use of a jury adds to this as the case is likely to last longer. At the end of the case the losing party will have to pay all the costs of the case which may amount to hundreds of thousands of pounds. As a result of this, the Lord Chancellor has introduced some reforms so that defamation actions will be less costly. First, with the increase in County Court jurisdiction, parties can now agree that their case should be transferred to the County Court. Here a jury of eight may be used and the trial is likely to be less expensive than one in the High Court. Second, the parties may also agree to the case being tried by a judge alone without a jury. The Defamation Act 1996 allows the claimant to seek a limited sum (up to £10,000) in a quick procedure dealt with by a judge. This allows those who want to clear their name and get immediate compensation at a lower cost to do so.

10.9 Alternatives to jury trial

Despite all the problems of using juries in criminal cases, there is still a strong feeling that they are the best method available. However, if juries are not thought suitable to try serious criminal cases, what alternative form of trial could be used?

10.9.1 Trial by a single judge

This is the method of trial in the majority of civil cases which is generally regarded as producing a fairer and more predictable result. Trial by a single judge was used for some criminal trials in Northern Ireland until 2007. These were called the Diplock courts and were brought in on the recommendation of Lord Diplock to replace jury trial because of the special problems of threats and jury nobbling that existed between the different sectarian parties.

There have recently been two provisions made in Acts of Parliament for trial by a single judge to take place in England and Wales.

In the Criminal Justice Act 2003 there is provision for the prosecution to apply for trial by a judge alone in:

- complex fraud cases, or
- where there has already been an effort to tamper with a jury in the case.

However, this is not yet in force and the provision is subject to an affirmative resolution. This means that it cannot be brought into effect without both Houses voting for it.

In the Domestic Violence, Crime and Victims Act 2004 there is provision for cases where there are a large number of counts on the indictment. This would allow a trial of sample counts with a jury and then, if the defendant was convicted on those, the remainder could be tried by a judge alone.

However, there appears to be less public confidence in the use of judges to decide all serious criminal cases. The arguments against this form of trial are that judges become case-hardened and prosecution-minded. They are also from a very elite group and would have little understanding of the background and problems of defendants. Individual prejudices are more likely than in a jury where the different personalities should go some way to eliminating bias. But, on the other hand, judges are trained to evaluate cases and they are now being given training in racial awareness. This may make them better arbiters of fact than an untrained jury.

10.9.2 A panel of judges

In some continental countries cases are heard by a panel of three or five judges sitting together. This allows for a balance of views, instead of the verdict of a single person. However, it still leaves the problems of judges becoming case-hardened, prosecution-minded and coming from an elite background. The other difficulty is that there are not sufficient judges and our system of legal training and appointment would need a radical overhaul to implement this proposal. It would also be expensive.

10.9.3 A judge plus lay assessors

Under this system the judge and two lay people would make the decision together. This method is used in the Scandinavian countries. It provides the legal expertise of the judge, together with lay participation in the legal system by ordinary members of the public. The lay people could either be drawn from the general public, using the same method as is used for selecting juries at present or a special panel of assessors could be drawn up as in tribunal cases. This latter suggestion would be particularly suitable for fraud cases.

10.9.4 A mini-jury

Finally, if the jury is to remain, then it might be possible to have a smaller number of jurors. In many continental countries when a jury is used there are nine members. For example, in Spain, which reintroduced the use of juries in certain criminal cases in 1996, there is a jury of nine. Alternatively a jury of six could be used for less serious criminal cases that at the moment have a full jury trial, as occurs in some American states.

Test Yourself

1. How are the names of potential jurors chosen?
2. What two types of vetting may take place?
3. When can a challenge be made to an individual juror?
4. What is the role of the jury in a criminal case?
5. What is meant by a majority verdict?
6. Which Act of Parliament makes it an offence for a juror to disclose what happened in the jury room?
7. Explain three advantages of using juries.
8. Explain three disadvantages of using juries.
9. Explain two problems of using a jury in a civil case.
10. State two alternative methods of trial other than trial by jury.

Examination questions

(b) Describe how jurors qualify and are selected to serve on a jury.

(c) Briefly discuss the disadvantages of using **lay persons** to decide criminal cases.

AQA LAW01 June 2009

NB The first part of this question can be found at the end of Chapter 8.

Examiner's tip

Read the question carefully. Look at part (c). First, note that it asks only for disadvantages. Also note that it requires you to discuss the use of 'lay persons'. So you must include comment on both juries and lay magistrates.

Chapter 11

The Legal Profession

In England and Wales there are two types of lawyers (barristers and solicitors) jointly referred to as the legal profession. Most countries do not have this clear-cut division among lawyers: a person will qualify simply as a lawyer, although, after qualifying, it will be possible for them to specialise as an advocate, or in a particular area of law. This type of system is also seen in this country in the medical profession, where all those wishing to become doctors take the same general qualifications. After they have qualified, some doctors will go on to specialise in different fields, perhaps as surgeons, and will take further qualifications in their chosen field.

In England and Wales, not only are the professions separate, but there is no common training for lawyers, although there have been increasing calls for this. As far back as 1971 the Ormrod Committee was in favour of a common education for all prospective lawyers. In 1994 the Lord Chancellor's advisory committee on legal education, under Lord Steyn, recommended that, instead of having separate training for barristers and solicitors, 'the two branches of the profession should have joint training. All those qualifying would then work for six months or a year at a solicitors', with those who wished to become barristers going on to do extra training at the Bar. Yet despite these recommendations, the training of the two professions remains separate.

11.1 Solicitors

There are over 110,000 solicitors practising in England and Wales and they are controlled by their own professional body, the Law Society. Of these, 83,000 are in private practice and the remainder are in employed work such as for local government or the Crown Prosecution Service.

11.1.1 Qualification

To become a solicitor it is usual to have a law degree, although those with a degree in a subject other than law can do an extra year's training in core legal subjects, and take the Common Professional Examination (CPE) or Graduate Diploma in Law (GDL). The next stage is the one-year Legal Practice Course. This is much more practically based than the previous Law Society Finals course and includes training in skills such as client-interviewing, negotiation, advocacy, drafting documents and legal research. There is also an emphasis on business management, for example, keeping accounts.

11.1.2 Training

Even when this course has been passed, the student is still not a qualified solicitor. He or she must next obtain a training contract under which they work in a solicitors' firm for two years, getting practical experience. This training period can also be undertaken in certain other legal organisations such as the Crown Prosecution Service, or the legal department of a local authority. During this two-year training contract the trainee will be paid, though not at the same rate as a fully qualified solicitor, and will do his

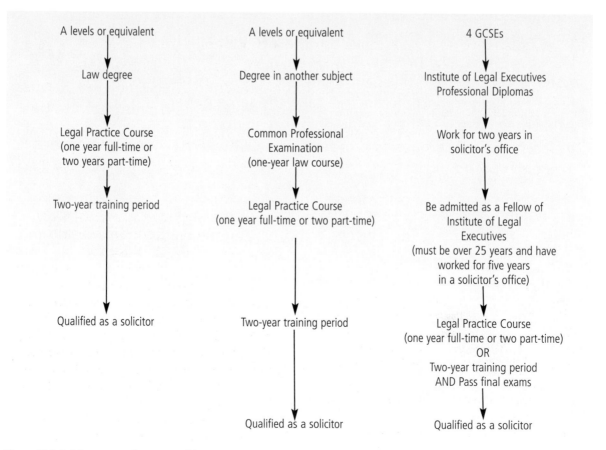

Figure 11.1 Training routes to become a solicitor

own work, supervised by a solicitor. He will also have to complete a 20-day Professional Skills Course which builds on the skills learnt on the LPC. At the end of the time, the trainee will be admitted as a solicitor by the Law Society and his name will be added to the roll (or list) of solicitors. Even after qualifying, solicitors have to attend continuing education courses to keep their knowledge up to date.

Non-graduate route

There is also a route under which non-graduates can qualify as solicitors by first becoming legal executives. This route is only open to mature candidates and takes longer than the graduate route. The three routes to becoming a solicitor are shown in Figure 11.1.

11.1.3 Criticisms of training

There are several criticisms of the training process.

The first of these is a financial problem, in that students will usually have to pay the fees of the Legal Practice Course (about £7,000) and support themselves during this year. If they have a degree in a subject other than law and have to do the CPE/GDL, they will also have had to pay for that course. This need to pay full fees is because the CPE/GDL and the LPC are post-graduate courses, so students must pay all the cost. The result of this policy is that students from poor families may not be able to afford to take the courses and may therefore be prevented from becoming solicitors, even though they have obtained a good degree. Other students may take out bank loans, so that although they qualify, they start the training period with a large debt. The problem has increased since universities started charging £3,000 or more a year. Would-be solicitors are likely to have debts of £20,000 or more by the time they start their training contract. This financial problem is also one faced by prospective barristers.

In order to try to help would-be solicitors, the CPE can be taken as a part-time course over two years, instead of the one-year full-time course. Doing the course part time allows students to work as well, easing their financial problems. Often this work will be as a para-legal in a law firm, so that the student is also getting practical experience at the same time.

A point common to barristers is that non-law graduates do only one year of formal law for the Graduate Diploma in Law. The Ormrod Committee which reported on legal education in 1971 thought that the main entry route should be via a law degree, but in practice 25 per cent of solicitors will not have taken a law degree. One critic posed the question of whether the public would be satisfied with doctors who have only studied medicine for one year, concentrating on only six subjects. Yet this is precisely what is occurring in the legal profession.

A third problem is one of over-supply, so that students who have passed the LPC may be unable to obtain a training contract. This was a real problem during the 1990s, but the number of places has increased. Even so, there will be some students who pass all their examinations but are unable to become solicitors because they cannot get a training contract.

11.1.4 Solicitors' work

The majority of those who succeed in qualifying as a solicitor will then work in private practice in a solicitors' firm. However, there are other careers available, and some newly-qualified solicitors may go on to work in the Crown Prosecution Service or for a local authority or government department. Others will become legal advisers in commercial or industrial businesses.

A solicitor in private practice may work as a sole practitioner or in a partnership. There are some 8,700 firms of solicitors, ranging from the small 'high street' practice to the big city firms. The number of partners is not limited, and some of the biggest firms will have over 100 partners as well as employing assistant solicitors.

The type of work done by a solicitor will largely depend on the type of firm he or she is working in. A small high street firm will probably be a general practice advising clients on a whole range of topics such as consumer problems, housing and business matters and family problems. A solicitor working in such a practice is likely to spend some of his time interviewing clients in his office and negotiating on their behalf, and a large amount of time dealing with paperwork. This will include:

- writing letters on behalf of clients;
- drafting contracts, leases or other legal documents;
- drawing up wills;
- dealing with conveyancing (the legal side of buying and selling flats, houses, office buildings and land).

The solicitor may also, if he wishes, act for some of his clients in court. Standing up in court and putting the client's case, and questioning witnesses is known as advocacy. Some solicitors will specialise in this and spend much of their time in court.

A solicitor with a client

Specialising

Although some solicitors may be general practitioners handling a variety of work it is not unusual, even in small firms, for a solicitor to specialise in one particular field. The firm itself may only handle certain types of cases (perhaps only civil actions) and not do any criminal cases, or a firm may specialise in matrimonial cases. Even within the firm the solicitors are likely to have their own field of expertise. In large firms there will be an even greater degree of specialisation with departments dealing with one aspect of the law. The large city firms usually concentrate on business and commercial law. Amounts earned by solicitors are as varied as the types of firm, with the top earners in big firms on £500,000 or more, while at the bottom end of the scale some sole practitioners will earn less than £30,000.

Conveyancing

Prior to 1985 solicitors had a monopoly on conveyancing: this meant that only solicitors could deal with the legal side of transferring houses and other buildings and land. This was changed by the Administration of Justice Act 1985 which allowed people other than solicitors to become licensed conveyancers. As a result of the increased competition in this area, solicitors had to reduce their fees, but even so they lost a large proportion of the work. This led to a demand for wider rights of advocacy.

Rights of advocacy

All solicitors have always been able to act as advocates in the Magistrates' Courts and the County Courts, but their rights of audience in the higher courts used to be very limited. Normally a solicitor could only act as advocate in the Crown Court on a committal for sentence, or on an appeal from the Magistrates' Court, and then only if he or another solicitor in the firm had been the

Key facts

Original rights	To present cases in County Court and Magistrates' Courts also at Crown Court on committal for sentence or appeal from Magistrates' Court
Practice Direction 1986	Following *Abse v Smith* allowed to make a statement in High Court in cases in which terms had been agreed
Courts and Legal Services Act 1990	Solicitors allowed to apply for certificate of advocacy to conduct cases in the higher courts. Must have experience of advocacy, take course and pass examinations
Access to Justice Act 1999	Possibility solicitors might have full rights of audience in the future – not yet in effect

Figure 11.2 Key facts chart on solicitors' rights of audience

advocate in the original case in the Magistrates' Court.

Until 1986 solicitors had no rights of audience in open court in the High Court, though they could deal with preliminary matters in preparation for a case. This lack of rights of audience was emphasised in *Abse v Smith* (1986) in which two Members of Parliament were contesting a libel action. They came to an agreed settlement, but the solicitor for one of them was refused permission by the judge to read out the terms of that settlement in open court. Following this decision the Lord Chancellor and the senior judges in each division of the High Court issued a Practice Direction, allowing solicitors to appear in the High Court to make a statement in a case that has been settled.

Certificate of advocacy

The first major alteration to solicitors' rights of audience came in the Courts and Legal Services Act 1990. Under this Act, a solicitor in private practice had the right to apply for a certificate of advocacy which enabled him to appear in the higher courts. Such a certificate was granted if the solicitor already had experience of advocacy in the Magistrates' Court and the County Court, took a short training course and passed examinations on the rules of evidence. The first certificates were granted in 1994 and by 2009 over 4,500 solicitors had qualified to be an advocate in the higher courts. Figure 11.2 sets out the changes to the rights of audience of solicitors.

Solicitors with an advocacy qualification are also eligible to be appointed as Queen's Counsel (see section 11.2.4) and also to be appointed to higher judicial posts.

The Access to Justice Act did have a provision that all solicitors could eventually be given full rights of audience. However, this provision has not yet been brought into effect.

Multi-discipline partnerships

Section 66 of the Courts and Legal Services Act 1990 allows solicitors to form partnerships with other professions, for example, accountants. This would give clients a wider range of expertise and advice in a 'one-stop shop'. However, the Law Society and the Bar Council have rules which prohibit the creation of multi-discipline partnerships, so that, as yet, 'one-stop' shops are not allowed. However, this will change under the Legal Services Act 2007 (see section 11.3).

11.1.5 The Law Society

The Law Society is the governing body of solicitors. It has a council elected by solicitors themselves. The head of the council is the President who is elected (and therefore changes) each year.

The Law Society's powers come from the Solicitors Act 1974. It sets down rules about qualifications and training. It is also responsible for disciplining solicitors.

11.1.6 Complaints against solicitors

A solicitor deals directly with clients and enters into a contract with them. This means that if the client does not pay, the solicitor has the right to sue for his fees. It also means that the client can sue his solicitor for breach of contract if the solicitor fails to do the work.

A client can also sue the solicitor for negligence in and out of court work. This happened in *Griffiths v Dawson* (1993) where solicitors for the claimant had failed to make the correct application in divorce proceedings against her husband. As a result the claimant lost financially and the solicitors were ordered to pay her £21,000 in compensation.

Other people affected by the solicitor's negligence may also have the right to sue in certain circumstances. An example of this was the case of *White v Jones* (1995) where a father wanted to make a will leaving each of his daughters £9,000. He wrote to his solicitors instructing them to draw up a will to include this. The solicitors received this letter on 17 July 1986 but had done nothing about it by the time the father died on 14 September 1986. As a result the daughters did not inherit any money and they successfully sued the solicitor for the £9,000 they had each lost.

Negligent advocacy

It used to be held that a solicitor presenting a case in court could not be sued for negligence. However, in *Hall v Simons* (2000), the House of Lords decided that advocates can be liable for negligence. This case is discussed more fully in section 11.2.6.

Complaints procedure

There have been problems with the complaints procedures operated by the Law Society. One of the main concerns has been that the Law Society was in the position of acting as a regulatory body to protect the interests of clients, while at the same time representing solicitors. This was seen as a conflict between the interest of the solicitor and the interest of the client who is complaining.

The other problem for those complaining about poor service by a solicitor was that the complaints bodies run by the Law Society have themselves frequently been criticised for delays and inefficiency.

Recent changes

In 2004 the Law Society created a new complaints body. This was the Consumer Complaints Service. An important feature of this is that there are several lay people on the board, so that it is not completely managed by solicitors.

However, this Consumer Complaints Service is still not as efficient as it should be. The Legal Service's Ombudsman's report for 2008–09 found that only two out of every three complaints were handled satisfactorily. The Ombudsman has in the past pointed out that 'the overall performance is well short of where a modern consumer-focused organisation should be'.

Future reforms

The Legal Services Act 2007 has provision for the creation of the Office for Legal Complaints. This will be completely independent of the Law Society and any other sector of the legal profession. The Office will have a non-lawyer as Chairman and the majority of members must also be non-lawyers. This Office will deal with complaints against solicitors and also all other sectors of the legal profession. It is likely to be set up by the end of 2010 (see section 11.3 for further detail).

The Legal Service Complaints Commissioner

The Legal Service Complaints Commissioner has the right to investigate the handling of complaints and to make recommendations about the arrangements for dealing with complaints. He or she can also impose targets for handling complaints and, if these are not met, can fine the professional body concerned.

In 2006 the Legal Services Complaints Commission fined the Law Society £250,000 for submitting an inadequate complaints-handling plan.

The post of Legal Services Complaints Commissioner will be abolished when the Office for Legal Complaints is set up.

The Legal Services Ombudsman

Under the Courts and Legal Services Act 1990, the post of Legal Services Ombudsman was created to examine complaints against solicitors, and also barristers and licensed conveyancers, where the professions' own regulatory bodies did not provide a satisfactory answer. Under the Access to Justice Act 1999 the Ombudsman has power to order that the solicitor concerned should pay compensation or that the Law Society itself should compensate the client.

The post of Legal Services Ombudsman will be abolished when the Office for Legal Complaints is set up in late 2010. It will be replaced by Office for Legal Complaints Ombudsman.

11.2 Barristers

There are about 12,000 barristers in independent practice in England and Wales. Collectively barristers are referred to as 'the Bar' and they are controlled by their own professional body – the General Council of the Bar. All barristers must also be a member of one of the four Inns of Court: Lincoln's Inn, Inner Temple, Middle Temple and Gray's Inn, all of which are situated near the Royal Courts of Justice in London.

11.2.1 Qualification

Entry to the Bar is normally degree-based, though there is a non-degree route for mature entrants, under which a small number of students qualify. As with solicitors, graduate students without a law degree can take the one-year course for the Common Professional Examination (Graduate Diploma in law) in the core subjects, in order to go on to qualify as a barrister. All student barristers have to pass the Bar Vocational Course. This course is being re-named as the Bar

Test Yourself

1. If a person has a non-law degree, what extra qualification must they take if they wish to become a lawyer?
2. What is the skills-based qualification which all would-be solicitors must pass?
3. What is a training contract?
4. What problems are there in respect of training to become a lawyer?
5. Explain three types of work that a solicitor's firm might do.
6. Apart from working in a solicitor's firm, what other legal careers are available to a qualified solicitor?
7. What is a certificate of advocacy?
8. Which body governs solicitors?
9. What complaints body is being set up under the provisions of the Legal Services Act 2007?
10. What is the role of the Legal Services Ombudsman?

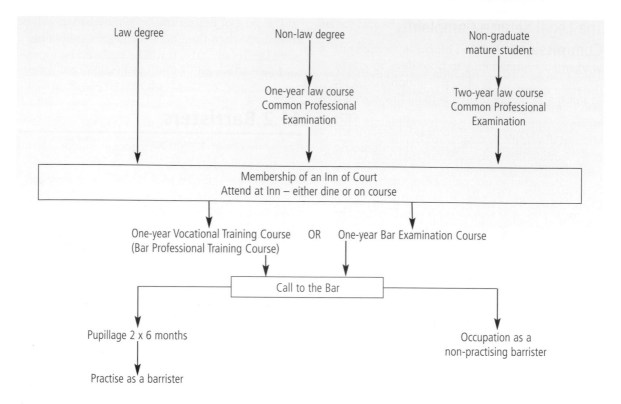

Figure 11.3 Training routes to become a barrister

Professional Training Course. On the course students study:

- case preparation;
- legal research;
- written skills;
- opinion-writing (giving written advice);
- drafting documents such as claim forms;
- conference skills (interviewing clients);
- negotiation;
- advocacy (speaking in court).

Students also study specific areas of law related to their future profession, such as civil litigation, criminal litigation and the law of evidence.

All student barristers must join one of the four Inns of Court and used to have to dine there 12 times before being called to the Bar. Students may now attend in a different way, for example, a weekend residential course. This helps students on courses outside London as travelling costs will be lower. The idea behind the rule requiring all

trainee barristers to dine was that they met senior barristers and judges and absorbed the traditions of the profession. In practice, few barristers dine at their Inns and students are unlikely to meet anyone except other students.

11.2.2 Training

Once a student has passed the Bar Vocational Course, he or she is then 'called to the Bar'. This means that they are officially qualified as a barrister. However, there is still a practical stage to their training which must be completed. This is called pupillage.

Pupillage

After the student has passed the Bar Vocational Course there is 'on the job' training where the trainee barrister becomes a pupil to a qualified barrister. This effectively involves 'work shadowing' that barrister, and can be with the same barrister for 12 months or with two different pupil masters for six months each. There is also a requirement that they take part in a programme of continuing education organised by the Bar Council. After the first six months of pupillage, barristers are eligible to appear in court and may conduct their own cases. During pupillage trainee barristers are paid a small salary, usually about half the amount paid to trainee solicitors.

The various training routes are shown in Figure 11.3.

11.2.3 Barristers' work

Barristers practising at the Bar are self-employed, but usually work from a set of chambers where they can share administrative expenses with other barristers. Most sets of chambers are fairly small comprising of about 15 to 20 barristers. They will employ a clerk as a practice administrator – booking in cases and negotiating fees – and they will have other support staff. One of the problems facing newly qualified barristers is the difficulty of finding a tenancy in chambers. Many will do a third six month pupillage and then 'squat' as an unofficial tenant before obtaining a place. The

A barrister

rule on having to practise from chambers has been relaxed, so that it is technically possible for barristers to practise from home. However, despite the fact that a tenancy in chambers is not essential, it is still viewed as the way to allow a barrister to build a successful practice.

The majority of barristers will concentrate on advocacy, although there are some who specialise in areas such as tax and company law, and who rarely appear in court. Barristers have rights of audience in all courts in England and Wales. Even those who specialise in advocacy will do a certain amount of paperwork, writing opinions on cases, giving advice and drafting documents for use in court.

Direct access

Originally it was also necessary for anybody who wished to instruct a barrister to go to a solicitor first. The solicitor would then brief the barrister. This was thought to create unnecessary expense for clients, as it meant they had to use two lawyers instead of one. As a result of criticism the Bar first of all started to operate a system called Bar Direct under which certain professionals such as accountants and surveyors could brief a barrister direct without using a solicitor. This was extended to other professionals and organisations. Then in September 2004 the Bar granted direct access to anyone (business or individual). It is no longer necessary to go to a solicitor in order to instruct a barrister in civil cases. However, direct access is still not allowed for criminal cases.

Cab rank rule

Normally barristers operate what is known as the cab rank rule under which they cannot turn down a case if it is on the area of law they deal with and they are free to take the case. However, where clients approach a barrister direct, the cab rank rule does not apply. Barristers can turn down a case which would require investigation or support services which they cannot provide.

Activity

Read the following article and answer the questions below.

Talent, not cash, should open the door to the Bar

The ancient buildings, paved courtyards and well-tended lawns of the Inns of Court shout privilege. But is the privilege of being a barrister one that anyone can attain – regardless of social background or wealth?

Concerns that it is now harder to enter the Bar have grown along with the costs of university and Bar training. Nearly one in three students arrive with debts of £20,000. The one-year vocational course can add another £15,000 – and non-law graduates have to fund an extra year on top of that.

But the barrier is not just financial. Geoffrey Vos, QC, whose father was a Bermondsey leather merchant, identifies other hurdles: lack of contacts or knowledge about the profession; its intimidating environment; the scramble to find a pupillage, or training place; and then the challenge of securing a seat in chambers. Finally, there is uncertainty of success or earning power.

The profession's entry profile is far more diverse that it was. But then what? Getting in is just the first hurdle. Perceived obstacles once inside can be a further deterrent. At the top the profession is still mostly male, white and privileged: 73 per cent of barristers in eight top commercial chambers went to private schools. At law firms, the proportion of women partners over ten years has risen slowly from 16.55 per cent to 23.2 per cent now. Women in the higher levels of the profession are nowhere near beginning to reflect the level of women entering the profession.

Adapted from an article by Frances Gibb, *The Times*, 3 April 2007. © The Times 2007/ nisyndication.com

Questions

1. The article mentions the Inns of Court. Name the four Inns of Court.
2. Briefly describe what the Bar Vocational Course consists of.
3. Why do non-law graduates have to do an extra year?
4. What financial barriers are there to becoming a barrister?
5. What other barriers are there to becoming a barrister?
6. In which area have the legal professions become more diverse?
7. What are the problems at the higher levels of the legal professions?

Employed barristers

The employed Bar, which includes those barristers working for the Crown Prosecution Service, have full rights of audience. They can appear in the Magistrates' Court, in the Crown Court, High Court or appellate courts.

11.2.4 Queen's Counsel

After at least 10 years as a barrister or as a solicitor with an advocacy qualification, it is possible to apply to the Lord Chancellor to become a Queen's Counsel (QC). About 10 per cent of the Bar are Queen's Counsel and it is known as 'taking silk'. QCs usually take on more complicated and high-profile cases than junior barristers (all barristers who are not Queen's Counsel are known as 'juniors'), and they can command higher fees for their recognised expertise. Often a QC will have a junior barrister to assist with the case.

New appointment system

Selection of new QCs is now made by an independent selection panel. Lawyers apply to become QCs. They have to pay a fee of £2,700. Applicants provide references (these can include references from clients) and are interviewed by members of the panel. The panel then recommends those who should be appointed to the Lord Chancellor.

The first appointments of QCs under the new system were made in 2006. 443 applied and 175 were appointed. Of these 33 were women, 10 from ethnic minorities and 4 were solicitors.

Since then the number of women appointed has been smaller but has reflected the number of women applying. In 2009 a total of 104 new QCs were appointed, about 40 per cent of applicants. Of these 104, 16 were women from the 29 women who had applied. Three out of the four solicitor applicants were also successful.

11.2.5 The Bar Council

The Bar Council is the governing body of barristers. Its full title is the General Council of the Bar. It is run by elected officials and is responsible for setting down rules for education and training, the Code of Conduct and disciplining barristers. The disciplinary body is the Senate of the Inns of Court which can disbar a barrister from practising.

The Bar Council also represents the interests of barristers in discussions with the government.

This means that it has two contradictory roles as it is a 'watchdog regulating practices and activities' but it is also a 'trade union pursuing the interests of the bar'.

@ Internet Research

The article on the previous page states that the profession's entry is far more diverse than it was.

Try to find out what the current figures are for entrants to the legal professions. Try the websites for the Law Society and the Bar Council: www.lawsociety.org.uk and www.barcouncil.org.uk.

11.2.6 Complaints against barristers

Where a barrister receives a brief from a solicitor, he or she does not enter into a contract with his client and so cannot sue if his fees are not paid. Similarly, the client cannot sue for breach of contract. However, they can be sued for negligence. In *Saif Ali v Sydney Mitchell and Co* (1980) it was held that a barrister could be sued for negligence in respect of written advice and opinions. In that case a barrister had given the wrong advice about who to sue, with the result that the claimant was too late to start proceedings against the right person.

In *Hall (a firm) v Simons* (2000) the House of Lords held that lawyers could also be liable for negligence in the conduct of advocacy in court. This decision overruled the earlier case of *Rondel v Worsley* (1969) in which barristers were held not to be liable because their first duty was to the courts and they must be 'free to do their duty fearlessly and independently'.

The Law Lords in *Hall (a firm) v Simons* felt that in light of modern conditions it was no longer in the public interest that advocates should have immunity from being sued for negligence. They pointed out that doctors could be sued and they had a duty to an ethical code of practice and might have difficult decisions to make when treating patients. There was no reason why advocates should not be liable in the same way.

They also pointed out that allowing advocates to be sued for negligence would not be likely to lead to the whole case being re-argued. If an

Key facts

	Solicitors	Barristers
Training	Degree, if not in law then must do Common Professional Examination or Graduate Diploma in Law	
	Legal Practice Course Training contract	Bar Vocational Course (Bar Professional Training Course) Must join one of the 4 Inns of Court Pupillage
Role	Private practice in solicitors' firm Wide variety of work Contracts, leases, wills, conveyancing etc. Direct access by clients	Self-employed in chambers Mostly court work Also write opinions and draft documents Since 2004 direct access by clients in civil cases
	May be employed in CPS, CDS, local authority etc. or private commercial business	
Advocacy	Automatic rights in magistrates' courts and County Court Advocacy certificate for higher courts (Courts and Legal Services Act 1990) Plans for full rights (Access to Justice Act 1999)	Full rights in all courts
Queen's Counsel	Selection is now by an independent QC selection panel Applicants will be judged on 7 competencies Applicants give referees and are interviewed by 2 members of the panel	
Supervision	Law Society Office for the Supervision of Solicitors – criticised for inefficiency	Bar Council Lay Complaints Commissioner + Bar Standards Board Complaints system working well with a high level of satisfaction
	Both the Office for the Supervision of Solicitors and the Bar Standards Board will be replaced in late 2010 by the Office for Legal Complaints	
	Legal Services Ombudsman Legal Services Complaints Commissioner Both these posts will be abolished and replaced in late 2010 by the Office for Legal Complaints Ombudsman	

Figure 11.4 Key facts chart comparing solicitors and barristers

action against an advocate was merely an excuse to get the whole issue litigated again, the matter would almost certainly be struck out as an abuse of process.

Bar Standards Board

Complaints against barristers are handled by the Bar Standards Board. If there was poor service, the Board can order the barrister to pay

Test Yourself

1. Name two of the Inns of Court.
2. What skills-based course must a would-be barrister pass?
3. What is pupillage?
4. What is meant by 'chambers'?
5. Explain two types of work a barrister might do.
6. What is meant by 'direct access' and which types of case is it NOT allowed for?

7. What is a QC?
8. Which body governs barristers?
9. Which case decided that barristers could be sued for negligence in their work?
10. Which body will take over handling complaints against the legal profession?

---

compensation of up to £15,000 to the client. The complaints process is overseen by an independent Lay Complaints Commissioner.

This system of handling complaints will be replaced by the Office for Legal Complaints in late 2010.

Legal Services Ombudsman

As set out earlier in section 11.1.6, there has been a Legal Services Ombudsman since 1991, whose work involves investigating complaints about all the legal professions. There are comparatively few complaints against barristers and the Ombudsman has found that the Bar Council handles 90 per cent of complaints satisfactorily.

This post will be abolished in late 2010 and replaced by the Office for Legal Complaints Ombudsman.

11.3 Legal Services Act 2007

11.3.1 Background

In 2001 a report by the Office of Fair Trading recommended that unjustified restrictions on competition in the legal profession should be removed.

In 2004 the Clementi Report into the legal profession was published (*Review of the Regulatory Framework for the Legal Services in England and Wales – Final Report*). The main recommendations were that:

- there should be a new complaints body that is independent of the professions;
- there should be a legal services board to be regulator over all the legal professional bodies;
- Legal Disciplinary Practices (LDPs) should be permitted where there are barristers, solicitors and non-lawyers working together in the same practice;
- non-lawyers should be allowed to own and manage LDPs, but there would be safeguards to make sure that they were 'fit to own' such a practice.

11.3.2 The Legal Services Act

The Government introduced this Bill into Parliament in the Autumn of 2006. It starts by setting out regulatory objectives for legal services. These are:

(a) supporting the constitutional principle of the rule of law;
(b) improving access to justice;
(c) protecting and promoting the interests of consumers;
(d) promoting competition in the provision of services;
(e) encouraging a strong, diverse and effective legal profession;
(f) increasing public understanding of the citizen's legal rights and duties;
(g) promoting and maintaining adherence to the professional principles.

Legal Services Board

The Act provides for the creation of the Legal
Services Board. The role of the Board is to have
independent oversight regulation of the legal
profession. It will consist of a Chairman and 7-10
members. The Lord Chancellor must consult with
the Lord Chief Justice on the appointment of
anyone to the Legal Services Board.

The Act also makes it clear that primary
responsibility for regulation rests with the
approved regulators, e.g. the Law Society or the
Bar Council. The Legal Services Board should only
interfere when the actions of an approved
regulator are palpably unreasonable.

Complaints about legal services

The Act has provision for establishing the Office
for Legal Complaints to handle all complaints in
respect of the legal profession. The Office will
have a Chairman and between 6 and 8 members.
The Chairman must be a non-lawyer and the
majority of members must also be non-lawyers.
The Office for Legal Complaints is due to start
work in late 2010.

The location of this Office is to be in the West
Midlands and staff will be drawn largely from the
Law Society's Consumer Complaints Service. This
is the organisation that has been frequently
criticised for its inefficient handling of complaints.

The Bar was concerned that their complaints
handling would be less efficient under the new
system. In fact, the Home Affairs Committee
reporting on the draft Bill had recommended that
approved regulators such as the Bar Standards
Board should have flexibility to handle service
and conduct of complaints. But the Government
rejected this recommendation and the Office for
Legal Complaints will deal with all complaints
about both solicitors and barristers and other
legal professionals such as legal executives.

11.3.3 Alternative Business Structures (ABSs)

Under the present system there are restrictions on
the types of business structures in the legal

profession. The main restrictions are:

- barristers and solicitors cannot operate from
  the same business;
- lawyers are not allowed to enter into
  partnership with non-lawyers;
- restrictions on non-lawyers being involved in
  the ownership or management of legal
  businesses;
- legal practices cannot operate as a companies.

So, generally, barristers and solicitors cannot work
together, nor can lawyers and non-lawyers work
together in legal businesses. The Legal Services
Bill will change this by allowing legal businesses
to include:

- lawyers and non-lawyers;
- barristers and solicitors;
- non-lawyers to own legal businesses;
- legal businesses will be able to operate as
  companies.

From 2010 solicitors will be allowed to form Legal
Disciplinary Practices (LDPs). In these up to 25
per cent of partners can be non-lawyers.

From 2011 Alternative Business Structures
(ABSs) will be allowed. These have to be given a
licence in order to operate. Access to justice must
be considered when such a licence is applied for.
This is to prevent commercial businesses
choosing only the most profitable areas of law
and possibly leaving an area without lawyers to
do the less profitable types of law.

@ Internet Research

Look up the Legal Services Act 2007 on
www.opsi.gov.uk. At the start of the
Act there is an index of contents. Use
this to find which part of the Act deals
with:

(a) The Legal Services Board
(b) Alternative Business Structures
(c) Legal complaints

11.4 Fusion

A major debate used to be whether the two professions should be merged into one profession. The advantages of fusion were thought to be:

- reduced costs as only one lawyer would be needed instead of a solicitor and a barrister;
- less duplication of work, because only one person would be doing the work, instead of a solicitor preparing the case and then passing it on to a barrister;
- more continuity as the same person could deal with the case from start to finish.

The disadvantages of fusion were seen as:

- a decrease in the specialist skills of advocacy;
- loss of the independent bar and the lack of availability of advice from independent specialists at the bar;
- less objectivity in consideration of a case; at the moment the barrister provides a second opinion;
- loss of the cab-rank principle under which barristers have to accept any case offered to them (except when they are already booked on another case for the same day). This principle allows anyone to get representation, even if their case is unpopular or unlikely to win.

The argument for fusion is no longer so important since the changes made by the Courts and Legal Services Act 1990 and the Access to Justice Act 1999 mean that barristers and solicitors can take a case from start to finish. Under the Access to Justice Act barristers have the right to do litigation (i.e. the preliminary work in starting a case) which has in the past always been done by solicitors. At the same time, solicitors have wider rights of advocacy and may represent clients in all courts, and clients may go directly to a barrister. In addition, the Legal Services Act 2007 allows solicitors and barristers to work together in the same business.

11.5 Women and ethnic minorities in the legal profession

The legal profession has an image of being white male-dominated. Both women and ethnic minorities are under-represented in the higher levels of the legal professions.

Women

Women make up an increasing number of entrants to the professions. They now account for over half of new solicitors and just over half of new entrants to the Bar. As a result of the increasing numbers of women studying law there are now greater numbers of women in both professions: 42 per cent of solicitors and 31 per cent of members of the Bar are female. Despite this there are very few women at the higher levels in either profession. For example, at the bar only about 10 per cent of QCs are women. Women solicitors tend to be in junior positions as assistant solicitors or junior partners.

One of the reasons put forward to explain this is that the increase in entrants is a fairly recent phenomenon. Twenty years ago there were comparatively few women going into the legal professions, and so it is not so surprising that there are correspondingly fewer women in senior positions.

In the solicitors' profession about 23 per cent of partners are women. This figure is increasing, but a survey in 2001 found that many women solicitors did not want to become partners.

Women also tend to earn less than their male counterparts, even when they do achieve higher status, especially in the solicitors' ranks. Women solicitors do not earn the same level of salary as male solicitors. Even the starting salaries of women are lower. The gap becomes bigger the higher up the profession, with men earning on average £15,000 more per year than women.

Ethnic minorities

Proportionate to the composition of the general population, ethnic minorities are well represented at the Bar. At the beginning of 2009, 15 per cent of practising barristers were from an ethnic minority. However, they experience even more difficulty in achieving higher positions than women do. There are still only a few Queen's Counsel of ethnic minority origin. This may reflect the fact that many of the ethnic minority at the Bar are fairly newly qualified, so that in time the number of QCs should increase.

In the solicitors' profession ethnic minorities are well represented. In the last few years the number of ethnic minority entrants has risen substantially. In 2008, 22.6 per cent of those admitted as solicitors were from ethnic minority backgrounds.

11.6 Legal executives

Legal executives work in solicitors' firms as assistants. They are qualified lawyers who have passed the Institute of Legal Executives' Professional Qualification in Law. They specialise in a particular area of law. There are over 22,000 legal executives practising.

Qualification and training

To become a legal executive it is necessary to pass the Professional Diploma in Law and the Professional Higher Diploma in Law. The Professional Diploma is set at A level standard and can be achieved in two ways:

● Mixed Assessment Route

This is by portfolio, case studies and one end of course examination which covers the English Legal System and essential elements of law and practice.

● Examination Route

The student has to sit four papers. These are normally taken over a two-year period. They

cover the English Legal System, Land Law, Criminal Law and Law of Tort in the first year and Consumer Law, Employment Law, Family Law, Wills & Succession in the second year. There is also an examination on practice and procedures dealing with matters such as conveyancing and procedure in civil and criminal cases.

The Professional Higher Diploma in Law (PHDL) is degree level and students have a choice of areas of law to study. In each area they learn the law and the practice side of that area of law.

As well as passing the PHDL examinations, it is also necessary to have worked in a solicitors' firm (or other legal organisation such as the Crown Prosecution Service or local government) for at least five years. When all the qualifications have been achieved the person becomes a Fellow of the Institute of Legal Executives.

A Fellow of the Institute of Legal Executives can go on to become a solicitor. In order to do this they will have to pass the Law Society's Legal Practice Course, but they may be given exemption from the two-year training contract.

Work

Legal executives specialise in a particular area of law. Within that area of law their day-to-day work is similar to that of a solicitor, though they tend to deal with the more straightforward matters. For example, they can:

● handle various legal aspects of a property transfer;
● assist in the formation of a company;
● draft wills;
● advise people with matrimonial problems;
● advise clients accused of serious or petty crime.

They also have some rights of audience. They can appear to make applications where the case is not defended in family matters and civil cases in the County Court and magistrates' courts.

Since 2008 legal executives have been able to do a course on advocacy and obtain wider rights of audience. There are three different practising certificates: a Civil Proceedings Certificate, a Criminal Proceedings Certificate and a Family Proceedings Certificate. These will allow legal executives to do such matters as make an application for bail or deal with cases in the Youth Court or the Family court of the Magistrates' courts.

Legal Executives are fee earners. This means that where a legal executive works for a firm of solicitors in private practice, that legal executive's work is charged an hourly rate directly to clients. In this way a legal executive makes a direct contribution to the income of the law firm. The partners of the firm are responsible for the legal executive's work.

Examination questions

1 (a) Outline how a barrister is trained and qualifies. (10 marks)

AQA Specimen Paper, part question

(see end of Chapter 12 for the other parts of the full question)

2 (a) Explain how a solicitor is trained and qualifies for entry to the profession. (10 marks)

AQA LAW01 June 2009, part question

Examiner's tip

Quite often examination questions will ask about just one branch of the legal profession. So make sure you are clear on the differences between solicitors and barristers.

Funding and Provision of Services

When faced with a legal problem, the average person will usually need expert help from a lawyer. Most often the need is just for advice, but some people may need help in starting court proceedings and/or presenting their case in court. For the ordinary person seeking legal assistance there are three main difficulties:

1. **Lack of knowledge**
   Many people do not know where their nearest solicitor is located or, if they do know this, they do not know which solicitor specialises in the law involved in their particular case.

2. **Fear of dealing with lawyers**
   People feel intimidated when dealing with lawyers.

3. **Cost**
   Solicitors charge from about £100 an hour for routine advice from a small local firm to over £600 an hour for work done by a top city firm of solicitors in a specialist field.

12.1 Access to justice

Where a person cannot get the help they need it is said they are being denied access to justice. Access to justice involves both an open system of justice and also being able to fund the costs of a case.

There have been various schemes aimed at making the law more accessible to everyone. One of the earliest was the Citizens' Advice Bureaux which started in 1939 and now operates in most towns.

However, the problem of cost still remains a major hurdle. The cost of civil cases in the High Court will run into thousands of pounds. Even in the cheaper County Court the cost will possibly be more than the amount of money recovered in damages. There is the additional risk in all civil cases that the loser has to pay the winner's costs.

In criminal cases a person's liberty may be at risk and it is essential that they should be able to defend themselves properly.

For these reasons the Government has run schemes to help those in lower income brackets with funding cases. The first scheme was started in 1949 and altered many times over the years. In 2000 a new scheme was started and this is the one currently in use.

12.2 The Legal Services Commission

The present funding scheme is overseen by the Legal Services Commission. This body was set up by the Access to Justice Act 1999. The Commission is responsible for identifying the needs and priorities of funding and developing the delivery of legal services in accordance with those needs.

In civil cases it is responsible for managing the Community Legal Service Fund which pays for legal funding in suitable cases. The Commission also has a role in respect of criminal legal aid managing the Criminal Defence Service.

For both civil and criminal cases the Legal Services Commission can make contracts with providers of legal services so that the providers can do legal work and be paid from Government funds. Providers include solicitors and not for profit organisations such as the Citizens Advice Bureaux offering advice on legal matters.

Figure 12.1 shows the organisation of the public funding under the Legal Services Commission.

As civil and criminal cases have separate funding and systems, we will consider the funding of civil matters in the next section and then the funding of criminal cases in section 12.4.

Figure 12.1 Public funding under the Legal Services Commission

12.3 Government funding in civil cases

The Community Legal Service is responsible for the funding of civil cases. It uses money from the Community Legal Service Fund for these cases.

12.3.1 The Community Legal Service

The Community Legal Service provides services for civil matters in the following ways:

- Legal Help – this covers advice but does not include issuing or conducting court proceedings;
- Help at Court – this allows help (i.e. advice) and advocacy at a court or tribunal, although without formally acting as legal representative in the proceedings;
- Legal representation – this covers all aspects of a case including starting or defending court proceedings and any advocacy needed in the case;
- Support Funding – this allows partial funding of cases which are otherwise being paid for privately, e.g. a very high cost case under a conditional fee agreement.

12.3.2 The Community Legal Service Fund

Each year, when the Government budget is drawn up, a set amount is given for helping people fund legal cases. The total amount of the legal aid budget is over £1.8 billion. Most of this will be spent on criminal cases, but some of the money goes to the Community Legal Service Fund to deal with civil matters.

There are two problems with this. First, there is a limit or cap on the amount given by the budget. When this runs out there is no more money. Second, criminal cases take priority on funding and so there may not be enough left for civil cases. This can lead to civil cases which have merit being refused funding just because the money has run out.

12.3.3 Funding criteria

In deciding whether a person should receive help with funding, two matters are taken into consideration. These are:

- the finances of the person (means test); and
- the merits of the case (merits test).

In addition there are general criteria that are considered such as the importance of the case.

Disposable income

The person's disposable income and disposable capital are considered. People receiving Income Support or Income Based Job Seekers' Allowance automatically qualify, assuming their disposable capital is below the set level.

For all other applicants their disposable income is calculated by starting with their gross income and taking away:

- tax and national insurance;
- housing costs;
- childcare costs or maintenance paid for children;
- an allowance for themselves and for each dependant.

If the amount left after making all deductions is below a minimum set by the Legal Services Commission, the applicant does not have to pay any contribution towards their funding. If the amount left is above a maximum set by the Legal Services Commission, the person will not qualify for help.

Where the income left is between the minimum level and the maximum level, the person applying for legal help has to pay a monthly contribution. The more in excess of the minimum the greater the amount of the contribution. Monthly disposable income is graded into bands. Those bands are:

Monthly disposable income	Monthly contribution
Band A	¼ of income in excess of the band
Band B	+ ⅓ of income in excess of the band
Band C	+ ½ of income in excess of the band

This idea of minimum and maximum levels is shown in Figure 12.2.

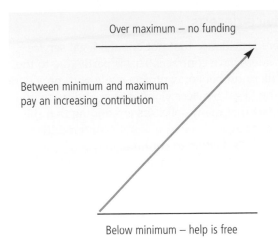

Figure 12.2 Minimum and maximum limits for legal aid

Disposable capital

Disposable capital is the assets of the person, such as money in a bank or savings account, stocks and shares or expensive jewellery. In order to qualify for funding to take a court case there is a minimum limit for disposable capital of £3,000 and a maximum of £8,000. If the assets are below £3,000, then no contribution is payable. If the person has over £3,000 but under £8,000 they will have to pay the extra above £3,000 as a contribution towards their funding. If they have more than £8,000 they must use their own money to fund any legal case, although once they have spent the money in excess of £8,000 they can become eligible for funding.

Where a person owns a home the value of that home is taken into account in deciding the disposable capital. This is so even though the person may have a large mortgage. Only the first £100,000 of any mortgage is deducted from the value of the home. This rule means that people are regarded as having too much disposable capital because of the value of the house, but in reality they have no spare money.

Merits test

In order to receive help with funding a court case, there must be a realistic chance of the case succeeding. Also the cost of bringing the case must not be greater than the likely damages (amount of money the court will award).

General criteria

As well as the means and merits test, there are other factors which will be considered. These include:

- the availability of money in the Community Legal Service Fund;
- the importance of the matters for the individual;
- whether the case can be funded in another way, such as through a conditional fee agreement (see section 12.7);
- the conduct of the individual;
- the public interest.

So even if a person is poor enough to qualify for help and has a very good chance of winning the case, they may still not get funding if there is not enough money in the Community Legal Service Fund or if they could use another way of resolving the dispute.

12.3.4 Excluded matters

Not every civil matter can qualify for public funding. Certain types of civil case are excluded from public funding. These are:

- Cases of negligence, even where the negligence caused death or serious injury. The only ones which can get public funding are cases of negligence by doctors or other health service workers.
- Conveyancing.
- Boundary disputes.
- Making of wills.
- Matters involving trust law.
- Cases of defamation or malicious falsehood.
- Company law, partnership law or anything arising from carrying on a business.

Funding is normally available on any other type of case in the courts. This covers the county court, the High Court and the appeal courts. The only exception is for claims of less than £5,000. These are dealt with as small claims and cannot receive public funding.

It is also not possible to get funding for most cases before tribunals. There are a few exceptions, such as mental health cases or asylum cases, where funding is available. This is because the cases involve the liberty of the individual, so public funding is allowed.

12.3.5 Advice in civil cases

The Community Legal Service allows service providers to give advice about legal matters. There are stricter financial limits than for getting help with a case at court. Funding is not available if the person has disposable capital worth more than £3,000.

However, the Community Legal Service does provide other services to try to make sure that advice is available. One of these is a telephone service, CLS Direct. This receives nearly a million calls a year. Many of the calls are from those in disadvantaged sections of society.

The Community Legal Service also has a website offering advice. This is at www.clsdirect.org.uk. This allows access to people in remote areas of the country and also to those who have difficulty travelling. As every public library has online computers available for people to use, it also means that the poorest in society can have access to advice on the website.

Community Legal Advice Centres

In 2006 Community Legal Advice Centres (CLAC) were started. These are a one-stop service providing advice on debt, welfare benefits, community care, housing and employment. The first two such centres were set up in Leicester and Gateshead. The Legal Services Commission intends that there will be eventually be about 75 CLACs.

12.3.6 Problems with funding of civil cases

Advice deserts

There is evidence that not enough legal service providers have contracts. This is partly due to the smaller numbers of contracts made with providers by the Legal Services Commission and partly to the fact that many solicitors are finding that the rates of pay are so low, it is not economically viable for solicitors to continue in the scheme. This is creating what have been called 'advice deserts'.

The problem of 'advice deserts' was considered by the Constitutional Affairs Select Committee in 2004. In the evidence to the Committee, even the Legal Services Commission acknowledged that: 'It is clear that there are parts of England and Wales in which the need for publicly funded legal services is not currently being met.'

In their report the select committee gave the position in Northumberland as an example. There were no housing law advisors and no one with a contract for immigration law in Northumberland. Furthermore, there were only two contracts for employment law in the area. People have to travel a long way to see a lawyer. This can be expensive and is difficult for people on low incomes, those caring for small children or those who have a disability which makes it difficult to travel.

Since 2004 the position has been getting worse as more solicitors have stopped doing Government-funded legal work. With so few legal service providers in certain areas, people who want help may have to travel long distances to find it.

Eligibility levels

Even where there are enough legal services providers in an area, only people with very low levels of income and capital can qualify for help. In 2004 the Select Committee on Constitutional Affairs which investigated the adequacy of the provision of civil legal aid pointed out that:

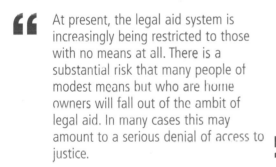

Key facts

Managing body	Community Legal Service
Different levels of help and representation available	● Legal Help—advice only ● Help at Court—advice and limited representation at court ● Legal Representation—covers all aspects of case ● Support Funding—partial funding of a very high cost case
Merits test for Legal Representation	Whether the case has a reasonable chance of success and the damages will be worth more than the costs. Other criteria including: ● can the matter be funded in another way? ● are there funds available?
Means test	Strict means test on gross income, disposable income and disposable capital
Problems	● number of solicitors is decreasing ● financial level of eligibility excludes people of modest means ● capping of fund together with increasing criminal expenditure means that less is available for civil cases ● not available for personal injury cases or employment tribunal cases

Figure 12.3 Key facts chart on public funding in civil cases

> At present, the legal aid system is increasingly being restricted to those with no means at all. There is a substantial risk that many people of modest means but who are home owners will fall out of the ambit of legal aid. In many cases this may amount to a serious denial of access to justice.

Lack of funds

The fact that there is a limit on the amount given by the budget means that some cases will not be funded as there is no money left for them. Also the fact that criminal cases take priority on funding means there may not be enough left for civil cases. This can lead to civil cases which have merited being refused funding just because the money has run out.

In 2009 the Government began a review on the possibility of separating the funds for civil and criminal cases. So, it is possible that in future civil funding will be protected and kept only for civil cases.

Non-availability

As set out in section 12.3.4, funding is not available for all civil claims. Claims for damages for personal injury are excluded from the scheme. Any such case has to be paid for privately or through a conditional fee agreement (see section 12.7). This works well where people have suffered minor injuries, but it can be argued that it creates difficulties for people who have been left with serious disabilities. They need all the help they can get to make sure they receive adequate compensation.

It can also be argued that people bringing employment claims against large companies are disadvantaged by being unable to receive public funding to bring their case. The company will be able to afford a lawyer and will be at an advantage in the case.

12.4 Government funding in criminal cases

12.4.1 The Criminal Defence Service

Under the Access to Justice Act 1999, the Legal Services Commission was required to establish a Criminal Defence Service. This service is aimed at:

> securing that individuals involved in criminal investigation or proceedings have access to such advice, assistance and representation as the interests of justice require.

The Criminal Defence Service offers the following schemes:

- duty solicitor schemes;
- advice and assistance;
- representation.

In order to get representation the defendant has to qualify under the interests of justice test. Also for cases in the magistrates' courts, the defendant is means tested.

Duty solicitors and advice and assistance schemes are explained in section 12.4.6.

12.4.2 The interests of justice test

A defendant will only get help with legal funding for representation in court if he can show that he comes within at least one of the five interests of

justice factors. These factors are:

- the individual would be likely to lose his liberty or livelihood or suffer serious damage to his reputation;
- the case will involve consideration of a point of law;
- the individual is unable to understand the proceedings in court or to state his own case;
- the case may involve the tracing, interviewing or expert cross-examination of witnesses;
- it is in the interests of another person that the individual is represented (e.g. in a rape case).

12.4.3 Means testing

As well as having to qualify under the interests of justice test, defendants who are being tried in the magistrates' courts are also means tested.

Those who are on income support, defendants under the age of 16 and those under 18 in full time education, automatically pass the means test. For everyone else the test starts with a first-stage simple means test which is calculated on gross annual income. If their income is too high on this test then the defendant does not qualify for legal aid. If a defendant's income is below a certain level they qualify. For those in the middle bracket, they are further means tested to calculate their disposable income.

The levels allowed are very low. This means that about three quarters of adults do not qualify for legal aid in criminal cases. This is particularly worrying as means testing for cases in the Crown Court will gradually come into operation during 2010. These are more serious cases and more expensive, so it is important that defendants should have access to legal help.

12.4.4 The Carter reforms

In July 2006 a report by Lord Carter, *Legal Aid – A Market-based Approach to Reform*, was published. The aim of this report is to reduce spending on criminal legal aid by more than 20 per cent over the next four years. This may seem a lot but comparative research by Carter on spending in other countries showed that the UK spends more than 10 times more than its nearest rival. There appeared to be no obvious reason for this difference.

Lord Carter's main proposals were:

- 'best-value' tendering for legal aid contracts based on quality, capacity and price;
- fixed fees for solicitors carrying out legal aid work in police stations (including cutting costs related to travelling and waiting times);
- revised graduated fees for Crown Court advocates – this will give junior barristers more for the 1 to 10 day case, but cut fees for longer cases;
- a new graduated fee scheme for Crown Court litigators to reward earlier preparation and resolution of cases.

The legal profession claim that these reforms will make Government-funded legal work uneconomic to do. There is a real risk the numbers of solicitors who do such work will be dramatically reduced. This will make it difficult for defendants to find a lawyer to represent them.

In 2010, the Government abandoned the idea of 'best value' tendering.

12.4.5 Public Defender Service

The Public Defender Service started in 2001. It has state-employed lawyers who represent defendants in criminal cases in four areas. There used to be eight offices, but four of them were closed in 2007 as they were not cost effective.

When the service started, critics pointed out that the system meant that the State, who was prosecuting the defendant (through the Crown Prosecution Service), was also defending the defendant (through the Public Defender Service). It has been suggested that this could mean that Public Defender Service lawyers might not be as independent as lawyers in private practice.

Evaluation

An evaluation of the PDS was published at the beginning of 2007. This found that there were positive aspects to the use of the PDS. In particular, lawyers from the service were more likely to attend at a police station to advise clients being held there. Where this happened, clients were less likely to be charged with an offence than those who used lawyers from private practice.

However, defendants who were charged and represented by the PDS were more likely to plead guilty in the magistrates' courts. This did not appear to have any advantage for the defendant in the way of pleading to a lower level or receiving a lesser sentence than those represented by private lawyers.

The evaluation found that the cost effectiveness of the PDS was not as good as for private firms. During the first three years of its operation the average case costs for the PDS ranged from between 40 per cent to just over 90 per cent higher than costs of private firms.

12.4.6 Advice in criminal cases

The two advice schemes run by the Criminal Defence Service are:

- duty solicitors;
- advice and assistance.

Duty solicitors

The Access to Justice Act 1999 states that the Legal Services Commission shall fund such advice and assistance as it considers appropriate for individuals who are arrested and held in custody at a police station or other premises. This provides those held at a police station with free legal advice.

This is an important right to protect the liberty of the individual. Originally this meant that anyone held was eligible to receive free advice from a duty solicitor.

However, since May 2004, they can no longer normally attend at a police station where the client is detained:

- for a non-imprisonable offence;
- on a warrant;

- in breach of bail conditions;
- for drink/drive offences.

A duty solicitor can still attend for the above in situations where the client is vulnerable; e.g. a youth, mentally ill, cannot speak English. They can also attend where the client complains of serious maltreatment by the police.

Telephone advice

One of the problems in the 1990s with duty solicitor schemes was that, in many cases, the solicitor did not attend at the police station but merely gave advice over the telephone. Although this was viewed as a defect in the scheme, telephone advice has now become the government's preferred method of action for duty solicitors. Since 2004 solicitors cannot claim for attending at the police station unless they can show that attendance was expected to 'materially progress the case'.

Advice and assistance

Advice and assistance is limited to one hour's work. Normally it is just for advice, but it can include advocacy if the solicitor has applied for a representation order which has been refused.

Normally there is a means test for advice and assistance and only those on low incomes will qualify. However, a duty solicitor at a magistrates' court can still see all defendants in custody under the advice and assistance scheme. For this there is no charge.

12.4.7 Problems with funding of criminal cases

Interests of justice test

This test is applied very strictly. Even where a defendant is charged with an offence for which a prison sentence can be given, for example theft, it does not necessarily mean that he will pass the

Key facts

Managing body	Criminal Defence Service
Different levels of help and representation available	<ul><li>duty solicitor at the police station</li><li>advice and assistance</li><li>legal representation</li></ul>
Merits test for representation	Whether it is in the interests of justice<ul><li>defendant at risk of losing liberty, livelihood or reputation</li><li>substantial point of law involved</li><li>defendant unable to understand proceedings</li><li>involves tracing, interview or expert cross-examination of witnesses</li><li>is in the interests of another person</li></ul>
Means test	Duty solicitor free of charge and not means tested Means testing for representation in magistrates' courts cases
Problems	<ul><li>strict application of interests of justice test</li><li>strict means test so that three-quarters of adults cannot qualify</li><li>lack of solicitors doing publicly-funded criminal law work</li><li>does the Public Defender Service give good service?</li></ul>

Figure 12.4 Key facts chart on public funding in criminal cases

interests of justice test. The rule is that there must be a real risk of imprisonment.

This has the effect that defendants who have several previous convictions for theft will qualify for legal help as they are likely to be imprisoned. However, someone with no previous convictions is not likely to be sent to prison. So, if they are pleading not guilty they will have to represent themselves or pay for private legal help.

Activity

Advise the people in the following scenarios whether publicly-funded help/representation is available and what problems they may encounter in trying to get funding.

1. Ali has been charged with theft of a laptop computer from a shop. He works as an IT specialist and has no previous convictions.
2. Bernice has been left paralysed from the waist down after being hit by a car when she was standing at a bus stop.
3. Connor believes he has been unfairly dismissed from his job. He wants to make a claim in an employment tribunal.
4. Davina has had building work done at her home. The company are in breach of contract and it has cost Davina £10,000 to have the work made good. She wishes to make a claim for this amount. She owns her house but has a mortgage of £140,000.

Means test

This is also a strict test. The levels of income allowed are very low. About three quarters of adults do not qualify for legal aid in criminal cases. With means testing being extended to the Crown Court where it is more expensive to defend a case, then there is a real risk of injustice due to lack of availability of legal help.

Lack of lawyers

The Government has cut the fees paid to lawyers for criminal cases. Fixed fees are being brought in which do not take account of the true amount of work that may need to be done. As a result fewer solicitors are taking on Government-funded legal work. This makes it more difficult for defendants to find a local solicitor to take their case.

Budget

The budget given by the Government for legal funding has not risen in line with inflation. This means that the Legal Services Commission has less money to allocate for funding.

12.5 Advice agencies

A number of different advice schemes are available. The main ones are Citizens' Advice Bureaux and law centres. However, there are other agencies which offer advice on specific legal topics. These include trade unions which will help members with work-related legal problems. There are also charities such as Shelter which offers advice to people with housing problems.

About 450 not-for-profit organisations have contracts from the Community Legal Service for providing advice.

12.5.1 Citizens Advice Bureaux

These were first set up in 1939 and today they give advice in over 3,000 locations. They give general advice free to anyone on a variety of issues mostly connected to social welfare problems and debt, but they also advise on some legal matters. They can also provide information on which local solicitors do legal aid work or give cheap or free initial interviews. Many have arrangements under which solicitors may attend at the bureau once a week or fortnight to give more qualified advice on legal matters.

As well as being available for anyone to get advice, the Legal Services Commission has awarded contracts for some Citizens Advice Bureaux to provide Government-funded advice.

12.5.2 Law centres

These offer a free, non means tested legal service to people in their area. The first law centre opened in North Kensington in 1970. This stated its aims as providing 'a first class solicitor's service to the people . . . a service which is easily accessible, not intimidating, to which they can turn for guidance as they would to their family doctor, or as someone who can afford it would turn to his family solicitor'.

Their aim is to provide free legal advice (and sometimes representation) in areas where there are few solicitors.

Funding is a major problem for Law Centres. However, the Community Legal Service has given funding for some centres.

12.5.3 Other advice agencies
Schemes run by lawyers

Some solicitors offer a free half an hour first interview. Local Citizens Advice Bureaux will have a list of solicitors who offer the service.

Key facts

Service	Community Legal Service	Criminal Defence Service	Privately paid lawyer
Types of case	Civil only	Criminal only	All types
Finance	Only available for those on low incomes	Means tested in magistrates' courts and only available for those on low incomes	Available to anyone who can afford to pay Conditional fee agreements can be used for civil cases
Availability	Not available for personal injury, defamation or small claims Not available for most tribunals	Free advice for anyone detained at a police station Representation only if it is in the interests of justice	
Merits	Must have a good chance of success **and** the cost must not be more than the likely damages	● risk of losing liberty, livelihood, reputation ● substantial point of law involved ● defendant unable to understand proceedings ● involves tracing, interviewing or expert cross-examination of witnesses ● is in the interests of another person	Will usually only take a case on a conditional fee if there is a very high chance of success
Comment	Set budget Only available if there are sufficient funds Decreasing number of solicitors	Lack of solicitors doing publicly-funded criminal law work	Expensive – £600 an hour for City lawyers Liable to pay other side's costs if lose case

Figure 12.5 Key Facts chart comparing sources of funding

Citizen's Advice Bureau logo

scheme barristers give their time free and represent clients in court at no cost. More than 2,000 cases are dealt with each year by the FRU.

Insurance

Another way of funding a court case is by legal insurance. Most motor insurance policies offer cover (for a small amount extra) for help with legal fees in cases arising from road accidents and there are also policies purely for insurance against legal costs.

12.6 Private funding

Anyone who can afford it can pay for a solicitor and/or a barrister to deal with a legal matter. There are firms of solicitors in most towns. However, some solicitors specialise in certain types of work. If your legal problem is on an unusual area of law, then it may be necessary to travel to another town to find a solicitor who can deal with it.

The bigger firms of solicitors work in the major cities, in particular London. They often specialise in commercial law and the majority of their clients are businesses.

Consulting a solicitor can be expensive. The average cost of a solicitor outside London is about £150 an hour. For a big London firm of solicitors the charges are usually at least £600 an hour and

Another service by solicitors is the Accident Legal Advice Service (ALAS) which is aimed at helping accident victims claim compensation. In addition, the Law Society runs Accident Line – a free telephone service to put accident victims in contact with solicitors who do personal injury work.

The Bar runs the Free Representation Unit (FRU) which helps people who are ineligible for legal aid present their case in court. Under this

Advice in civil cases	Advice in criminal cases
Publicly funded ● CLS Direct by telephone ● CLS website ● Community Legal Advice Centres ● Advice from a service provider	Publicly funded ● At police station – usually by telephone ● Duty solicitor at magistrates' courts ● Advice and assistance scheme
Private ● Citizens Advice Bureaux ● Law Centres ● Solicitors' schemes such as ALAS ● Free Representation Unit (barristers) ● Insurance	Private ● Paying for advice from a solicitor

Figure 12.6 Availability of advice in civil and criminal cases

can be as much as £1,000 an hour.

On issues of civil law it is also possible to consult a barrister directly, without going to a solicitor first. This can be cheaper than using a solicitor because barristers do not have such high business expenses as solicitors.

12.7 Conditional fee agreements (CFAs)

One of the main problems of taking a case to court is that it is difficult to estimate how long it will last or how much it will cost. If a person is funding their own case, this is a major problem for them. Also if they lose the case they may have to pay the costs of the other party. The combined costs of the case can be many thousands of pounds. In order to overcome these problems, a conditional fee agreement (CFA) can be used in all civil cases except family cases.

CFAs cannot be used in criminal cases.

12.7.1 How CFAs work

The solicitor and client agree on the fee that would normally be charged for such a case. The agreement will also set out what the solicitor's success fee will be if he wins the case.

Many conditional fee agreements will be made on the basis that if the case is lost, the client pays nothing. Because of this sort of agreement, the scheme is often referred to as 'no win, no fee'. However, some solicitors may prefer to charge a lower level fee, for example half the normal fee, even if the case is lost.

If the case is won the client has to pay the normal fee plus the success fee.

12.7.2 Success fee

The success fee can be up to 100% of the normal fee. However, most agreements will include a 'cap' on the success fee, which prevents it from being more than 25 per cent of the damages (amount of money) that the client wins as compensation. This protects the client from

having to pay more than he or she won as compensation. Even so, it can mean that the client is left with very little of their damages. This is easier to understand by looking at the examples given in Figure 12.7.

When conditional fee agreements were first allowed by the Courts and Legal Services Act 1990, the client had to pay the success fee themselves and could not claim it back from the other side as part of their cost of the case. This meant that clients often ended up with very little even though they had won the case, so the Access to Justice Act 1999 changed the rules to allow reasonable levels of success fees to be claimed as costs from the losing party.

What level of success fee that could be claimed back as costs has been the subject of many disputes. Eventually rules set down what level could be claimed. These depend on when the case is settled. If the case is settled at an early stage then the defendant (or in most cases, his insurers) will only have to pay 12.5 per cent of any success fee. This can mean that the successful claimant has to pay the rest of the success fee to his own solicitor. It will depend on what was agreed in the conditional fee agreement.

However, if the other side refuses to settle and then loses the case in court, the rules allow the claimant to get back 100 per cent of the success fee as costs from the other side.

Case example

An example of a case in which a success fee of 100 per cent was ordered to be paid by the losing party is *Campbell v Mirror Group Newspapers Ltd (No 2)* (2005).

In this case the model Naomi Campbell successfully sued the *Daily Mirror* for libel and breach of privacy when the paper published an article and photos of her. She was awarded £3,500 in damages. The case had been originally tried in the High Court and then appealed to the Court of Appeal. For both these court actions Campbell had paid her lawyers' legal costs in the ordinary way.

Agreement

Normal fee	£4,000
Fee if case is lost NIL	
Success fee	£2,000
Cap on success fee	25% of damages

Possible results of case	Client pays	
Case is lost	Nothing	
Case is won: client gets £50,000 damages	£6,000	(£4,000 + £2,000)
Case is won: client gets £6,000 damages	£5,500	(£4,000 + £1,500*)

*This £1,500 is because the success fee cannot be more than 25% of the damages

Figure 12.7 Illustration of conditional fees

When the case went to the House of Lords, Campbell entered into conditional fee agreements with both her solicitors and the barrister who represented her in the House of Lords. The agreements allowed for success fees of 95 per cent and 100 per cent respectively. Campbell won the case in the House of Lords and then claimed the success fees as part of her costs from Mirror Group Newspapers (MGN). The success fees came to almost £280,000 and this added to the normal fees made the total bill for her costs over £1 million. MGN challenged the amount of the success fees on two points:

1. the amount was disproportionate; and
2. the risk of having to pay large sums in costs was an infringement of the human right to freedom of expression: it effectively acted as a 'gag' on the media as it could prevent them from publishing items.

In the House of Lords, the Law Lords ruled that the cost of the success fees was proportionate because it reflected the reality of conditional fee agreements. Successful cases had to be paid more to allow for losses in other cases. If this was not so, then solicitors would not be able to take on cases where winning was not virtually certain. It promoted access to justice.

They also held that success fees did not infringe the media's freedom of expression. Using CFAs with a success fee was the only way most people could bring defamation cases against newspapers. If success fees were not allowed then the media would be free to make defamatory statements as those affected could not afford to bring cases against them.

12.7.3 Insurance premiums

Although the client will often not have to pay anything to his own lawyer if the case is lost, they will usually have to pay the costs of the other side. This can leave the client with a very large bill to pay. To help protect against this, it is possible to insure against the risk. This type of insurance is known as 'after the event' insurance. So, if the case is lost your insurers will pay the other side's costs.

In order to get insurance it is necessary to pay a premium (a sum of money) to the insurance company. Premiums for 'after the event' insurance are usually quite expensive. This premium usually has to be paid in advance of the decision in the case. This can cause problems to people who cannot afford the cost of the premium. Also, until the Access to Justice Act 1999, the insurance premium could not be claimed as costs from the losing party.

Matters have now improved as the law allows the premium to be claimed from the losing party. Also some solicitors have made arrangements with insurance companies that the premium need not be paid in advance.

12.7.4 Advantages of conditional fee agreements

CFAs provide access to justice. They allow people who could not afford to pay their own legal fees to bring cases. This is particularly important for personal injury cases as government legal aid is not available for such cases. It is also important in defamation cases as these will also not normally be given government funding.

This access to justice is shown by the fact that thousands of claims have been brought using CFAs.

Allowing a successful claimant using a CFA to reclaim the success fee and the insurance premium makes CFAs fairer. Previously people found that a large proportion of the damages they won as compensation for injuries was taken up by having to pay the success fee and the insurance premium.

As the solicitor only gets the fee if the case is won, the client will feel confident in the solicitor's commitment to the case. The solicitor benefits from winning the case.

Solicitors will not want to take on cases which have no chance of success. This should prevent hopeless cases being started and wasting court time.

12.7.5 Disadvantages of conditional fee agreements

Surveys and research into CFAs suggests that there are still problems with such agreements. Research in 1998 by Sheffield University found that:

● The poorest clients could not afford to pay insurance premiums or other expenses such as a payment for a medical report. These normally have to paid for at the beginning of a case and, although they can be claimed back if the case is won, that may be two or three years later.
● Those with cases which were not certain to win found it difficult to find a solicitor prepared to take on the case.
● The amount of work needed to be done on some types of personal injury case, especially accidents at work, made it difficult to estimate the cost. In such cases solicitors found that the case had cost them more than the combined fee plus success fee.

In 2004 a report, *'No Win, No Fee, No Chance'* by James Sandbach published by Citizens Advice Bureaux identified several problems with CFAs. These included:

Test Yourself

1. Which body oversees the public funding scheme for civil and criminal cases?
2. Which service provides publicly funded advice and representation in civil cases?
3. What is meant by 'disposable income'?
4. Explain two problems with public funding of civil cases.
5. Which service provides publicly funded advice and representation in criminal cases?
6. What is the 'interests of justice test'?
7. Give two publicly funded advice schemes which are available in criminal cases.
8. Give two ways in which you could get advice in a civil case.
9. Briefly explain what a conditional fee agreement is.
10. Explain two disadvantages of conditional fee agreements.

Key facts

How conditional fee agreements work	● the client and solicitor agree on the normal fee and on a success fee if the case is won ● the success fee can be up to 100% of the normal fee ● if the case is lost most clients will pay nothing to their own solicitor ● after-the-event insurance is usually taken out to protect against the risk of paying the other's costs if the case is lost
Advantages of CFAs	● provide access to justice for those who cannot get government funding and cannot afford to pay in the normal way ● client will feel confident in solicitor's commitment to case ● hopeless cases will not be taken on, saving court time
Disadvantages of CFAs	● clients cannot afford to pay insurance premiums or other expenses ● consumers may be subjected to high-pressure sales tactics ● consumers do not understand the risks and liabilities of CFAs and may be misled by sales persons ● some claims end in 'zero-gain' ● solicitors do not want to take on high-risk claims or low-value claims: this can deny access to justice

Figure 12.7 Key facts chart on conditional fee agreements

● Consumers are subjected to high-pressure sales tactics, including salesmen approaching accident victims in hospital.
● Few consumers seem to understand the risks and liabilities of CFAs. These are not properly explained to them and they may be misled into thinking the system is genuinely 'no win, no fee' but can then find that there are hidden and unpredictable costs.
● Where insurance premiums are paid for with loan finance, this in addition to other legal costs, can be more than the compensation awarded. In some cases consumers even owe money at the end of the process. The whole claims process is turned into a 'zero-gain' for consumers and denies effective access to compensation.
● Solicitors do not want to take on high-risk claims or low-value claims. This can deny people access to justice, especially as government funding is no longer available for personal injury cases.

@ Internet Research

Find websites of solicitors' firms in which they explain how conditional fee agreements work. You should be able to find such sites by entering the phrase 'conditional fee agreement' in Google or another search engine.

When you have found the sites, look at two different ones and compare what they say about CFAs.

Examination questions

(b) Paveen has been injured in an accident. Explain from whom she could get advice about a possible claim. (10 marks)

(c) Briefly discuss advantages and disadvantages of both private funding and of 'no-win – no fee' arrangements in a civil claim. (10 marks)

AQA Specimen Paper, part question

(see end of Chapter 11 for first part of question)

Examiner's tip

Sometimes examination questions will ask you to tell a person how they can get legal help. If you look at part (b) of the Examination questions you will see this.

It is important to identify whether you are being asked to explain about a civil case or a criminal case.

In the question above the sentence 'Paveen has been injured in an accident' is enough to identify this as a civil case. So you should only include information about advice in a civil case.

Chapter 13

The Judiciary

When speaking of judges as a group they are referred to as the judiciary. There are many different levels of judges, but their basic function is the same. Their main role is to make decisions in respect of disputes. This they must do in a fair, unbiased way, applying the law and the legal rules of England and Wales.

The judiciary is divided into what are known as 'superior' judges (those in the High Court and above) and 'inferior' judges (those in the lower courts). This distinction affects training, work and, in particular, the terms on which they hold office. So it is important to start by understanding which judges sit in which court.

13.1 Types of judges

13.1.1 Superior judges

Superior judges are those in the Supreme Court, the Court of Appeal and the High Court. They are:

- the Justices of the Supreme Court;
- the Lord Justices of Appeal in the Court of Appeal;
- High Court judges (also known as puisne (pronounced 'pew-nay') judges) who sit in the three divisions of the High Court: judges in the Queen's Bench Division of the High Court also sit to hear serious cases in the Crown Court.

The head of the judiciary is the Lord Chief Justice. As well as being head of the whole judiciary, this judge is also head of the Criminal Division of the Court of Appeal.

There are also senior judges who head the Civil Division of the Court of Appeal and the divisions of the High Court. These are:

- The Master of the Rolls who is head of the Civil Division of the Court of Appeal;
- The President of the Queen's Bench Division of the High Court;
- The Chancellor of the High Court who is head of the Chancery Division;
- The President of the Family Division of the High Court.

The parade of judges and silks on the first day of the legal year

13.1.2 Inferior judges

The inferior judges include:

- Circuit judges who sit in both the Crown Court and the County Court;
- Recorders who are part-time judges who usually sit in the Crown Court, though some hear cases in the County Court;
- District judges who hear small claims and other matters in the County Court;
- District judges (Magistrates' Courts) who sit in magistrates' courts in London and other major towns and cities;
- Tribunal judges.

13.2 Qualifications

The relevant qualifications for the different judicial posts are set out in the Courts and Legal Services Act 1990 as amended by the Tribunals, Courts and Enforcement Act 2007. Qualifications to become a judge are based on legal qualifications plus relevant legal experience.

Before 1990, only barristers who had practised at the bar for at least ten years could become High Court judges or above. The 1990 Act allowed solicitors to become High Court judges. The Tribunals, Court and Enforcement Act 2007 further widened the pool of potential applicants. Under this Act it is necessary for applicants for judicial posts to have the relevant legal qualification. This is normally barrister or solicitor, but for some levels the Act has opened up judicial posts beyond solicitors and barristers for the first time. Fellows of the Institute of Legal Executives (ILEX) and Registered Patents Attorneys and Trade Mark Attorneys may apply for certain posts such as Deputy District judge or Tribunal Judge.

The Tribunals, Court and Enforcement Act 2007 also widened the ways in which applicants may have gained experience in law. As well as practising or teaching law, such activities as acting as an arbitrator or mediator, advising on law or drafting legal documents are also methods by which an applicant can gain experience in law.

These changes have helped to widen the pool of potential candidates for judgeships.

The qualifications for each level of judge are set out below.

13.2.1 Justices of the Supreme Court

These are appointed from those who hold high judicial office, for example as a judge in the Court of Appeal, or from those who have been qualified to appear in the Senior Courts for at least 15 years. This can be as a practising lawyer or as an academic who holds the necessary qualification to practise. As the Supreme Court is the final appellate court for Scotland and Northern Ireland as well, judges can also be appointed from those who have practised (or been qualified to practise) as an advocate in Scotland for at least 15 years or as a member of the Bar in Northern Ireland for at least 15 years or held high judicial office in their own legal system. There are 12 Justices of the Supreme Court.

All judgments by the Justices of the Supreme Court are put on their website (www.supremecourt.gov.uk).

Note that the most senior court in the UK used to be the Appellate Committee of the House of Lords. The Constitutional Reform Act 2005 abolished this and replaced it with the Supreme Court. The changeover occurred in October 2009. Judgments by the House of Lords for cases between 1996 and 2009 can be found on the website for Parliament (www.parliament.uk).

13.2.2 Lords Justices of Appeal

These must be qualified as a barrister or solicitor and have seven years' relevant legal experience or be an existing High Court judge. In practice nearly all Lords Justices of Appeal have been appointed from existing High Court judges. Up to 2006 all Lords Justices of Appeal had been qualified as barristers, but in 2007 the first solicitor Lord Justice of Appeal was appointed.

13.2.3 High Court judges

In order to be eligible to be appointed as a High Court judge it is necessary to be a barrister or solicitor and have seven years' relevant legal experience. Prior to the Courts and Legal Services Act 1990 only those who had practised as a barrister for at least 10 years were eligible. The present qualification routes give solicitors the chance to become High Court judges. This can be either by promotion from a circuit judgeship or by holding a certificate of advocacy for 10 years. So far there have only been two solicitors appointed to the High Court. The first was in 1993 and the second in 2000. This second solicitor judge (Sir Lawrence Collins) has since been promoted to the Court of Appeal.

13.2.4 Circuit judges

There are different routes to becoming a Circuit judge. The candidate must be qualified as a barrister or solicitor and have seven years' relevant legal experience. About 17 per cent of circuit judges are solicitors. The Courts and Legal Services Act 1990 also allowed for promotion after being a district judge or a tribunal judge for at least three years. These provisions widened the pool of potential judges and are starting to lead to a better cross-section amongst the judges.

13.2.5 Recorders

This is a part-time post. The applicant must be qualified as a barrister or solicitor and have seven years' relevant legal experience. Recorders sit as a judge for 20 days in the year, the rest of the time they do their own work. The appointment is for five years and most recorders work in the Crown Court hearing criminal cases, though some are appointed as civil recorders and sit in the County Court to hear civil cases.

13.2.6 District judges

These need to be qualified as a barrister or solicitor and have five years' relevant legal experience. This means they can be appointed from either barristers or solicitors, but in practice the vast majority of district judges are solicitors. They work in the County Court and are concerned only with civil cases.

Under the Tribunals, Courts and Enforcement Act 2007, ILEX Fellows are now eligible to be appointed as Deputy District judges.

13.2.7 District judges (magistrates' courts)

At this level an applicant must have been qualified as a barrister, solicitor and have gained experience in law for at least five years or to have been a Deputy District judge. It is usual to have sat part-time as a Deputy District judge before

being considered for the position of District judge in the Magistrates' courts. Under the Tribunals, Courts and Enforcement Act 2007, ILEX Fellows are now eligible to be appointed as Deputy District judges.

13.3 Selection

13.3.1 History

Until 2005, the Lord Chancellor was the key figure in the selection of superior judges. The Lord Chancellor's Department would keep information on all possible candidates. These files would contain confidential information and opinions from existing judges on the suitability of each person. The contents of these files were secret.

When there was a vacancy for a judicial position in the former Appellate Committee of the House of Lords, the Court of Appeal or the High Court, the Lord Chancellor would consider the information in these files and decide which person he thought was the best for the post. That person would then be invited to become a judge.

Not surprisingly, this system of selection was seen as secretive. It was also felt that it favoured white males, as there were few women in the higher ranks of the judiciary.

Matters improved for High Court judgeships as, from 1998, vacancies were advertised and any qualified person could apply. However, even then, the Lord Chancellor continued to invite people to become judges, rather than appoint solely from those who applied.

The major role of the Lord Chancellor in appointment was very controversial as the Lord Chancellor is a political appointment. It was thought that the appointment of judges should be independent from any political influence. So the method of appointment was changed by the Constitutional Reform Act 2005 and a Judicial Appointments Commission created to deal with selection of judges.

SUPERIOR JUDGES

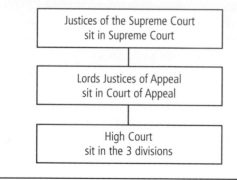

INFERIOR JUDGES

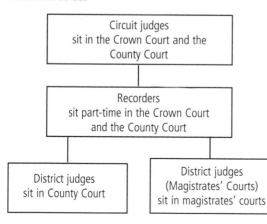

Figure 13.1 The hierarchy of judges

13.3.2 The Judicial Appointments Commission

Virtually all judges are now selected by the Judicial Appointments Commission. This was created under the Constitutional Reform Act and started work in April 2006. The Commission is responsible for selecting between about 500 and 700 people for appointment to judicial posts each year.

There are 15 members of this Commission. There must be:

- 6 lay members
- 5 judges – 3 of these from the Court of Appeal or High Court plus 1 circuit judge and 1 district judge or equivalent;
- 1 barrister;
- 1 solicitor;
- 1 magistrate;
- 1 tribunal member.

The key features of the new process for appointing judges are:

- appointments are made solely on merit;
- the Commission is entirely responsible for assessing the merit of the candidates and selecting candidates for appointment;
- no candidate can be appointed unless recommended by the Commission;

- the Commission must consult with the Lord Chief Justice and another judge of equivalent experience before recommending a candidate for appointment;
- the Lord Chancellor has limited powers in relation to each recommendation for appointment. He can reject a candidate once or ask the Commission to reconsider once but he must give reasons in writing for this.

The power of the Lord Chancellor to reject a candidate or ask the Commission to reconsider has been criticised.

Judicial qualities

The Commission have listed five qualities that are desirable for a good judge. These are:

- intellectual capacity;
- personal qualities including integrity, independence of mind, sound judgment, decisiveness, objectivity and willingness to learn;
- ability to understand and deal fairly;
- authority and communication skills;
- efficiency.

The process

Positions are advertised widely in newspapers, legal journals and also online.

	Facts	Comment
Previous system	Superior judges were selected by Lord Chancellor	• Lord Chancellor had too much power • risk of political bias • relied on secret files • led to a predominately white male judiciary
	Inferior judges applied for posts but final selection relied on Lord Chancellor	
Present system	Selection carried out by the Judicial Appointments Commission • all positions are advertised • candidates must apply giving references • candidates are short-listed and interviewed	• selection is on merit • allows a wider group to be considered for judgeships • this should lead to a more representative judiciary • Lord Chancellor can reject first choice of JAC: this is criticised as it still gives the Lord Chancellor power over appointments

Figure 13.2 Comment on the systems of selection of judges

All candidates have to fill in an application form. Candidates are also asked to nominate between three and six referees. In addition, the Commission has published a list of people whom it may consult about candidates. These include existing judges.

For lower level posts, applicants are also asked to write an essay or do a case study.

The Commission then selects the best candidates to be interviewed. The interview process may include role play or taking part in a formal, structured discussion. After the interviews, the final selections are made and recommended to the Lord Chancellor for appointment.

In 2006, the first vacancies for High Court judgeships were advertised through this system. There were 129 applicants, but only 18 of these were women and all the applicants were white.

The Judicial Appointments Commission has tried to encourage a wider range of candidates to apply by running roadshows and other outreach events designed to communicate and explain the appointments system to potential applicants.

More information can be found on the Judicial Appointments Commission's website at www.judicialappointments.gov.uk.

 Internet Research

Look at the Commission's website to see if any judicial posts are being currently advertised.

13.3.3 Justices of the Supreme Court

When the Supreme Court was established in 2009, all existing Law Lords from the House of Lords automatically became judges in the new court. Judges for new appointments after that are selected according to the method set out in Part 3 of the Constitutional Reform Act 2005. This states that when there is a vacancy, the Lord Chancellor must set up a Supreme Court selection commission to select the best candidate.

This commission must include the President and the Deputy President of the Supreme Court and one member of the Judicial Appointments Commission. As the Supreme Court is also the final court of appeal for Scotland and Northern Ireland, the commission must also include a member of the Judicial Appointments Board for Scotland and the Northern Ireland Judicial Appointments Commission.

The commission will decide the selection process to be used. It will then use that process to select a candidate and report that selection to the Lord Chancellor.

Under s 29 of the Constitutional Reform Act 2005, the Lord Chancellor can reject that candidate or ask the commission to reconsider. This can only be done if the Lord Chancellor is of the opinion that the person selected is not suitable for the office or that there is evidence that the person is not the best candidate on merit. The Lord Chancellor must give his reasons for rejecting a candidate or asking the commission to reconsider in writing.

Once the Lord Chancellor has accepted the commission's nomination, he then notifies the Prime Minister and the Prime Minister must recommend to the Queen that she appoints that person. The Prime Minister will not be able to recommend another person for appointment.

13.4 Appointment

Once a candidate has been selected and that selection accepted by the Lord Chancellor, then the appointment is made by the Queen for all judicial posts from District Judges up to the Supreme Court.

13.5 Judicial roles

The work that a judge does depends on the level of court in which he or she works.

13.5.1 Justices of the Supreme Court

Judges in the Supreme Court hear about 70 cases each year. These are appeals. They can be in civil or criminal cases. However, there are always far

Activity

Below is the advertisement of a vacancy which appeared in October 2009. Read it and answer the questions below.

Justice of The Supreme Court

An ad hoc selection commission has been established under section 27 and schedule 8 of the Constitutional Reform Act 2005 to select a candidate to be recommended for appointment as a Justice of the Supreme Court. The vacancy arises as a result of Lord Neuberger's appointment as Master of the Rolls.

The statutory minimum qualification for appointment is to have held high judicial office for a period of at least two years, or to have satisfied the judicial appointment eligibility condition on a 15-year basis or to have been a qualifying practitioner for a period of at least 15 years.

The selection commission invites applications from all eligible candidates who fulfil one of the above statutory requirements.

Additional information on the qualifications, the criteria and the selection process can be found in the Information Pack which is available from Grainne Hawkins (grainne.hawkins@supremecourt.gsi.gov.uk tel: 020 7960 1906).

The closing date for applications is 5pm Monday 26 October.

Applications should be sent to:

**Jenny Rowe
Chief Executive
UK Supreme Court
Parliament Square
LONDON SW1P 3BD**

Advert in The Times 8 October 2009

Questions

1. Under which section of which Act has a selection commission been established?
2. What is the role of the selection commission?
3. If the candidate has held high judicial office in other courts, what is the minimum period of time must they have held that office?
4. If the candidate has not held high judicial office, what qualification(s) do they need?

more civil appeals each year. A case can only be appealed to the Supreme Court if there is a point of law involved. Often civil cases involve complicated and technical areas of law such as planning law or tax law.

The Justices of the Supreme Court must sit as an uneven number panel (minimum three judges) to hear a case.

Any decision the Supreme Court makes on a point of law becomes a precedent for all lower

The new Supreme Court

courts to follow. You can find reports of cases decided by the Supreme Court at www.supremecourt.gov.uk.

13.5.2 Lords Justices of Appeal

There are some 37 Lords Justices of Appeal. They sit in both the civil and criminal divisions of the Court of Appeal, so they deal with both civil and criminal cases. Their workload is much heavier than the Supreme Court.

On the criminal side they will hear over 7,000 applications for leave to appeal against sentence or conviction. These are dealt with by one judge. Only about a quarter of these get leave to appeal, so the full court then has about 1,800 criminal appeals to hear. In addition, they hear over 3,000 civil appeals. These may be appeals against the finding of liability or an appeal about the remedy awarded, e.g. the amount of money given as damages.

Court of Appeal judges usually sit as a panel of three to hear cases. On rare occasions in important cases, there may be a panel of five. Decisions by the Court of Appeal on points of law become precedents which lower courts must follow.

Because the workload of the Court of Appeal is so large, High Court judges are often used to

form part of the panel. This means there may be one Lord Justice of Appeal sitting with two High Court judges.

In law reports Court of Appeal judges are referred to as Lord Justice or Lady Justice, but when their judgments are being quoted it is usually abbreviated to the surname, followed by LJ, for example, Arden LJ.

13.5.3 High Court judges

Each judge in the High Court will be assigned to one of the Divisions. There are 72 judges in the Queen's Bench Division, 17 in the Chancery Division and 18 in the Family Division.

There are also Deputy High Court judges who sit to help with the workload.

The main function of High Court judges is to try cases. These are cases at first instance because it is the first time the case has been heard by a court. They will hear evidence from witnesses, decide what the law is and make the decision as to which side has won the case. If the claim is for damages (an amount of money) the judge decides how much should be awarded to the winning claimant. When hearing first instance cases, judges sit on their own. In some rare cases in the Queen's Bench Division there may be a jury.

High Court judges also hear some appeals.

Key facts

Court	Judges	Qualifications	Role
Supreme Court	Justices of the Supreme Court	15-year Senior Courts qualification or have held high judicial office	Hear appeals on points of law Civil and criminal cases
Court of Appeal	Lords Justices of Appeal	barrister or solicitor with seven years' legal experience or be an existing High Court judge	Hear appeals Criminal cases against conviction and/or sentence Civil cases on the finding and/or the amount awarded
High Court	High Court judges Also known as puisne judges	barrister or solicitor with seven years' legal experience or be a Circuit judge for 2 years	Sit in one of the 3 Divisions Hear first instance cases and decide liability and remedy Some appeal work
Crown Court	High Court judges Circuit judges Recorders	See above barrister or solicitor with seven years' legal experience or be a recorder or District judge for 2 years barrister or solicitor with five years' experience	Try cases with a jury Decide the law Pass sentence on guilty defendants
County Court	Circuit judges District judges	See above barrister or solicitor with five years' experience	Civil cases – decide liability and remedy District judges hear small claims
Magistrates' Courts	District judges (Magistrates' Courts)	barrister or solicitor with five years' experience ILEX fellows can be appointed as Deputy District Judges	Criminal cases – decide law and verdict Pass sentence on guilty defendants Some family work

Figure 13.3 Key facts chart on judges

These are mainly from civil cases tried in the County Court. The judges in the Queen's Bench Division also hear criminal appeals from the magistrates' courts by a special case stated method. These are appeals on law only. When sitting to hear appeals, there will be a panel of two or three judges.

Judges from the Queen's Bench Division also sit in the Crown Court to hear criminal trials. When they do this they sit with a jury. The jury decide the facts and the judge decides the law. Where a defendant pleads guilty or is found guilty by a jury, the judge then has to decide on the sentence.

In law reports High Court judges are referred to as Mr Justice or Mrs Justice, but when their judgments are being quoted it is usually abbreviated to the surname, followed by J, for example, Dobbs J.

13.5.4 Inferior judges

Circuit judges sit in the County Court to hear civil cases and also in the Crown Court to try criminal cases. In civil cases they sit on their own (it is very rare to have a jury in a civil case in the County Court). They decide the law and the facts. They make the decision on who has won the case.

In criminal cases they sit with a jury. The jury decide the facts and the judge decides the law. Where a defendant pleads guilty or is found guilty by a jury, the judge then has to decide on the sentence.

Recorders are part-time judges who are appointed for a period of five years. They are used mainly in the Crown Court to try criminal cases, but some sit in the County Court to help with civil cases.

District Judges sit in the County Court to deal with small claims cases (under £5,000) and can also hear other cases for larger amounts.

District Judges (magistrates' courts) try criminal cases in the magistrates' courts. They sit on their own and decide facts and law. When a defendant pleads guilty or is found guilty, they also have to decide on the sentence.

They may also sit to hear family cases, but this will usually be with two lay magistrates.

@ Internet Research

Look up law reports on the Internet. Try www.bailii.org.

TRY TO FIND:

1. A law report in which there was a female judge.

2. A report of the Court of Appeal in which one at least of the judges is only of High Court level.

3. A report from the High Court in which the judge sitting is only a Deputy High Court judge.

13.6 Training

The training of judges is carried out by the Judicial Studies Board. Most of the training is, however, focused at the lower end of the judicial scale, being aimed at recorders. Once a lawyer has been appointed as an assistant recorder, they go on a one-week course run by the Judicial Studies Board, then they shadow an experienced judge for a week. After this they will sit to hear cases, though there will be one-day courses available from time to time, especially on the effect of new legislation.

Critics point out that the training is very short and that, even if all the trainee judges are experienced lawyers, this does not mean that they have any experience of doing such tasks as summing up to the jury or sentencing. There is also the fact that some recorders will not have practised in the criminal courts as lawyers, so their expertise is limited and a one-week course is a very short training period.

There is no compulsory training given to new High Court judges, although they are invited to attend the courses run by the Judicial Studies Board. The attitude of the judiciary to training has changed considerably over the last 20 years. Training used to be seen as insulting to lawyers who had spent all their working lives in the courts building up expertise in their field. It was also seen as a threat to judicial independence. However, the need for training is now fully accepted.

Human awareness training

Since 1993 all judges have to attend a course designed to make them aware of what might be unintentionally discriminatory or offensive, such as asking a non-Christian for their Christian name. The Judicial Studies Board has also introduced training in human awareness, covering gender awareness, and disability issues. The training explores the perceptions of unrepresented parties, witnesses, jurors, victims and their families, and tries to make judges more aware of other people's viewpoints.

13.6.1 Should there be a 'career' judiciary?

In many continental countries becoming a judge is a career choice made by students once they have their basic legal qualifications. They will usually not practise as a lawyer first, but instead are trained as judges. Once they have qualified as a judge they will sit in junior posts and then hope for promotion up the judicial ladder. This has two distinct advantages over the system in use in this country:

● The average age of judges is much lower, especially in the bottom ranks. In this country a recorder will normally be in their late 30s/early 40s when appointed, while the average age for appointment to the High Court bench tends to be late 40s/early 50s.
● Judges have had far more training in the specific skills they need as judges.

The disadvantage of the continental system is that judges may be seen as too closely linked to the government as they are civil servants. In this country judges are generally considered as independent from the government. This point of judicial independence is explored more fully at section 13.10.

13.7 Dismissal and retirement

It is important that judges should be impartial in their decisions. In particular it is important that the government cannot force a judge to resign if that judge makes a decision with which the government of the day disagrees. In this country judges are reasonably secure from political interference.

13.7.1 Security of tenure of superior judges

Superior judges have security of tenure in that they cannot be dismissed by the government. This right originated in the Act of Settlement 1701

Key facts

Judges	Court/s	Tenure
Justices of the Supreme Court	Supreme Court	'whilst of good behaviour' (Constitutional Reform Act s 33)
Lords Justices of Appeal	Court of Appeal	'whilst of good behaviour' (Senior Courts Act 1981, s 11(3))
High Court judges (puisne judges)	High Court Crown Court for serious cases	'whilst of good behaviour' (Senior Courts Act 1981, s 11(3))
Circuit judges	Crown Court County Court	Can be dismissed by Lord Chancellor for incapacity or misbehaviour (Courts Act 1971, s 17(4))
District judges	County Court Magistrates' Court	Can be dismissed by the Lord Chancellor
Recorders	Crown Court Some may sit in County Court	Appointed for period of five years; Lord Chancellor can decide not to reappoint

Figure 13.4 Key facts chart on judges and their tenure

which allowed them to hold office whilst of good behaviour. Before 1700 the Monarch could dismiss judges at will. The same provision is now contained in the Senior Courts Act 1981 for High Court judges and Lords Justices of Appeal, and in the Constitutional Reform Act 2005 for the Justices of the Supreme Court. As a result they can only be removed by the Monarch following a petition presented to her by both Houses of Parliament. This gives superior judges protection from political whims and allows them to be independent in their judgments.

This power to remove a superior judge has never been used for an English judge, though it was used in 1830 to remove an Irish judge, Jonah Barrington, who had misappropriated £700 from court funds.

There have, however, been occasions when pressure has been put on unsatisfactory High Court judges to resign. The first of these was in 1959 when the Lord Chancellor asked Mr Justice Hallett to resign and the second in 1998 when Mr Justice Harman resigned after criticisms by the Court of Appeal.

Activity

Read the following newspaper article and answer the questions below.

'Do you fancy being a High Court judge? Forget the whisper over a drink at your Inn of Court or the traditional "tap on the shoulder". Dust off your CV and send in an application. And then prepare yourself for an "interview" with a selection panel. This is the new world of appointing judges. . .

The selection process will be undertaken by the Judicial Appointments Commission, the independent body set up under the Constitutional Reform Act in 2005 to take over responsibility for selecting judges from the Lord Chancellor's officials.

There has been advertising for High Court judges before – but they were selected on paper. This time, the candidates will undergo a face-to-face discussion – and that, with references and their own application form, will combine to inform the selection.

Baroness Usha Prashar, who is chairman of the 15 lay and judicial commissioners and 105 staff, will now be responsible for 500 to 700 appointments a year, including the High Court.

The aim she says is for a much more transparent process that will encourage a greater diversity of candidates. "Up to now the process was perceived to be very secretive and not very open. There was a view that it was those who you knew who counted – and that probably deterred a lot of people who felt they would not get a fair deal. This will be objective and transparent and hopefully that will encourage more people to apply.'

Taken from an article by Frances Gibb
The Times, 31 October 2006. © The Times 2006/nisyndication.com

Questions

1. Who was responsible for appointing judges under the old system?
2. Who is responsible for appointing judges now?
3. Describe the problems with the old system of appointing judges.
4. Describe how the new system operates.
5. Explain whether you think that the new system will encourage a wider range of applicants for judeships.

13.7.2 Tenure of inferior judges

These do not have the same security of tenure of office as superior judges. The Lord Chancellor has the power to dismiss inferior judges for incapacity or misbehaviour. A criminal conviction for dishonesty would obviously be regarded as misbehaviour and would lead to the dismissal of the judge concerned. This has happened only once in the case of Bruce Campbell, a circuit judge, who was convicted of evading customs duty on cigarettes and whisky.

13.7.3 Retirement

Since the Judicial Pensions and Retirement Act 1993 all judges now have to retire at the age of 70, though there are some situations in which authorisation can be given for a judge to continue beyond that age. Prior to this Act judges in the High Court and above could remain sitting as judges until they were 75. All inferior judges also now retire at 70.

13.8 Composition of the judiciary

One of the main criticisms of the bench is that it is dominated by elderly, white, upper class males. There are few women judges and even fewer judges from ethnic minorities. Also, women and ethnic minorities who are appointed tend to be in the lower ranks of the judiciary. It is unusual for any judge to be appointed under the age of 40 with superior judges usually being well above this age.

13.8.1 Women in the judiciary

The number of women in judicial posts is small, although there has been an improvement in recent years.

During the 1990s there was an increase in the number of women appointed to the High Court. Before 1992 all women judges in the High Court were appointed to the Family Division. However, the first woman judge in the Queen's Bench Division was appointed in 1992 and the first in the Chancery Division in 1993. In 2009 there were 15 female judges in the High Court out of a total of over 100 judges.

The first woman in the Court of Appeal was appointed in 1988. It was not until 1999 that a second woman was appointed to the Court of Appeal, and a third in 2000. In February 2001 the first all-female Court of Appeal panel sat. The first, and so far only, woman judge in the House of Lords (now Supreme Court) was appointed in 2004. In 2009 there were three female judges in the Court of Appeal and just one in the Supreme Court.

Lower down the judicial ladder there are slightly more women being appointed than in the past. In 2009, 14 per cent of Circuit Judges and 13 per cent of Recorders were female. The highest percentages of women were for District Judges (27 per cent).

13.8.2 Ethnic minorities

In 2004 the first ethnic minority judge (mixed race) was appointed to the High Court. There are no ethnic minority judges in the Court of Appeal or Supreme Court. Even at the lower levels, ethnic minorities are still poorly represented. In 2009 less than 1 per cent of Circuit Judges and 2.7 per cent of Recorders were from a black or Asian ethnic minority. These percentages have not changed much over the past five years. It will be interesting to see if the new appointments system leads to greater diversity.

13.8.3 Educational and social background

At the higher levels judges tend to come from the upper levels of society, with many having been educated at public school and nearly all attending Oxford or Cambridge University.

Judges, especially superior judges, will have spent at least 20 years working as barristers and mixing with a small group of like-minded people. As a result judges are seen as out of touch with society. Occasionally the media report actions or comments which appear to support this view, for example where a judge said of an eight-year old

On the Internet look up the judicial website www.judiciary.gov.uk. Select Key Facts and go to the Senior Judiciary Biographies.

Choose any two judges and look at their biographies. Find out the following matters:

(a) Which school did they go to?

(b) At which university did they get their degree?

(c) When did they first become a judge?

(d) What was their first judicial post?

(e) When were they appointed to their present position?

Now go to Statistics on the same site and:

1. Find out how many women judges there are in the Court of Appeal.

2. Find out how many ethnic minority judges there are in the High Court.

rape victim that she 'was no angel'. Since 1995 training in human awareness has been given to prevent this type of offensive remark.

Lord Taylor, a former Lord Chief Justice and who was one of the few senior judges who had attended a state school, pointed out that judges do live in the real world and do ordinary things like shopping in supermarkets.

13.9 The doctrine of the separation of powers

The theory of separation of powers was first put forward by Montesquieu, a French political theorist, in the eighteenth century. The theory states that there are three primary functions of the state and that the only way to safeguard the liberty of citizens is by keeping these three functions separate. These functions are:

- Legislative;
- Executive;
- Judiciary.

As the power of each is exercised by independent and separate bodies, each can keep a check on the others thus limiting the amount of power wielded by any one group. Ideally this theory requires that individuals should not be members of more than one 'arm of the state'.

Some countries, for example the United States of America, have a written constitution which embodies this theory. In the United Kingdom we have no such written constitution, but even so the three organs of State are roughly separated. However, there is some overlap, especially in the fact that the Lord Chancellor is involved in all three functions of the state. However, the Lord Chancellor's role in relation to the judiciary is now much reduced.

The three arms of the State identified by Montesquieu are:

1. **The legislature**
   This is the law-making arm of the State and in our system this is Parliament.
2. **The executive** or the body administering the law.
   Under the British political system this is the government of the day which forms the Cabinet.
3. **The judiciary**
   This is the judges and they apply the law.

There is an overlap between the executive and the legislature in that the ministers forming the government also sit in Parliament and are active in the law-making process. With the exception of the Lord Chancellor, there is very little overlap between the judiciary and the other two arms of the state.

This is important because it allows the judiciary to act as a check and ensure that the executive does not overstep its constitutional powers. This is in accordance with Montesquieu's theory. However, it is open to debate whether the judiciary is truly independent from the other organs of government.

13.10 Independence of the judiciary

As already stated an independent judiciary is seen as important in protecting the liberty of the individual from abuse of power by the executive. Judges in the English system can be thought of as being independent in a number of ways.

13.10.1 Independence from the legislature

Judges generally are not involved in the law-making functions of Parliament. Full-time judges are not allowed to be members of the House of Commons, although the rule is not as strict for part-time judges so that recorders and assistant recorders can be Members of Parliament. There used to be judges in the House of Lords when the Appellate Committee of the House of Lords was the final court of appeal. The main reason for the creation of the Supreme Court in 2009 was to separate the judiciary from the legislature.

13.10.2 Independence from the executive

Superior judges cannot be dismissed by the government and in this way they can truly be said to be independent of the government. They can make decisions which may displease the government without the threat of dismissal. The extent to which judges are prepared to challenge or support the government is considered at section 13.10.4

Judicial independence is now guaranteed under s 3 of the Constitutional Reform Act 2005. This states that the Lord Chancellor, other Ministers in the government and anyone with responsibility for matters relating to the judiciary or the administration of justice must uphold the continued independence of the judiciary.

The section also specifically states that the Lord Chancellor and other Ministers must not seek to influence particular judicial decisions.

Ministry of Justice

In 2007 a Ministry of Justice was created to bring together all the key elements of the justice system under one ministry. Previously two ministries, the Department for Constitutional Affairs and the Home Office, had had responsibility for separate parts of the justice system.

The Ministry of Justice has responsibility for:

- the civil courts;
- the criminal courts;
- the judiciary;
- legal aid and funding of cases;
- prisons;
- the probation service;
- sentencing.

There are fears that the budget of the new department will not be sufficient for all this and that prisons will take a large part of the budget. This could result in there not being enough money for the courts service.

Test Yourself

1. Give the types of superior judge.
2. Give the types of inferior judge.
3. What qualification(s) does a High Court judge need?
4. Which body makes the selection of potential judges?
5. What power does the Lord Chancellor have in relation to the selection of judges?
6. What is the role of the judges in the Supreme Court?
7. Which body carries out the training of judges?
8. How can a superior judge be dismissed?
9. How can an inferior judge be dismissed?
10. Briefly explain the theory of the separation of powers.

Judges are also worried about the effect of the change on their independence. The Minister for Justice is also the Lord Chancellor. As the Minister for Justice is a key role in the executive, it is difficult to see how he can also maintain the independence of the judiciary.

13.10.3 Freedom from pressure

There are several ways in which judges are protected from outside pressure when exercising their judicial functions.

1. They are given a certain degree of financial independence, as judicial salaries are paid out of the consolidated fund so that payment is made without the need for Parliament's authorisation. This does not completely protect them from parliamentary interference with the terms on which they hold office. As already seen, changes can be made to retirement ages and qualifying periods for pensions.
2. Judges have immunity from being sued for actions taken or decisions made in the course of their judicial duties. This was confirmed in *Sirros v Moore* (1975) and is a key factor in ensuring judicial independence in decision-making.
3. As already noted, the security of tenure of the superior judges protects them from the threat of removal.

13.10.4 Independence from political bias

This is the area where there is most dispute over how independent the judiciary are. Writers, such as Professor Griffith, have pointed out that judges are too pro-establishment and conservative with a small 'c'.

Pro-government decisions

Griffith cited cases such as the 'GCHQ case' in showing that judges tend to support the establishment. This case, *Council of Civil Service Unions v Minister for the Civil Service* (1984),

concerned the minister for the Conservative Government withdrawing the right to trade union membership from civil servants working at the intelligence headquarters in Cheltenham. The House of Lords upheld the minister's right, and the decision was seen as anti-trade union.

Anti-government decisions

There is, however, evidence that judges are not as pro-establishment as sometimes thought. Lord Taylor, when giving the Dimbleby Lecture in 1992, pointed out that this could be seen in the case of the Greenham Common women who had camped by an RAF base in protest against nuclear missiles. In *DPP v Hutchinson* (1990) some of the women were prosecuted under a by-law for being on Ministry of Defence property unlawfully. The case went all the way to the House of Lords which ruled in the women's favour, holding that the Minister had exceeded his powers in framing the by-law so as to prevent access to common land.

Human rights

More recently, the courts have upheld challenges by asylum seekers and by those held under the Anti-Terrorism, Crime and Security Act 2001. In *R (on the application of Q) v Secretary of State for the Home Department* (2003) Collins J in the High Court declared that the Home Secretary's power to refuse to provide assistance to asylum seekers who had not immediately, on their entry to this country, declared their intention to claim asylum was unlawful. The Court of Appeal upheld this decision, although they did suggest how the relevant Act could be made compatible with human rights.

In *A and another v Secretary of State for the Home Department* (2004) the House of Lords declared that the Anti-Terrorism, Crime and Security Act 2001 was incompatible with the Convention. The Act allowed foreign nationals to be detained indefinitely without trial where there was suspicion that they were involved in terrorist activity. The Lords held that this breached both

Article 5 (the right to liberty) and Article 14 (no discrimination on basis of nationality). This decision forced the government to change the law.

With the Human Rights Act 1998 incorporating the European Convention on Human Rights, judges can declare that an Act is incompatible with the Convention. This puts pressure on the government to change the law. The first case in which this happened was *H v Mental Health Review Tribunal* (2001). The courts also have a duty to interpret laws in a way which is compatible with the Convention.

So, while it is true that judges are still predominantly white, male, middle-class and elderly, it is possible to argue that they are no longer so out of touch with the 'real world', and that they are increasingly prepared to challenge the establishment.

13.10.5 Independence from case

Judges must not try any case where they have any interest in the issue involved. The Pinochet case in 1998 reinforced this rule. In that case the House of Lords judges heard an appeal by the former head of the state of Chile. There was a claim to extradite him to Chile to face possible trial for crimes involving torture and deaths which had occurred there while he was head of state.

Amnesty International, the human rights movement, had been granted leave to participate in the case. After the House of Lords ruled that Pinochet could be extradited, it was discovered that one of the judges, Lord Hoffmann, was an unpaid director of Amnesty International Charitable Trust. Pinochet's lawyers asked for the decision to be set aside and to have the case re-heard by a completely independent panel of judges.

The Law Lords decided that their original decision could not be allowed to stand. Judges had to be seen to be completely unbiased. The fact that Lord Hoffmann was connected with Amnesty meant that he might be considered not to be completely impartial. The case was retried with a new panel of judges.

Human rights

The test for bias has been influenced by the European Convention on Human Rights. In *Re Medicaments (No 2), Director General of Fair Trading v Proprietary Association of Great Britain* (2001) the Court of Appeal followed decisions of the European Court of Human Rights. The court said that the test was an objective one of whether the circumstances were such as to lead a fair-minded and informed observer to conclude that there was a real possibility of bias.

Examination questions

(a) Briefly explain how inferior and superior judges are selected and appointed. (10 marks)

(b) Explain how inferior and superior judges can be dismissed from office. (10 marks)

(c) Consider why it is difficult to dismiss a judge from office. (10 marks)

AQA LAW01 January 2009

Examiner's tip

Make sure you are clear on the differences between superior judges and inferior judges. Also make sure that you write about both superior judges and inferior judges for parts (a) and (b). Remember that if you write only about one you cannot get into the top mark bands.

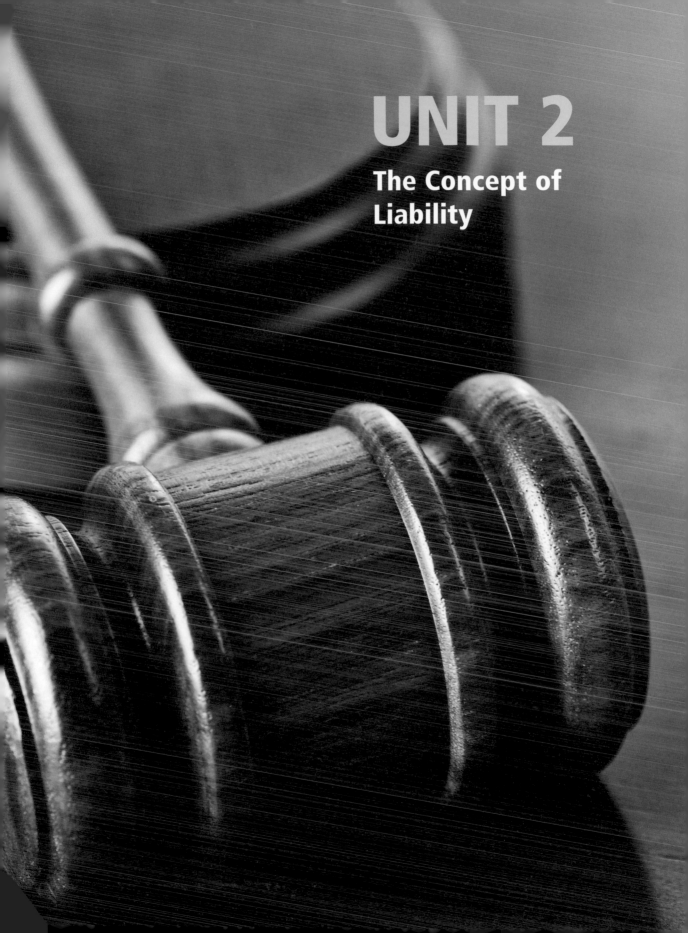

UNIT 2

The Concept of Liability

Chapter 14

Introduction to Criminal Law

In most crimes there are two elements which must be proved to show that the defendant is guilty. These two elements are known as the *actus reus* and the *mens rea*. The *actus reus* is the physical element of the crime, i.e. what the defendant has done or not done. *The mens rea* is the mental element of the crime, i.e. what the defendant is intending or thinking or failing to think about when the crime is committed.

Each crime has its own *actus reus* and *mens rea*. For example, in theft the defendant must 'appropriate' property belonging to another for the *actus reus*; and do this dishonestly and intend to permanently deprive the other of it for the *mens rea*. For battery the *actus reus* is applying unlawful force to another person. This can be any act such as punching, kicking, stabbing or hitting with a weapon. It can be an indirect act such as setting up a booby trap, so that when the trap is sprung something hits the victim. In some circumstances it can even be a failure to act. The *mens rea* for battery is intending to apply the force or being reckless as to whether force is applied.

Although each crime has its own *actus reus* and *mens rea* there are certain general rules which apply and these are explained in the rest of this chapter.

14.1 *Actus reus*

As already stated the *actus reus* is the physical element of a crime. It can be:

- an act, or
- a failure to act (an omission), or
- a state of affairs.

For some crimes the *actus reus* must have an act or omission and also result in a consequence. This can be seen in an assault occasioning actual bodily harm (s 47 Offences Against the Person Act 1861). There must be the threat or the use of force and there must be a consequence of 'actual bodily harm', in other words some injury to the victim. This could be just a bruise or it could be a broken nose or broken arm. It could even be psychiatric injury.

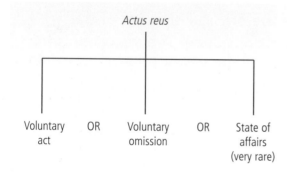

Figure 14.1 *Actus reus*

14.1.1 Voluntary nature of *actus reus*

The act or omission must be voluntary on the part of the defendant. If the defendant has no control over his actions then he has not committed the *actus reus*. In *Hill v Baxter* (1958) the court gave examples where a driver of a vehicle could not be said to be doing the act of driving voluntarily. These included where a driver lost control of his vehicle because he was stung by a swarm of bees, was struck on the head by a stone or had a heart attack while driving.

Involuntary acts and assaults

Involuntary conduct can occur in assaults. One example is where one person pushes another causing them to bump into the victim. In this situation the act of the person who has been pushed is involuntary. They will not be guilty of any assault. However, it is possible (depending on whether they have the necessary *mens rea*) that the person who did the pushing will be guilty of assaulting the person they pushed and also of assaulting the person who was bumped into.

Another example of an involuntary act is where the defendant hits another person due to a reflex action or a muscle spasm.

These examples show that the criminal law is concerned with fault on the part of the defendant. Where there is an absence of fault then the defendant is usually not liable.

State of affairs cases

However, there are some rare instances in which the defendant has been convicted even though he or she did not act voluntarily. These situations involve what are known as state of affairs cases. In *Larsonneur* (1933) the defendant had been ordered to leave the United Kingdom. She decided to go to Eire, but the Irish police deported her and took her back to the UK. She did not wish to go back and was certainly not doing this voluntarily. When she landed in the UK she was immediately arrested and charged with 'being an alien to whom leave to land in the UK had been refused, was found in the UK'. She was convicted because she was an alien who had been refused leave to land and she was found in the UK. It did not matter that she had been brought back by the Irish police against her will (see also section 14.4 on strict liability).

14.1.2 Omissions as *actus reus*

The normal rule is that an omission cannot make a person guilty of an offence. This was explained by Stephen J, a nineteenth-century judge, in the following way: 'A sees B drowning and is able to save him by holding out his hand. A abstains from doing so in order that B may be drowned. A has committed no offence'.

Exceptions to the rule

There are exceptions to the rule that an omission cannot make a person guilty of an offence. In some cases it is possible for a failure to act (an omission) to be the *actus reus*. An Act of Parliament can create liability for an omission. Examples include the offences of failing to report a road traffic accident and of failing to provide a specimen of breath.

For common law crimes an omission is only sufficient for the *actus reus* where there is a duty to act. There are five ways in which such a duty exists.

Read the following scenario and discuss whether you think Zoe should be guilty of an offence.

Scenario

Zoe is sitting by a swimming pool in the grounds of a hotel. Jason is swimming in the pool. He is the only person in the water and there are no other people near the pool. Jason gets out of the pool and, while walking around it, slips and falls into the water. He is knocked unconscious. Zoe sees this happen but she does nothing. Jason drowns.

Would it make any difference to your answer if:

(a) Zoe could not swim.
(b) Zoe was a qualified lifeguard.
(c) Jason was aged 3.
(d) Jason was aged 3 and Zoe was his mother.

1. **A contractual duty**
   In *Pittwood* (1902) a railway crossing keeper omitted to shut the gates so that a person crossing the line was struck and killed by a train. The keeper was guilty of manslaughter. A more modern example would be of a lifeguard at a beach who leaves his post unattended. His failure to do his duty could make him guilty of an offence if a swimmer was injured.

2. **A duty because of a relationship (usually parent and child)**
   In *Gibbins and Proctor* (1918) a child's father and his mistress failed to feed the child, so that it died of starvation; they were guilty of murder.

3. **A duty which has been taken on voluntarily**
   In *Stone and Dobinson* (1977) Stone's elderly sister came to live with the defendants. She became ill and unable to care for herself. She died. The two defendants were convicted of manslaughter through failing to care for her or summon help when she became helpless.

4. **A duty through one's official position**
   In *Dytham* (1979) a police officer witnessed a violent attack on the victim, but took no steps to intervene or summon help; instead he drove away from the scene. The officer was guilty of wilfully and without reasonable excuse neglecting to perform his duty.

5. **A duty which arises because the defendant has set in motion a chain of events**
   In *Miller* (1983) a squatter accidentally started a fire. When he realised this he left the room and went to sleep in another room. He did not attempt to put out the fire or summon help. He was guilty of arson.

Doctors' duties

If discontinuance of medical treatment is in the best interests of the patient then this is not an omission which can form the *actus reus*. This was decided in *Airedale NHS Trust v Bland* (1993) in

which the NHS Trust was given permission to stop artificial feeding of a man who had been in a persistent vegetative state (PVS) for over three years.

14.1.3 Causation

Where a consequence must be proved, then the prosecution has to show that:

- the defendant's conduct was the factual cause of that consequence, and
- the defendant's conduct was in law the cause of that consequence, and
- there was no intervening act which broke the chain of causation.

Factual cause

The defendant can only be guilty if the consequence would not have happened 'but for' the defendant's conduct. In *Pagett* (1983) the defendant used his pregnant girlfriend as a shield while he shot at armed policemen. The police fired back and the girlfriend was killed. Pagett was convicted of her manslaughter. She would not have died 'but for' him using her as a shield in the shoot out.

The opposite situation was seen in *White* (1910) where the defendant put cyanide in his mother's drink intending to kill her. She died of a heart attack before she could drink it. The defendant did not cause her death; he was not guilty of murder, though he was guilty of attempted murder.

Cause in law

There may be more than one person whose act may have contributed to the consequence. The defendant can be guilty even though his conduct was not the only cause of the consequence. The rule is that the defendant's conduct must be more than a 'minimal' cause, but it need not be a substantial cause.

Key facts

Source	Explanation	Examples
Act of Parliament	Parliament can word an Act so that it is an offence not to do something	Failing to provide a specimen of breath (s 6 Road Traffic Act 1988)
A duty at common law	• Under a contract especially of employment • Because of a relationship such as parent and child • A duty voluntarily undertaken, e.g. care of an elderly relative • Because of a public office, e.g. police officer • As a result of a dangerous act or omission	*Pittwood* *Gibbins & Proctor* *Stone & Dobinson* *Dytham* *Miller*

Figure 14.2 Key facts chart of when omissions can be *actus reus*

The defendant must also take the victim as he finds him. This is known as the 'thin skull rule'. It means that if the victim has something unusual about his physical or mental state which makes an injury more serious, then the defendant is liable for the more serious injury. So this means that if the victim has an unusually thin skull which means that a blow to his head gives him a serious injury, then the defendant is liable for that injury. This is so even though that blow would have only caused bruising in a 'normal' person.

An example is the case of *Blaue* (1975) where a young woman was stabbed by the defendant. She was told she needed a blood transfusion to save her life but she refused to have one as she was a Jehovah's witness and her religion forbade blood transfusions. She died and the defendant was convicted of her murder. The fact that she was a Jehovah's witness made the wound fatal, but the defendant was still guilty because he had to take his victim as he found her.

Chain of causation

There must be a direct link from the defendant's conduct to the consequence This is known as the chain of causation. In some situations something else happens after the act (or omission) by the defendant which, if it is sufficiently separate from the defendant's actions, may break the chain of causation. The extra happening is called an intervening act.

An example is where the defendant has injured the victim, who needs to be taken to hospital. On the way the ambulance is involved in a crash and the victim receives serious injuries from which he dies. Under the 'but for' test it could be argued that the victim would not have been in the ambulance and involved in the accident but for the injuries caused by the defendant's conduct. However, the accident is such a major intervening act that the defendant would not be liable for the death of the victim. The chain of causation has been broken as shown in Figure 14.3.

The chain of causation can be broken by:

- an act of a third party;
- the victim's own act;
- a natural but unpredictable event.

In order to break the chain of causation so that the defendant is not responsible for the consequence, the intervening act must be both sufficiently independent of the defendant's conduct and sufficiently serious enough.

Figure 14.3 Breaking the chain of causation

Medical treatment

Medical treatment is unlikely to break the chain of causation unless it is so independent of the defendant's acts and 'in itself so potent in causing death' that the defendant's acts are insignificant The following three cases show this.

- *Smith* (1959). Two soldiers had a fight and one was stabbed in the lung by the other. The victim was carried to a medical centre by other soldiers, but was dropped on the way. At the medical centre the staff gave him artificial respiration by pressing on his chest. This made the injury worse and he died. Had the proper treatment been given, his chance of recovering would have been as high as 75 per cent. Despite this, the original attacker was still guilty of his murder. This was because the stab wound was the overwhelming cause of the death.
- *Cheshire* (1991): The defendant shot the victim in the thigh and the stomach. The victim had problems breathing and was given a tracheotomy (i.e. a tube was inserted in his throat to help him breath). The victim died

from rare complications of the tracheotomy, which were not spotted by the doctors. By the time he died the original wounds were no longer life-threatening. The defendant was still held to be liable for his death.

- *Jordan* (1956): The victim had been stabbed in the stomach. He was treated in hospital and the wounds were healing well. He was given an antibiotic but suffered an allergic reaction to it. One doctor stopped the use of the antibiotic but the next day another doctor ordered that a large dose of it be given. The victim died from the allergic reaction to the drug. In this case the actions of the doctor were held to be an intervening act which caused the death. The defendant was not guilty of murder.

Switching off a life support machine when a patient is brain dead does not break the chain of causation. This was decided in *Malcherek* (1981).

Victim's own act

If the defendant causes the victim to react in a foreseeable way, then any injury to the victim will have been caused by the defendant. This occurred in *Roberts* (1971) where a girl jumped from a car in order to escape from sexual advances. The car was travelling at between 20 and 40 mph and the girl was injured through jumping from the car. The defendant was held to be liable for her injuries.

However, if the victim's reaction is unreasonable, then this may break the chain of causation. In *Williams* (1992) a hitch-hiker jumped from Williams' car and died from head injuries caused by his head hitting the road. The car was travelling at about 30 mph. The prosecution alleged that there had been an attempt to steal the victim's wallet and that was the reason for his jumping from the car. The Court of Appeal said that the victim's act had to be foreseeable and also had to be in proportion to the threat. The question to be asked was whether the victim's conduct was:

> " within the ambit of reasonableness and not so daft as to make his own voluntary act one which amounted to a *novus actus interveniens* (an intervening act) and consequently broke the chain of causation. "

Activity

Read the following situations and explain whether causation would be proved.

1. Adam has been threatened by Ben in the past. When Adam sees Ben approaching him in the street, Adam runs across the road without looking and is knocked down and injured by a car. Would Ben be liable for his injuries?
2. Toyah stabs Steve in the arm. His injury is not serious but he needs stitches, so a neighbour takes Steve to hospital in his car. On the way to the hospital the car crashes and Steve sustains serious head injuries. Would Toyah be liable for the head injuries?
3. Lewis has broken into Katie's third floor flat. He threatens to rape her and in order to escape from him she jumps from the window and is seriously injured. Would Lewis be liable for her injuries?
4. Ross stabs Paul in the chest. Paul is taken to hospital where he is given a blood transfusion. Unfortunately, he is given the wrong blood and he dies. Would Ross be liable for Paul's death?

14.2 *Mens rea*

Mens rea is the mental element of an offence. Each offence has its own *mens rea* or mental element. The only exceptions are offences of strict liability. These offences do not require proof of mental element in respect of at least part of the *actus reus*.

There are different levels of *mens rea*. To be guilty the accused must have at least the minimum level of *mens rea* required by the offence.

The highest level of *mens rea* is intention. This is also referred to as specific intention. The other main types of *mens rea* are recklessness and negligence.

14.2.1 Intention

In the case of *Mohan* (1975) the court defined intention as 'a decision to bring about, in so far as it lies within the accused's power [the prohibited consequence], no matter whether the accused desired that consequence of his act or not'.

This makes it clear that the defendant's motive or reason for doing the act is not relevant. The important point is that the defendant decided to bring about the prohibited consequence.

This can be illustrated by looking at the offence set out in s 18 of the Offences Against the Person Act 1861. For this offence the defendant must wound or cause grievous bodily harm. The *mens rea* is that the defendant must intend to cause grievous bodily harm or intend to resist arrest or prevent the apprehension or detainer of another person. If the defendant did not intend one of these then he or she cannot be guilty of this offence. For example, if a person opens a door very suddenly and hits and seriously injures someone on the other side of the door that they did not know was there, then they do not intend to 'bring about' the prohibited consequence.

In most cases, the defendant's intention is clear. For example, where D deliberately punches another person, then he has an intention to use unlawful force on the victim. This is also known as direct intent.

Foresight of consequences

The main problem with proving intention is in cases where the defendant's main aim was not the prohibited consequences, but, in achieving the aim, the defendant foresaw that he would also cause those consequences. This is referred to as 'foresight of consequences'.

The first rule about foresight of consequences is that it not the same as intention but can be evidence of intention. A jury may use this evidence to find that the defendant had intention, but only where the harm caused as a result of the defendant's actions was a virtual certainty and the defendant realised that this was so.

This was explained in *Woollin* (1998) where the defendant threw his three-month-old baby towards his pram which was against a wall some

Key facts

Type of *mens rea*	Comment	Explanation	Case
Intention	Highest level of *mens rea*	Intention to bring about a particular consequence	*Mohan*
Foresight of consequences as intention	It is only evidence from which intention can be found	The consequence must be a virtual certainty **and** the defendant must realise this is so	*Woollin*
Recklessness	A lower level of *mens rea* than intention	The defendant must realise there is a risk of the consequence happening and decide to take that risk	*Cunningham*

Figure 14.4 Key facts chart for *mens rea*

three or four feet away. The baby suffered head injuries and died. The court ruled that the consequence must be a virtual certainty and the defendant must realise this. Where the jury were satisfied on both these two points, then there was evidence on which the jury could find intention.

Another example is where the defendant decides to set fire to his shop in order to claim insurance. His main aim is damaging the shop and getting the insurance. Unfortunately he starts the fire when staff are working in the shop and some of them are seriously injured. Has the defendant the intention for a section 18 offence of causing grievous bodily harm? Only if serious injury was a virtual certainty and he realised this. This is also known as oblique or indirect intent and is shown in Figure 14.5.

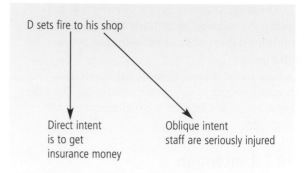

Figure 14.5 Direct and oblique intent

Recklessness is the minimum level of *mens rea* required by all assaults except for the section 18 offence discussed in section 14.2.1. Don't forget that if the defendant has the higher level of intention he will, of course, be guilty.

For example, if the defendant intends to punch the victim in the face, that defendant has the higher level of intention and is guilty of a battery (see section 15.2). It is only when the defendant does not have the higher level that recklessness has to be considered.

Cunningham

The explanation of recklessness comes from the case of *Cunningham* (1957). In *Cunningham* the defendant tore a gas meter from the wall of an empty house in order to steal the money in it. This caused gas to seep into the house next door, where a woman was affected by it. Cunningham was charged with an offence against s 23 of the Offences Against the Person Act 1861 of maliciously administering a noxious thing. It was held that he was not guilty since he did not realise the risk of gas escaping into the adjacent house. He had not intended to cause the harm, nor had he taken a risk he knew about.

The offence involved in *Cunningham* uses the word 'maliciously' to indicate the *mens rea* required. The court held this word to mean that to have the necessary *mens rea* the defendant must either intend the consequence or realise that there was a risk of the consequence happening and decide to take that risk.

Activity

In each of the following situations explain whether the defendant has the required intention for a section 18 offence (Offences Against the Person Act 1861).

1. Kyle dislikes Vince and decides to attack him. Kyle uses an iron bar to hit Vince on the head. Vince suffers serious head injuries.
2. Scott throws a large stone into a river to see how much of splash it will make. Jake is swimming in the river and is hit by the stone and seriously hurt.
3. Diane throws a large stone from a bridge onto the motorway below. It is rush hour and there is a lot of traffic on the motorway. The stone smashes through the windscreen of Ashley's car and causes him serious injury.

14.2.2 Recklessness

This is a lower level of *mens rea* than intention. Recklessness is the taking of an unjustifiable risk. It has to be proved that the defendant realised the risk, but decided to take it.

The case of *Savage* (1991) confirmed that the same principle applies to all offences where the definition in an Act of Parliament uses the word 'maliciously'. The Law Lords said that 'maliciously' was a term of legal art. In other words it has a special meaning when used in an Act of Parliament, not its normal dictionary definition. It means doing something intentionally or being reckless about the risk involved.

14.2.3 Transferred malice

This is the principle that the defendant can be guilty if he intended to commit a similar crime but against a different victim. An example is aiming a blow at one person with the necessary *mens rea* for an assault causing actual bodily harm but actually hitting another person. This occurred in *Latimer* (1886) where the defendant aimed a blow with a belt at a man in a pub after that man had attacked him. The belt bounced off the man and struck a woman in the face. Latimer was guilty of an assault against the woman, although he had not meant to hit her.

However, where the *mens rea* is for a completely different type of offence then the defendant may not be guilty. This was the situation in *Pembliton* (1874) where the defendant threw a stone intending it to hit people with whom he had been fighting. The stone hit and broke a window. The intention to hit people could not be transferred to the window.

General malice

In some cases the defendant may not have a specific victim in mind, for example, a terrorist who plants a bomb in a pub intending to kill or injure anyone who happens to be there. In this case the defendant's *mens rea* is held to apply to the actual victim.

14.3 Coincidence of *actus reus* and *mens rea*

In order for an offence to take place, both the *actus reus* and the *mens rea* must be present at the same time. For example, if you decide to go round to your next door neighbour intending to assault them, but when you get to their house you change your mind and do not actually assault them, you cannot be guilty of an assault even though you had the *mens rea*.

If, two hours later, you are driving your car out of your driveway and knock down your neighbour because you did not see them, you have now done what could be the *actus reus* for an assault. However, you are not guilty of any criminal offence since at the moment you hit your neighbour you did not have the necessary *mens rea*. The *mens rea* and the *actus reus* were not present at the same time. (Although there is no crime, there may be the tort of negligence; see Chapter 18.)

Continuing act

Where there is a continuing act for the *actus reus* and, at some point while that act is still going on the defendant has the necessary *mens rea*, then

Activity

Explain in the following situations whether there is *actus reus* and *mens rea* present. (Do not forget that there may be transferred malice.)

1. Bart has had an argument with Cara. He aims a punch at her head, but Cara dodges out of the way and Bart hits Homer who was standing behind Cara.
2. Desmond is sitting in a lecture. He pushes his chair back, but does not realise that one of the chair legs is pressing on to Mark's foot. Mark asks Desmond to move the chair, but Desmond thinks what has happened is funny and does not move but sits there laughing for several minutes.
3. Sara throws a stone at a cat. Her aim is very poor and the stone hits Marge who is standing several feet away.

the two do coincide and the defendant will be guilty.

This is illustrated by the case of *Fagan v Metropolitan Police Commissioner* (1968). Fagan was told by a police officer to park by a kerb. In doing this Fagan drove on to the policeman's foot without realising he had done so. Initially Fagan refused to move the car. The policeman pointed out what had happened and asked Fagan several times to move the car off his foot. Eventually Fagan did move the car.

The Court of Appeal held that once Fagan knew the car was on the police officer's foot he had the required *mens rea*. As the *actus reus* (the car putting force on the foot) was still continuing the two elements were then present together.

14.4 Strict liability

Offences of strict liability are those where the defendant is guilty because he or she did the *actus reus*. There is no need to prove any *mens rea*. This can seem unfair since the defendant will be guilty even though they had no intention of committing any offence.

An extreme situation is the case of *Larsonneur* (1933) which we have already considered in section 14.1.1. The defendant had been ordered to leave the United Kingdom. She decided to go to Eire, but the Irish police deported her and took her back to the UK. She did not want to return to the UK. She had no *mens rea*.

Another example of a strict liability offence is *Harrow London Borough Council v Shah* (1999). The defendants owned a newsagent's business where lottery tickets were sold. They had told their staff not to sell tickets to anyone under 16 years old and had also put up notices in the shop stating this. They told their staff that if there was any doubt about a customer's age, the staff should ask for proof of age, and if still in doubt should refer the matter to the defendants. One of their staff sold a lottery ticket to a 13-year-old boy without asking for proof of age. The salesman mistakenly believed the boy was over 16 years old.

The defendants were found guilty of selling a lottery ticket to a person under 16. The offence did not require any *mens rea*. The act of selling the ticket to someone who was actually under 16 was enough to make them guilty, even though they had done their best to prevent this happening in their shop.

14.4.1 Which offences are strict liability?

The judges often have difficulty in deciding whether an offence is one of strict liability or not. The first rule is that where an Act of Parliament includes words indicating *mens rea* (e.g. knowingly, intentionally, maliciously or permitting), the offence requires *mens rea* and is not one of strict liability. However, if an Act of Parliament makes it clear that *mens rea* is not required, the offence will be one of strict liability.

The presumption of *mens rea*

The problem arises where an Act of Parliament does not include any words indicating *mens rea*. In this situation the judges will start by presuming that all criminal offences require *mens rea*. This was made clear in the case of *Sweet v Parsley* (1970). In this case the defendant rented a farmhouse and let it out to students. The police found cannabis at the farmhouse and the defendant was charged with 'being concerned in the management of premises used for the purpose of smoking cannabis resin'. The defendant did not know that cannabis was being smoked there. It was decided that she was not guilty as the court presumed that the offence required *mens rea*.

Although judges start by presuming that an offence has to have the element of *mens rea*, it is possible for them to decide that an offence is one of strict liability. The only situation in which the presumption can be displaced is usually where the statute involves an issue of social concern. This most often occurs in offences which are

Test Yourself

1. Briefly explain what is meant by *actus reus*.
2. Give three situations where an omission can be sufficient for the *actus reus*.
3. Explain the 'but for' test in causation.
4. Give two examples of events that can break the chain of causation.
5. Give a case in which it was held that the chain of causation was not broken by medical treatment.
6. What is meant by *mens rea*?
7. What is meant by 'foresight of consequences'?
8. In criminal law when is a defendant reckless?
9. What is meant by an offence of strict liability?
10. Explain a justification for having strict liability offences.

regulatory in nature as these are not thought of as being truly criminal matters. This includes offences such as breaches of regulations for selling food or alcohol or lottery tickets (as in *Harrow London Borough Council v Shah* (1999)) or causing pollution.

Where an offence is 'truly criminal' such as being involved with drugs as in *Sweet v Parsley* or a sex offence as in *B v DPP*, then it is unlikely that the judges will decide it is a strict liability offence. This is particularly so where it could lead to the defendant being sent to prison.

14.4.2 Justification for strict liability

The main justification is that strict liability offences help protect society by promoting greater care over matters of public safety. It encourages higher standards in such matters as hygiene in processing and selling food. It makes sure that businesses are run properly.

On the practical side, it is easier to enforce as there is no need to prove *mens rea*.

It also saves court time as people are more likely to plead guilty. The fact that the defendant is not blameworthy can be taken into account when sentencing.

14.4.3 Arguments against strict liability

The main argument against strict liability is that it makes people who are not blameworthy guilty. Even those who have taken all possible care will be found guilty and can be punished. This happened in the case of *Harrow London Borough Council v Shah* (1999) where the defendants were guilty even though they had done their best to prevent sales of lottery tickets to anyone under the age of 16.

Examination questions

Jenny had an argument with her boyfriend, David. This resulted in David hitting Jenny with a cricket bat. Jenny suffered a very badly broken leg that needed surgery. David, who has several previous convictions for violence, denies that he was involved.

(a) Criminal offences usually require *actus reus* and *mens rea*, although some crimes are crimes of strict liability.
   (i) Explain, using examples, the meaning of the term *actus reus*.
   (ii) Explain, using examples, the meaning of the term *mens rea*.
   (iii) Explain, using examples, the meaning of the term strict liability.

(b) (i) Taking into account the explanations given in your answer to (a), discuss the criminal liability of David for the injuries suffered by Jenny.
   (ii) Outline the procedure that would be used following David's arrest and charge up to the start of the trial.

(c) (i) Briefly explain the range of sentences available to the criminal courts if David were to be convicted of an offence.
   (ii) Briefly describe the range of factors the court may take into account before he is sentenced.
                              AQA Unit 2 Specimen Paper

Examiner's tip

Part (a) of the question on criminal law in Unit 2 usually asks for knowledge of the concepts and terms used in criminal law. These are explained in this chapter. So make sure you know and understand the material in this chapter, including being able to use cases and/or examples to explain.

Chapter 15

Offences Against the Person

There are many different types of offence against the person. For this book we shall look at four of the main non-fatal offences. These are common assault, assault occasioning actual bodily harm (s 47), maliciously inflicting grievous bodily harm or wounding (s 20) and causing grievous bodily harm or wounding with intent (s 18). The last three offences are set out in the Offences Against the Person Act 1861.

15.1 Common assault

The word assault has two meanings: the first is the general term for a physical attack on another person; the second is a specific type of offence.

Common assault is the lowest level of offence against the person. It is not defined in any Act of Parliament but has been built up through cases and judge-made law. There are two types of common assault. These are:

- assault;
- battery.

15.1.1 Assault

To commit this offence the defendant must intentionally or subjectively recklessly cause another person to fear immediate unlawful personal violence.

Actus reus of assault

The *actus reus* of an assault requires some act or words. There is no need for physical contact. The *actus reus* is completed when the defendant does any act or says something which causes the victim to believe that unlawful force is about to be used against him or her. Examples include:

- raising a fist as though about to hit the victim;
- throwing a stone at the victim which just misses;
- pointing a loaded gun at someone within range;
- making a threat by saying 'I am going to hit you'.

However, there must be some act or words for an assault; an omission or failure to act is not enough.

Fear of violence

The important point is that the act or words must cause the victim to fear that immediate force is going to be used against them. There is no assault if the situation is such that it is obvious that the defendant cannot actually use force, for example, where the defendant shouts threats from a passing train. Also, it has been decided that pointing an unloaded gun at someone who knows that it is unloaded cannot be an assault. This is because the other person does not fear immediate force. If the other person thought the gun was loaded then this could be an assault.

Where violence is possible in the immediate future, then the *actus reus* for an assault can exist. For example, an assault can take place even though it is through a closed window. This was decided in *Smith v Chief Constable of Woking* (1983). In this case the defendant entered a private garden at night and looked through the bedroom window of the victim. She was terrified and thought that he was about to enter the room. This was enough for an assault.

Words as an assault

Words are sufficient for an assault. The judges in the case of *Ireland* (1998) pointed out that a man in a dark alley saying to a woman 'Come with me or I will stab you' would cause her to fear immediate personal violence. Even silent telephone calls have been held to be an assault. This was in the case of *Ireland* (1998) where the defendant made several silent phone calls to three different women. The victim may fear that the purpose of the call is to find out if she is at home and that the caller is about to come to her home immediately after the call.

However, where the defendant says something which indicates there will be no violence, then these words can prevent an act from being an assault. This happened in the old case of *Tuberville v Savage* (1669) where a man put his hand on his sword and said, 'If it were not assize-time, I would not take such language from you'. Although the man had done an act which could have made the victim fear immediate violence, the words showed that no violence was going to be used.

The level of force need not be serious. Fear of any unwanted touching is sufficient.

Mens rea of assault

The *mens rea* of an assault must be either an intention to cause another to fear immediate unlawful personal violence or recklessness as to whether such fear is caused. To be reckless the defendant must realise the risk that his acts and/or words could cause another to fear unlawful personal violence.

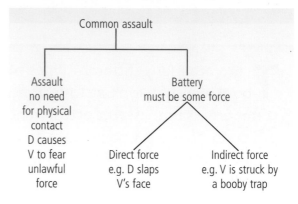

Figure 15.1 Common assault

15.1.2 Battery

This is the stage beyond an assault where the defendant intentionally or subjectively recklessly applies unlawful force to another. In many situations there will be an assault followed quickly by a battery. This is what happens where the defendant raises his fist to hit the victim in the face and then actually punches him. The raising of the fist is an assault; the punch connecting with the victim's face is the battery. It is possible, however, to have a battery without an assault. This will happen if the victim does not know that force is about to be used, as where someone hits you from behind.

Actus reus of battery

There must be some force. This can be the slightest touching, such as a hand on one's

Actus reus of assault	Smith v Chief Constable of Woking (1983) Ireland (1999) Tuberville v Savage (1669)	Can be through a window; being in a private garden looking in and frightening victim Silent telephone calls Putting hand on sword can be actus reus BUT in this case negatived by words
Actus reus of battery	Fagan v Metropolitan Police Commander (1969) DPP v K (1990) Haystead (2000)	Can be a continuing act, e.g. leaving car wheel on foot Can be an indirect act, e.g. putting acid in a hand drier e.g. child dropping to floor because of punch to the person holding them

Figure 15.2 Case chart for *actus reus* of assault and battery

shoulder. The force may be through a continuing act, as in *Fagan v Metropolitan Police Commander* (1968) where the defendant parked his car with one of the tyres on a police officer's foot and left it there for several minutes.

A battery can also be through an indirect act such as a booby trap. In this situation the defendant causes force to be applied, even though he does not personally touch the victim. This occurred in *DPP v K* (1990) where the defendant put acid into a hot air hand drier in a cloakroom so that the next person to use the drier would be

sprayed by the acid. Another example of indirect force occurred in *Haystead* (2000) where the defendant caused a child to fall to the floor by punching the person holding the child.

Mens rea for battery

The *mens rea* for battery must be either an intention to apply unlawful physical force or recklessness that the force will be applied. Where the recklessness is relied on, it is a subjective test, in other words the defendant must realise the risk of physical contact and take that risk.

Activity

Explain in each of the following situations whether there has been an assault and/or a battery.

1. Jane and Sue are having an argument. During the argument, Jane says 'If you don't shut up I'll thump you'.
2. Ray sneaks up behind Karen and hits her on her back.
3. Miles throws a stone at Tanya, but misses. Tanya is very angry at this and picks up the stone and throws it at Miles, hitting him in the face.
4. Grant turns round quickly without realising that Harry is standing just behind him and bumps into Harry. Harry shouts at him, 'If you were not wearing glasses, I would hit you in the face'.

15.2 Assault occasioning actual bodily harm

This is an offence under s 47 of the Offences Against the Person Act 1861.

For the *actus reus* of s 47 there must be an assault or a battery and this must cause actual bodily harm.

Actual bodily harm

Actual bodily harm is 'any hurt or injury calculated to interfere with the health or comfort' of the victim. This is very wide and covers such injuries as bruises, scratches, a broken nose or finger or any other injury. It also includes psychiatric injury, but not 'mere emotions such as fear, distress or panic'. In *T v DPP* (2003) it was held that loss of consciousness, even

Key facts

Offence	*Actus reus*	Injury required	*Mens rea*
Assault	Causing V to fear immediate unlawful force	None	Intention of, or subjective recklessness as to, causing victim to fear immediate unlawful violence
Battery	Application of unlawful force	None	Intention of, or subjective recklessness as to, applying unlawful force
Section 47 OAPA 1861	An assault or battery	Actual bodily harm (e.g. bruising) This includes psychiatric harm	Intention or subjective recklessness as to causing fear of unlawful violence or of applying unlawful force
Section 20 OAPA 1861	A direct or indirect act or omission No need to prove an assault	A wound (a cutting of the whole skin) **or** Grievous bodily harm (really serious harm) which includes psychiatric harm	Intention or subjective recklessness as to causing some injury (though not serious)
Section 18 OAPA 1861	A direct or indirect act or omission which causes V's injury	A wound or grievous bodily harm (as above)	Specific intention to cause grievous bodily harm or to resist or prevent arrest

Figure 15.3 Key facts chart on assault offences

momentarily, was actual bodily harm. The victim was chased by the defendant. He fell to the ground and was kicked by the defendant. This caused him to lose consciousness for a brief period.

Although technically, actual bodily harm includes even a small bruise, the Crown Prosecution Service will not charge a defendant with a s 47 offence. There must be some higher degree of injury than just a bruise under the CPS charging standards.

If an injury is serious then, although the defendant could be charged with this offence of occasioning actual bodily harm, it is more likely that the offence will be a more serious one (see section 15.3).

Mens rea of an assault occasioning actual bodily harm

The defendant must intend to subject the victim to unlawful force or be reckless with regard to whether the victim fears or is subjected to unlawful force. This is the same *mens rea* as for an assault or a battery. There is no need for the defendant to intend or be reckless as to whether actual bodily harm is caused. In *Roberts* (1971) the defendant, who was driving a car, touched the girl in the passenger seat. She feared that he was going to commit a more serious assault and jumped from the car while it was travelling at about 30 miles per hour. As a result of this she was slightly injured. He was found guilty of assault occasioning actual bodily harm even though he had not intended any injury or realised there was a risk of injury.

This was confirmed in *Savage* (1991) where a woman in a pub threw beer over another woman. In doing this the glass slipped from the defendant's hand and the victim's hand was cut by the glass. The defendant said that she had only intended to throw beer over the woman. She had not intended her to be injured, nor had she realised that there was a risk of injury. The court found that she was guilty of a s 47 offence (assault occasioning actual bodily harm). The fact that she intended to throw the beer over the other woman was sufficient for the *mens rea* of the offence.

15.3 Wounding and grievous bodily harm

There are two offences which involve wounding or grievous bodily harm. These are s 20 and s 18 of the Offences Against the Person Act 1861. The *actus reus* is almost the same for the two offences. Section 20 requires that the defendant wounds or 'inflicts' grievous bodily harm to the victim. Section 18 requires that the defendant wounds or 'causes' grievous bodily harm to the victim.

There appears to be very little difference between the two words 'inflict' and 'cause'. The word 'cause' is very wide so that it is only necessary to prove that the defendant's act was a substantial cause of the wound or grievous bodily harm. It is possible that it is wider than the word 'inflict', but in *Burstow* (1998) it was decided that 'inflict' does not require a technical assault or a battery. This decision means that there appears to be little, if any, difference in the *actus reus* of the two offences.

Both offences require the consequence of a wound or grievous bodily harm.

Wound

Wound means a cut or a break in the continuity of the whole skin. A cut of internal skin, such as

Mens rea for section 47 (abh)	*Roberts* (1971) *Savage* (1991)	Must intend or be reckless as to an assault or battery: BUT No need to intend or be reckless as to injury e.g. intending to touch victim (who was so frightened she jumped out of car) or intending to throw drink over victim
Mens rea for section 20	*Parmenter* (1991)	Must intend some injury or realise risk of injury (but not serious injury). Defendant not guilty of s 20 because did not realise risk of injury when throwing and catching baby
Actual bodily harm	*DPP v Santana-Bermudez* (2003) *T v DPP* (2003)	Slight injury sufficient e.g. needle running into finger causing bleeding Momentary unconsciousness is abh
Wound	*JCC v Eisenhower* (1983)	Must be a cut of the whole skin An internal injury, such as bleeding in eye is not a wound
Grievous bodily harm	*Bollom* (2004) *Dica* (2004)	Severe bruising may be gbh: must consider effect on health of victim Disease such as HIV can be gbh

Figure 15.4 Case chart for actual bodily harm (abh), wounding and grievous bodily harm (gbh)

in the cheek, is sufficient, but internal bleeding where there is no cut of the skin is not sufficient. In *JCC v Eisenhower* (1983) the victim was hit in the eye by a shotgun pellet. This did not penetrate the eye but did cause severe bleeding under the surface. As there was no cut, it was held that this was not a wound.

Grievous bodily harm

Grievous bodily harm means 'really serious harm' but the harm does not have to be life threatening. Serious psychiatric injury can also be grievous bodily harm.

In *Bollom* (2003) the defendant had caused several severe bruises to a 17-month-old child. The Court of Appeal held that the victim's age and health were relevant when deciding whether an injury amounted to grievous bodily harm. There had to be an assessment of the effect of the harm to the particular victim. This ruling means that severe bruising may be grievous bodily harm where the victim is a young child or a frail elderly person.

A disease can be grievous bodily harm. In *Dica* (2004) the defendant was charged with two offences of causing grievous bodily harm under s 20 of the Offences Against the Person Act 1861. He had had sexual intercourse with two women when he knew that he was HIV positive. Both women contracted HIV. It was accepted that this was grievous bodily harm.

Mens rea

The important difference between the two offences is in the *mens rea* required. Section 18 requires a higher level of *mens rea* than s 20. This difference is explained in sections 15.3.1 and 15.3.2.

15.3.1 Section 20 offence

This is an offence under s 20 of the Offences Against the Person Act 1861.

This states:

> Whosoever shall unlawfully and maliciously wound or inflict any grievous bodily harm upon any other person, either with or without a weapon or instrument, shall be guilty of an offence.

For the *mens rea* the defendant must intend to cause another person some harm or be subjectively reckless as to whether he suffers some harm.

There is no need for the defendant to foresee serious injury but he must realise the risk of some injury. In *Parmenter* (1991) the defendant injured his three-month-old baby when he threw the child in the air and caught him. Parmenter said that he had often done this with slightly older children and did not realise that there was risk of any injury. He was found not guilty of the s 20 offence but guilty of assault occasioning actual bodily harm under s 47.

15.3.2 Section 18 offence

This is an offence under s 18 of the Offences Against the Person Act 1861. This states:

> Whosoever shall unlawfully and maliciously by any means whatsoever wound or cause any grievous bodily harm to any person, with intent to do some grievous bodily harm to any person, or with intent to resist or prevent the lawful apprehension or detainer of any person, shall be guilty of an offence.

It is considered a much more serious offence than s 20, as can be seen from the difference in the maximum punishments. Section 20 has a maximum of five years' imprisonment whereas the maximum for s 18 is life imprisonment.

Section 18 is a specific intent offence. For the *mens rea* of wounding or causing grievous bodily harm with intent the defendant must be proved to have intended to:

- do some grievous bodily harm, or
- resist or prevent the lawful apprehension or detainer of any person.

The concept of foresight of consequences as already explained at section 14.2.1 applies to s 18. So, if the act that the defendant does is virtually certain to cause grievous bodily harm and the defendant realises that this is so, then there is evidence that the defendant had the necessary *mens rea* for a s 18 offence.

To help you with the differences between the offences see Figure 15.3. Also, Figure 15.5 helps you to decide which offence is the most appropriate when looking at scenarios.

Activity

Explain in each of the situations below, what type of offence may have been committed.

1. In a football match Danny is kicked by Victor. This causes bruising to Danny's leg. Danny is annoyed at this and punches Victor in the face causing a cut to his lip.
2. Anish is walking along a canal bank. Kim, who is in a hurry, pushes past him, knocking him into the canal. Anish hits his head on the side and suffers a fractured skull.
3. Karl waves a knife at Emma, saying 'I am going to cut that silly smile off'. Emma is very frightened and faints. She falls against Nita, who is knocked to the ground and suffers bruising.

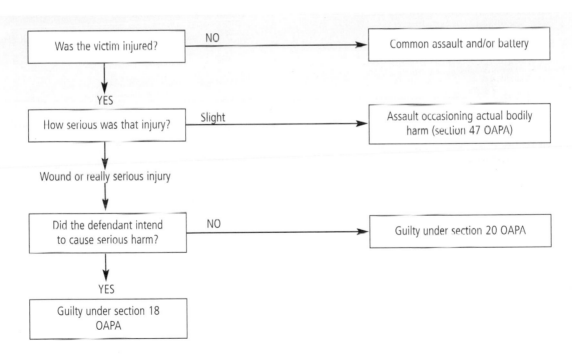

Figure 15.5 Flow chart for serious offences

Examination questions

Andy saw Bilal standing at a bus stop as he drove past. Andy immediately stopped his car and, in an aggressive manner, ran over to Bilal shouting racist abuse and accusing him (falsely) of being involved in the kidnapping of a child. Andy then punched Bilal, knocking him to the ground. Andy then hit Bilal repeatedly with a rubbish bin which Andy had ripped from the bus stop.

Bilal's injuries included a fractured cheekbone and jaw, and severe cuts to his face from which he lost a lot of blood. Bilal needed major surgery to rebuild his face. Unfortunately, whilst Bilal was undergoing the surgery, the oxygen tube became disconnected and, as a result, he suffered significant brain damage.

(a) Criminal offences require an *actus reus* which may include voluntary acts and omission and causation.
(i) Explain, using cases and/or examples, the meaning of 'voluntary acts and omissions'. (7 marks)

(ii) Explain, using cases and/or examples, the meaning of 'causation'. (7 marks)

(b) (i) Discuss the criminal liability of Andy for his behaviour before he punched Bilal. (7 marks)
(ii) Discuss the criminal liability of Andy for the initial injuries to Bilal's face. (7 marks)
(iii) Taking into account the explanations given in your answers to (a) and (b)(ii) discuss whether Andy would be found to have caused Bilal's brain damage. (7 marks)

(c) (i) Outline the procedure that would be followed up to Andy's trial. (5 marks)
(ii) Assuming that Andy is found guilty of any offence, outline the range of factors that the court may take into account before he is sentenced. (7 marks)

AQA LAW02 January 2009

Examiner's tip

For parts b(i) and b(ii) to help you decide which offence may have been committed, try writing down what Andy did at each stage and whether there were any injuries as a result of what he did. See the example below. Now work out which offences may have been committed.

Actions	Injuries	Possible offence
Andy ran over to Bilal in an aggressive manner, shouting	No injuries	
Andy hit Bilal repeatedly with a rubbish bin	Fractured cheekbone and jaw, and severe cuts	

You can check if you are right by looking at the completed chart on page 266

Chapter 16

Criminal Procedure

We have already looked at the criminal courts in Unit 1 (see Chapter 8). For Unit 2 you need to know what happens in criminal cases from the moment the police charge the defendant to the start of the trial.

The type of offence will make a difference as to the procedure for the case. We have already looked at this in Chapter 8, but it is included again to make this chapter complete.

16.1 Classification of offences

Criminal offences are divided into three categories. These are:

- summary offences;
- triable either way offences;
- indictable offences.

16.1.1 Summary offences

These are the least serious offences. They are always tried in the Magistrates' Court. They include nearly all driving offences. Common assault, which you will study in this unit, is a summary offence.

16.1.2 Triable either way offences

These are the middle range of crimes. As the name implies, these cases can be tried in either the Magistrates' Court or the Crown Court. They include a wide range of offences such as theft and assault causing actual bodily harm (s 47) and the offence under s 20 of the Offences Against the Person Act 1861.

The pre-trial procedure for triable either way cases is more complicated than for summary or indictable offences as it has to be decided where the case will be dealt with. This procedure is explained in section 16.5.

16.1.3 Indictable offences

These are the most serious crimes. Section 18 of the Offences Against the Person Act 1861 is an indictable offence. The first preliminary hearing for such an offence will be at the Magistrates' Court, but then the case is transferred to the Crown Court. All indictable offences must be tried at the Crown Court by a judge and jury.

16.2 Charge or summons

In order for a criminal case to come to court, the defendant must be either summoned for an offence or charged with an offence.

A summons is a document that is sent to the defendant by post setting a date when he must attend the magistrates' court. This is used for minor offences, especially driving offences. It is also the method most likely to be used for an offence of common assault.

A charge is made where the defendant has been arrested by the police and the matter investigated by police, including interviewing the defendant. The police send the evidence to the Crown Prosecution Service (see section 16.4). A Crown prosecutor decides if there is enough evidence for the defendant to be charged with an offence. The charge is done verbally by the police and the defendant is also given a written record of it. This is the method used for more serious crimes.

16.3 Bail

An important pre-trial matter to be decided is whether the defendant should stay in custody while awaiting their trial or whether bail should be granted. A person can be released on bail at any point after being arrested by the police. Being given bail means that the person is allowed to be at liberty until the next stage in the case.

16.3.1 Police powers to grant bail

The police may release a suspect on bail while they make further inquiries. This means that the suspect is released from police custody on the condition that they return to the police station on a specific date in the future.

The police can also give bail to a defendant

who has been charged with an offence. In this case the defendant is bailed to appear at the local Magistrates' Court on a set date. If any person granted bail by the police fails to surrender to that bail (i.e. attend at the next stage of the case) then the police are given the right to arrest them. About 84 per cent of those charged with offences are given bail by the police.

Conditional bail

The police have the power to impose conditions on a grant of bail. The types of conditions include asking the suspect to surrender his passport, report at regular intervals to the police station or get another person to stand surety for him. These conditions can be only imposed in order to make sure that the suspect surrenders to bail, does not commit an offence while on bail and does not interfere with witnesses or interfere in any other way with the course of justice.

No police bail

Where the police are not prepared to allow bail, they must bring the defendant in front of the Magistrates' Court at the first possible opportunity. If (as usually happens) the magistrates cannot deal with the whole case at that first hearing, the magistrates must then make the decision as to whether the defendant should be given bail or remanded in custody.

16.3.2 The Bail Act 1976

This Act starts with the assumption that an accused person should be granted bail, though this right is limited for certain cases (see section 16.3.3). Section 4 of the Bail Act 1976 gives a general right to bail. However, the court need not grant a defendant bail if it is satisfied that there are substantial grounds for believing that the defendant, if released on bail, would:

1. Fail to surrender to custody.
2. Commit an offence while on bail.
3. Interfere with witnesses or otherwise obstruct the course of justice.

Key facts

Bail can be granted by	• police • magistrates • Crown Court
Bail Act 1976	There is a presumption in favour of bail BUT • for an offence while already on bail, bail can only be given if the court is satisfied there is no significant risk of further offending • must be exceptional circumstances for bail to be granted for murder, attempted murder, manslaughter, rape or attempted rape where the defendant has already served a custodial sentence for such an offence
In all cases bail can be refused if there are reasonable grounds for believing the defendant:	• would fail to surrender • would commit further offences • would interfere with witnesses
Conditions can be imposed	• sureties • residence in bail hostel • curfew • hand in passport, etc.
Comment	Many of those in prison are awaiting trial and could have been given bail Problem of balancing this against need to protect public

Figure 16.1 Key facts chart on bail

The court can also refuse bail if it is satisfied that the defendant should be kept in custody for his own protection.

In deciding whether to grant bail, the court will consider various factors including:

- The nature and seriousness of the offence (and the probable method of dealing with it).
- The character, antecedents (that is, past record), associations and community ties of the defendant.
- The defendant's record as respects the fulfilment of his obligations under previous grants of bail in criminal proceedings; in other words has he turned up (surrendered to his bail) on previous occasions.
- The strength of the evidence against him.
- If a defendant is charged with an offence which is not punishable by imprisonment, bail can only be refused if the defendant has previously failed to surrender to bail and there are grounds for believing that he will not surrender on this occasion.

Conditions

A court can make conditions for the granting of bail. These are similar to conditions which can be set by the police and may include the surrender of passport and/or reporting to a police station. The court can also make a condition as to where the accused must reside while on bail; this could be at a home address or at a bail hostel.

The court can also order that the defendant is placed on a curfew. This means that he has to be at his home address at set times, for example for the evening and night. As part of the curfew order the defendant is usually required to wear an electronic tag so that his whereabouts is known at all times.

Sureties

The court (and the police) can require a surety for bail. A surety is another person who is prepared to promise to pay the court a certain sum of money if the defendant fails to attend court. Note that no money is paid unless the defendant fails to answer to his bail. This system is different from that of other countries. For example, in the US the surety must pay the money into court before the defendant is released on bail, but gets the money back when the defendant attends court as required.

16.3.3 Restrictions on bail

The right to liberty is a human right and the right to bail is therefore part of that right. This means that even for serious offences, bail must be available in suitable cases. However, in some situations the public need to be protected from a potentially dangerous person. In such circumstances the right to bail is restricted. The main situations where bail is restricted are where:

- the defendant is charged with murder, attempted murder, manslaughter, rape or attempted rape and they have already served a custodial sentence for a similar offence, they only have the right to bail if the court thinks that there are exceptional circumstances;
- the defendant was on bail when the present alleged offence was committed then he may not be granted bail unless the court is satisfied that there is no significant risk of his committing an offence on bail (whether subject to conditions or not;
- the defendant has tested positive for certain Class A drugs and is charged on a drugs related offence and refuses to take part in an assessment of his drug-dependency, the court may not grant bail unless the court is satisfied that there is no significant risk of the defendant committing an offence on bail.

16.4 Crown Prosecution Service (CPS)

Once the police have charged a defendant they have to pass the case to the Crown Prosecution Service.

16.4.1 Organisation of the CPS

The head of the CPS is the Director of Public Prosecutions (DPP), who must have been qualified as a lawyer for at least 10 years. The DPP is appointed by, and is subject to supervision by, the Attorney-General. Below the DPP are Chief Crown Prosecutors who each head one of the 42 areas into which the country is divided up. Each area is subdivided into branches, each of which is headed by a Branch Crown Prosecutor. Within the branches there are several lawyers and support staff, who are organised into teams and given responsibility for cases.

16.4.2 The functions of the CPS

These involve all aspects of prosecution and can be summarised as:

- Deciding on what offence(s) should be charged. This used to be done by the police, but sometimes inappropriate charges were brought which meant that the case had to be discontinued.
- Reviewing all cases passed to them by the police to see if there is sufficient evidence for a case to proceed, and whether it is in the public interest to do so; this is to avoid weak cases being brought to court.
- Being responsible for the case after it has been passed to them by the police.
- Conducting the prosecution of cases in the Magistrates' Court; this is usually done by lawyers working in the Crown Prosecution Service as Crown Prosecutors or lay presenters.

Conducting cases in the Crown Court. This can either be by instructing an independent lawyer to act as prosecuting counsel at court or a Crown Prosecutor with the appropriate advocacy qualification.

On a practical level, once a defendant has been charged or summonsed with an offence the police role is at an end. They must send the papers for each case to the CPS – each case is then assigned to a team in the local branch of the CPS, and that team will be responsible for the case throughout the prosecution process.

16.5 Plea and sending for trial

16.5.1 Summary offences

It is possible for cases to be dealt with on a first appearance in court but often an adjournment

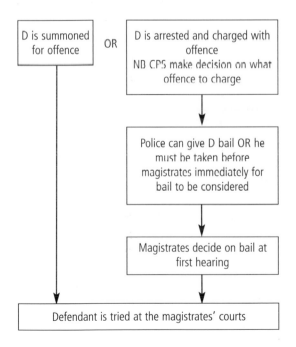

Defendant is tried at the magistrates' courts

Figure 16.2 Pre-trial procedure for a summary offence

may be needed. This could be because the Crown Prosecution Service has not got all the information required to complete the case, or because the defendant wants to get legal advice. Another reason for adjourning a case is where the magistrates want pre-sentence reports on a defendant who pleads guilty, before they decide what sentence to impose.

When a defendant wishes to plead not guilty, there will almost always have to be an adjournment, as witnesses will have to be brought to court. One of the main points to be decided on an adjournment is whether the defendant should be remanded on bail or in custody (see section 16.3).

Common assault is a summary offence and will always be tried in the magistrates' courts.

16.5.2 Pre-trial procedure for triable either way offences
Plea before venue

The plea before venue procedure applies only to triable either way offences. Under this procedure, the defendant is first asked whether he or she pleads guilty or not guilty. If the plea is guilty then the defendant has no right to ask for the case to be heard at the Crown Court. However, the magistrates may decide to send the defendant to the Crown Court for sentence.

Mode of trial

If the defendant pleads not guilty then the magistrates must carry out 'mode of trial' proceedings to decide whether the case will be tried in the Magistrates' Court or the Crown Court.

The magistrates first decide if they think the case is suitable for trial in the Magistrates' Court and whether they are prepared to accept jurisdiction (they have the power to deal with the case). In making the decision, the magistrates must consider the nature and seriousness of the

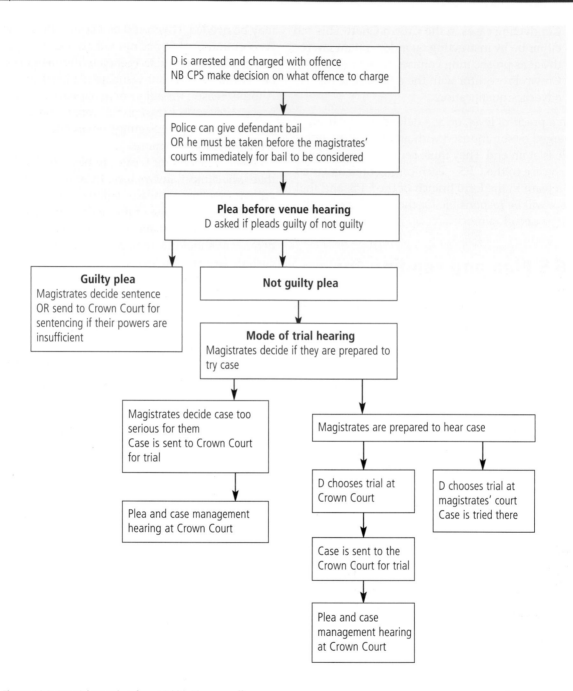

Figure 16.3 Pre-trial procedure for a triable either way offence

case, their own powers of punishment and any representations of the prosecution and defence.

Cases involving complex questions of fact or law should be sent to the Crown Court. Other relevant factors which may make a case more suitable for trial at the Crown Court include:

- where there was a breach of trust by the defendant;
- where the crime was committed by an organised gang;

- where the amount involved is more than twice the amount that the magistrates can fine the defendant.

Defendant's election

If the magistrates are prepared to accept jurisdiction, the defendant is then told he has the right to choose trial by jury, but may be tried by the magistrates if he agrees to this course. However, he is also warned that if the case is tried by the magistrates and at the end of the case he is found guilty, the magistrates can send him to the Crown Court for sentence if they feel their powers of punishment are insufficient.
Section 47 and s 20 offences are triable either way offences. They can be tried in either the magistrates' court or the Crown Court.

A main point for discussion is whether defendants should be allowed to choose where they will be tried. This involves the right to trial by jury.

16.5.3 The right to trial by jury

Cases where the defendant pleads not guilty to a summary offence can never be tried by a jury. These are always tried by magistrates.

Cases where the defendant pleads not guilty to an indictable offence are always tried by jury.

The only offences for which there is a choice of who should try the case are triable either way offences. The choice is made at the mode of trial proceedings (explained at section 16.4.2) in cases where the defendant is pleading not guilty to a triable either way offence. If the magistrates decide that the case is suitable for them to try, then they must offer the defendant the choice of court for the trial.

In this type of case most defendants choose to be tried by magistrates in the Magistrates' Courts. However, there are some reasons why defendants may prefer to be tried by a jury in the Crown Court.

Reasons for choosing trial by jury

Defendants are more likely to be acquitted (that is, found not guilty) at the Crown Court than in the

Magistrates' Court. Only 20 per cent of defendants who plead not guilty in the Magistrates' Courts are found not guilty. At the Crown Court over 60 per cent of defendants are acquitted.

An interesting point on the number of acquittals in the Crown Court is that most are as a result of the judge discharging the case or directing that the defendant be found not guilty. This will happen where the prosecution drop the case or witnesses fail to attend court, so there is no evidence against the defendant.

However, juries do acquit in more cases than magistrates. They acquit in about 35 per cent of cases compared to the 20 per cent acquittal rate in the Magistrates' Courts.

Research conducted into the reasons why defendants chose trial at the Crown Court found that most did so on the advice of their lawyers. The main factor in the choice was the higher chance of an acquittal.

However, there were other factors influencing the choice, including (where defendants were held in custody awaiting trial) a wish to serve part of the sentence in a remand prison!

Another reason for choosing trial at the Crown Court is that the defendant is more likely to get legal aid. This means that the State will pay for his legal representation.

The legal representative at the Crown Court must have a certificate of advocacy giving the right to do cases at the Crown Court. This is likely to mean that the lawyer is more experienced at presenting cases in court.

Disadvantages of trial by jury

There will be usually be a longer wait before the case is dealt with than for cases in the Magistrates' Courts. If the defendant is not given bail, this waiting period is spent in prison. However, waiting times for trials in the Crown Court have been reduced in recent years. Nearly half of cases where the defendant is pleading not guilty are now dealt with within 16 weeks from the case being sent to the Crown Court.

The costs of the case are much greater than those in the Magistrates' Court. If the defendant has to pay for their own lawyers, this will be expensive. In addition, if the defendant is ordered to pay part of the prosecution costs, this will be more than in the Magistrates' Court.

The other disadvantage is that, for defendants who are found guilty, the judge at the Crown Court has the power to give a greater sentence than the magistrates.

Plea and case management hearing

If the case is sent to the Crown Court for trial, there will first be a 'plea and case management' hearing in front of a judge at the Crown Court. This is to make sure that all necessary preparation is taken for the case to be ready for trial.

The defendant will be asked what he pleads to the charges – guilty or not guilty. If the defendant pleads guilty the judge can sentence him immediately. If the defendant pleads not guilty, then the prosecution and defence must provide the judge with information about such matters as:

- which witnesses are needed to attend the trial;
- what documents and exhibits, such as any weapon, will be produced at the trial;
- any points of law that will be raised at the trial.

16.5.4 Pre-trial procedure for indictable offences

Even for the most serious offences the first hearing is in the magistrates' court. This deals with

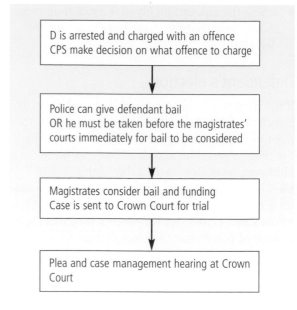

Figure 16.4 Pre-trial procedure for an indictable offence

whether the defendant wants to apply for legal aid and issues of bail. All indictable offences are then sent to the Crown Court immediately after the early administrative hearing in the magistrates' court. A s 18 offence is an indictable offence. It always has to be tried in the Crown Court.

Plea and case management hearing

All other pre-trial matters are dealt with by a judge at the Crown Court in a 'plea and case management' hearing in the same way as for a triable either way offence (see 16.5.3).

Test Yourself

1. What is meant by a summary offence? Give an example.
2. What is meant by an indictable offence? Give an example.
3. What other category of offence is there?
4. Who can grant bail?
5. What assumption is the starting point for considering bail?

6. When can a defendant be refused bail?
7. Who makes the decision on what offence the defendant should be charged with?
8. When does a mode of trial hearing take place in the magistrates' court?
9. What is a plea and case management hearing?
10. What is the standard of proof in criminal cases?

16.6 Burden and standard of proof

An accused person is presumed innocent until proven guilty. This means that the burden of proof is on the prosecution. They must prove the case by proving both the required *actus reus* and the required *mens rea* of the offence charged.

The standard of proof necessary in order for the defendant to be found guilty is 'beyond reasonable doubt'. This is usually explained by the judge telling the jury that they should only convict the defendant if they are sure of the defendant's guilt.

Examination questions

For part questions see the end of Chapter 14, Question (b)(ii) and see the end of Chapter 15, Question c(i).

Examiner's tip

Read the question carefully. Which part of the procedure does it ask about? If you look back to the question at the end of Chapter 14, it asks for the procedure following (that is after) arrest and up to the start of the trial. This will depend on what offence has been committed. The following chart helps you know which procedure is relevant for the different offences.

Offence	Category	Tried in	What happens
Common assault	Summary offence	Magistrates' court	All procedure is in the magistrates' court
s 47	Triable either way offence	Magistrates' court or Crown Court	Decision has to be made on where trial will be held D has choice
s 20	Triable either way offence	Magistrates' court or Crown Court	
s 18	Indictable offence	Crown Court	Will go to magistrates' court for first hearing but will then be transferred to Crown Court

Chapter 17

Sentencing

Whenever a person pleads guilty, or is found guilty of an offence, the role of the court is to decide what sentence should be imposed on the offender. Judges and magistrates have a fairly wide discretion as to the sentence they select in each case, although they are subject to certain restrictions. Magistrates can only impose a maximum of six months' imprisonment for one offence (12 months' for two) and a maximum fine of £5,000. The Criminal Justice Act 2003 has provision for these sentencing powers to increase to 12 months for one offence and 15 months for two or more offences. Judges in the Crown Court have no such limits; they can impose up to life imprisonment for some crimes and there is no maximum figure for fines. Figure 17.1 shows the percentages of different sentences imposed in Magistrates' Courts and at the Crown Court in 2007. The differing percentages of offenders given an immediate custodial sentence stresses that the Crown Court is dealing with more serious offences.

17.1 Aims of sentencing

When judges or magistrates have to pass a sentence they will not only look at the sentences available, they will also have to decide what they are trying to achieve by the punishment they give. Section 142 of the Criminal Justice Act 2003 sets out the purposes of sentencing for those aged 18 and over saying that a court must have regard to:

- the punishment of offenders;
- the reduction of crime (including its reduction by deterrence);
- the reform and rehabilitation of offenders;
- the protection of the public; and
- the making of reparation by offenders to persons affected by their offences.

Punishment is often referred to as retribution. In addition to the purposes of sentencing given in the 2003 Act, denunciation of crime is also recognised as an aim of sentencing. Each of the aims will now be examined in turn.

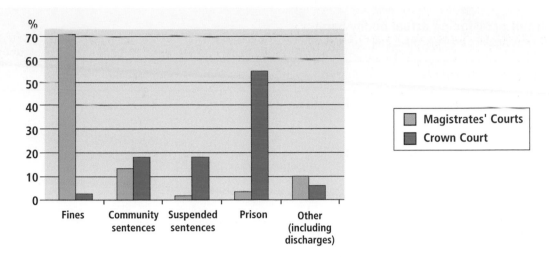

Figure 17.1 Sentencing in the Magistrates' Courts and Crown Court
Source: Sentencing Statistics England and Wales, 2007

17.1.1 Retribution/punishment

Retribution is based on the idea of punishment. The offender deserves punishment for his or her acts. This aim of sentencing does not seek to reduce crime or alter the offender's future behaviour. A judge using this aim is only concerned with the offence that was committed and making sure that the sentence given is in proportion to that offence.

The crudest form of retribution can be seen in the old saying 'an eye for an eye and a tooth for a tooth and a life for a life'. This was one of the factors used to justify the death penalty for the offence of murder.

Tariff sentences

Retribution, today, is based more on the idea that each offence should have a certain tariff or level of sentencing. The Sentencing Guidelines Council produces guidelines for this. For example, for s 20 offences the Council gives the chart on the next page showing the tariffs for adult offenders.

17.1.2 Deterrence

This can be individual deterrence or general deterrence. Individual deterrence is intended to ensure that the offender does not re-offend, through fear of future punishment. General deterrence is aimed at preventing other potential offenders from committing crimes. Both are aimed at reducing future levels of crime.

Individual deterrence

There are several penalties that can be imposed with the aim of deterring the individual offender from committing similar crimes in the future. These include a prison sentence, a suspended sentence or a heavy fine. However, prison does not appear to deter as about 55 per cent of adult prisoners re-offend within two years of release. With young offenders, custodial sentences have even less of a deterrent effect. Over 70 per cent of young offenders given a custodial sentence re-offend within two years.

General deterrence

The value of this is even more doubtful as potential offenders are rarely deterred by severe sentences passed on others. However, the courts do occasionally resort to making an example of an offender in order to warn other potential offenders of the type of punishment they face.

Assault occasioning actual bodily harm
Offences Against the Person Act 1861 (section 47)

Type/nature of activity	Starting point	Sentencing
Pre-meditated assault **EITHER** resulting in injuries just falling short of GBH **OR** involving the use of a weapon	30 months custody	2–4 years custody
Pre-meditated assault resulting in relatively serious injury	12 months custody	36 weeks – 2 years custody
Pre-meditated assault resulting in minor, non-permanent injury	24 weeks custody	12–36 weeks custody
Other assault resulting in minor, non-permanent injury	Community Order (HIGH)	Community Order (MEDIUM) – 26 weeks custody

Additional aggravating factors	Additional mitigating factors
	1. Provocation 2. Unintended injury

Figure 17.2 Sentencing Council's Guidelines on s 20 offences

General deterrence is in direct conflict with the principle of retribution, since it involves sentencing an offender to a longer term than is deserved for the specific offence. It is probably the least effective and least fair principle of sentencing.

17.1.3 Reform/rehabilitation

Under this aim of sentencing the main aim of the penalty is to reform the offender and rehabilitate him or her into society. It is a forward-looking aim, with the hope that the offender's behaviour will be altered by the penalty imposed, so that he or she will not offend in the future (it aims to reduce crime in this way).

Reformation is a very important element in the sentencing philosophy for young offenders, but it is also used for some adult offenders. The court will be given information about the defendant's background, usually through a pre-sentence report prepared by the probation service. Where relevant, the court will consider other factors, such as school reports, job prospects, or medical problems.

Offenders will usually be given a community order with various requirements aimed at rehabilitating them.

17.1.4 Protection of the public

The public need to be protected from dangerous offenders. For this reason life imprisonment or a long term of imprisonment are given to those

Key facts

Theory	Aim of theory	Suitable punishment
Retribution/ Punishment	Punishment imposed only on ground that an offence has been committed	• Tariff sentences • Sentence must be proportionate to the crime
Deterrence	Individual – the offender is deterred through fear of further punishment General – potential offenders warned as to likely punishment	• Prison sentence • Heavy fine • Long sentence as an example to others
Rehabilitation	Reform offender's behaviour	• Individualised sentence • Community order
Protection of the public	Offender is made incapable of committing further crime Society is protected from crime	• Long prison sentences • Tagging • Banning orders
Reparation	Repayment/reparation to victim or to community	• Compensation order • Unpaid work • Reparation schemes
Denunciation	Society expressing its disapproval Reinforces moral boundaries	• Reflects blameworthiness of the offence

Figure 17.3 Key facts chart on aims of sentencing

who commit murder or other violent or serious sexual offences.

The Criminal Justice Act 2003 introduced a provision for serious offences that where the court is of the opinion that there is a significant risk to members of the public of serious harm being caused by the defendant in the future, the court must send the defendant to prison for the protection of the public.

The Criminal Justice Act 2003 also has provision for extended sentences to be given where it is thought necessary to protect the public. This adds an extra period to the defendant's sentence during which he is freed on licence.

For less serious offences there are other ways in which the public can be protected. For example, dangerous drivers are disqualified from driving. Another method is to include an exclusion order as a requirement in a community order. This will ban the offender from going to places where he is most likely to commit an offence. The use of such a banning order is shown in the case of *R v Winkler* (2004).

In this case the defendant committed an affray in Manchester when attending a football match in which Oldham Athletic, the team he supported, was playing. The judge banned the defendant from going into Oldham town centre on home match days and also banned him from approaching within half a mile of any football stadium. Both bans were for a period of six years.

Another method of protecting the public is to impose a curfew order on the offender ordering him to remain at home for certain times of the day or night. The curfew can be monitored by an electronic tag, which should trigger an alarm if the offender leaves his home address during a curfew period.

17.1.5 Reparation

This is aimed at compensating the victim of the crime usually by ordering the offender to pay a sum of money to the victim or to make restitution, for example, by returning stolen property to its rightful owner. The courts are required to consider ordering compensation to the victim of a crime, in addition to any other penalty they may think appropriate. There are also projects to bring offenders and victims together, so that the offenders may make direct reparation.

The concept of restitution also includes making reparation to society as a whole. This can be seen mainly in the use of an unpaid work requirement where offenders are required to do so many hours work on a community project under the supervision of the probation service.

17.1.6 Denunciation

This is society expressing its disapproval of criminal activity. A sentence should indicate both to the offender and to other people that society condemns certain types of behaviour. It shows people that justice is being done.

Activity

Read the following article and answer the questions following it.

'Tougher jail terms DO deter criminals, admits Home Office'

A Home Office report has concluded that stiffer prison sentences deter crime ... the study found that convicts jailed for less than a year are almost 50 per cent more likely to commit a fresh crime within two years of their release than those locked up for between one and four years.

And they are twice as likely to break the law as those jailed for at least four years.

The report is embarrassing for the Government. Only this month [May 2007], Lord Falconer, newly-created Justice Secretary, announced that tens of thousands of burglars and other thieves would receive community punishments instead of jail sentences under plans to ease chronic prison overcrowding.

In March [2007] the Prime Minister signalled that there should be greater emphasis on rehabilitating offenders, tougher community sentences and crime prevention ...

Figures show that 70 per cent of convicts jailed for under 12 months re-offended within two years, compared with 49 per cent of those convicted to between one and four years and 36 per cent of those serving as least four years.

The report said prisoners released from longer sentences were less likely to reoffend because they were older, had time to be rehabilitated and had been convicted of more serious "one-off" offences.

Taken from an article by Ian Drury in the *Daily Mail*, 19 May 2007

Questions

1. What sentencing aim does this article suggest that stiffer prison sentences promotes?
2. What sentencing aim did the Prime Minister want emphasised?
3. What sentencing aim does the Home Office Report say had an effect on longer term prisoners?
4. Name and explain two other sentencing aims.

Inside of a prison

Denunciation also reinforces the moral boundaries of acceptable conduct and can mould society's views on the criminality of particular conduct – for example, drink driving is now viewed by the majority of people as unacceptable behaviour. This is largely because of the changes in the law and the increasingly severe sentences that are imposed. By sending offenders to prison, banning them from driving and imposing heavy fines, society's opinion of drink driving has been changed.

17.2 Sentences available for adults

17.2.1 Custodial sentences

A custodial sentence is the most serious punishment that a court can impose. Custodial sentences range from a few weeks to life imprisonment. They include:

- mandatory and discretionary life sentences;
- fixed-term sentences;
- custody plus (short-term sentence);
- suspended sentences.

Custodial sentences are meant to be used only for serious offences. The Criminal Justice Act 2003 says that the court must not pass a custodial sentence unless it is of the opinion that the offence (or combination of offences):

 was so serious that neither a fine alone nor a community sentence can be justified.

Mandatory life sentences

For murder the only sentence a judge can impose is a life sentence. However, the judge is allowed to state the minimum number of years' imprisonment that the offender must serve before being eligible for release on licence. This minimum term is now governed by the Criminal Justice Act 2003. This gives judges clear starting points for the minimum period to be ordered. The starting points range from a full life term down to 12 years.

Discretionary life sentences

For other serious offences such as an offence under s 18 of the Offences Against the Person Act

1861 the maximum sentence is life imprisonment, but the judge does not have to impose it. The judge has discretion in sentencing and can give any lesser sentence where appropriate. This can even be a fine or a discharge.

Fixed-term sentences

For other crimes, the length of the sentence will depend on several factors, including the maximum sentence available for the particular crime, the seriousness of the crime and the defendant's previous record. Imprisonment for a set number of months or years is called a 'fixed-term' sentence.

Prisoners do not serve the whole of the sentence passed by the court. Anyone sent to prison is automatically released after they have served half of the sentence. Only offenders aged 21 and over can be given a sentence of imprisonment.

Prison population

A problem is that prisons in England and Wales are overcrowded. There has been a big increase in the number of people in prison and there are not enough prison places. Figure 17.5 shows the increase in the prison population between 1951 and 2009.

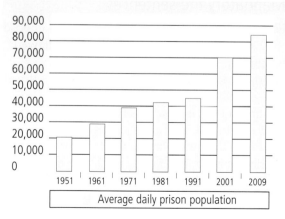

Figure 17.5 Bar chart of average daily prison population for England and Wales 1951–2009

 Internet Research

Look up the current weekly prison population on the Internet. It can be found at www.hmprisonservice.gov.uk.

Suspended prison sentences

An adult offender may be given a suspended prison sentence of up to two years (six months maximum in the Magistrates' Court). This means that the sentence does not take effect immediately. The court will fix a time during which the sentence is suspended; this can be for any period up to two years. If, during this time, the offender does not commit any further offences, the prison sentence will not be served. However, if the offender does commit another offence within the period of suspension, then the prison sentence is 'activated' and the offender will serve that sentence together with any sentence for the new offence.

A suspended sentence should only be given where the offence is so serious that an immediate custodial sentence would have been appropriate, but there are exceptional circumstances in the case that justify suspending the sentence.

17.2.2 Community orders

The Criminal Justice Act 2003 created one community order under which the court can combine any requirements they think are necessary. These requirements are listed below. The sentencers can 'mix and match' requirements allowing them to fit the restrictions and rehabilitation to the offender's needs. The sentence is available for offenders aged 16 and over. The full list of requirements available to the courts is set out in s 177 of the Criminal Justice Act 2003. This states:

 177(1) Where a person aged 16 or over is convicted of an offence, the court by or before which he is convicted may make an order imposing on him any one or more of the following requirements:

(a) an unpaid work requirement
(b) an activity requirement
(c) a programme requirement
(d) a prohibited activity requirement
(e) a curfew requirement
(f) an exclusion requirement
(g) a residence requirement
(h) a mental health treatment requirement
(i) a drug rehabilitation requirement
(j) an alcohol treatment requirement
(k) a supervision requirement, and
(l) in the case where the offender is aged under 25, an attendance centre requirement.

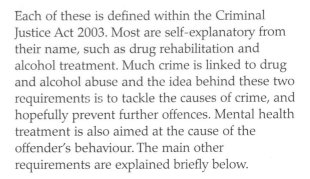

Each of these is defined within the Criminal Justice Act 2003. Most are self-explanatory from their name, such as drug rehabilitation and alcohol treatment. Much crime is linked to drug and alcohol abuse and the idea behind these two requirements is to tackle the causes of crime, and hopefully prevent further offences. Mental health treatment is also aimed at the cause of the offender's behaviour. The main other requirements are explained briefly below.

Unpaid work requirement

This requires the offender to work for between 40 and 300 hours on a suitable project organised by the probation service. The exact number of hours will be fixed by the court, and those hours are then usually worked in eight-hour sessions, often at weekends. The type of work involved will vary, depending on what schemes the local probation service have running. The offender may be required to paint school buildings, help build a play centre or work on conservation projects.

Prohibited activity requirement

This requirement allows a wide variety of activities to be prohibited. The idea is to try to prevent the defendant from committing another crime of the type he has just been convicted of. Often the defendant is forbidden to go into a certain area where he has caused trouble. In some cases the defendant has been banned from wearing a 'hoodie'. In 2006, a defendant who was found guilty of criminal damage was banned from carrying paint, dye, ink or marker pens.

Curfew requirement

Under these, an offender can be ordered to remain at a fixed address for between 2 and 12 hours in any 24-hour period. This order can last for up to six months and may be enforced by electronic tagging (where suitable). Courts can only make such an order if there is an arrangement for monitoring curfews in their area. Such monitoring can be done by spot-checks,

THIS IS THE GOVERNMENT'S LATEST IDEA FOR A COMMUNITY SENTENCE

Read the following extract from an article in the *New Law Journal* and answer the questions below.

Taking responsibility

Fifty-eight per cent of all prisoners and three in four young offenders are re-convicted within two years of release, write *Finola Farrant* and *Joe Levenson*. Why is this and what can be done?

Prisoners have many of the characteristics of social exclusion:

- 26 per cent have spent time in care as a child;

- 47 per cent of women in prison have no educational qualifications;

- 66 per cent of men in prison do not have a job at the time of their conviction; and

- eight per cent of female prisoners have previously been admitted to a psychiatric hospital...

The Prison Reform Trust recently published *Barred Citizens: Volunteering and Active Citizenship by Prisoners*, which examined and identified the benefits of volunteering and active citizenship by prisoners. Volunteering can offer a means of improving the employment prospects of prisoners by providing work experience, improving skills and confidence and enabling prisoners to gain a work reference ...

Prisoners currently face great difficulties finding employment after release because of low educational attainment, health problems, a lack of suitable housing and obsolete skills. Ex-prisoners also frequently face discrimination from employers ...

Volunteering, especially when it involves undertaking community placements, allows prisoners to build or maintain links with the outside world.

Taken from 'Taking Responsibility' by Finola Farrant and Joe Levenson, *New Law Journal*, 6 August 2002, LexisNexis Butterworths

Questions

1. What percentage of prisoners re-offend within two years of release?
2. What problems do many of those who are convicted have prior to their conviction?
3. What problems are faced by prisoners when they finish their sentence?
4. What solution does the article suggest for some of these problems?
5. Suggest other ways in which offenders could be prepared to reintegrate into society.

The article above refers to the work of the Prison Reform Trust. Look up this organisation on the Internet at www.prisonrefomtrust.org.uk.

with security firms sending someone to make sure that the offender is at home or offenders may be electronically tagged. There are also pilot schemes on using satellite technology to track those who are tagged.

Supervision requirement

For this requirement the offender is placed under the supervision of a probation officer for a period of up to three years. During the period of supervision the offender must attend appointments with the supervising officer or with any other person decided by the supervising officer.

17.2.3 Fines

This is the most common way of disposing of a case in the Magistrates' Court where the maximum fine is £5,000 for an individual offender. The magistrate can impose a fine of up to £20,000 on businesses who have committed offences under certain regulations, such as health and safety at work. In the Crown Court only a small percentage of offenders are dealt with by way of a fine.

17.2.4 Discharges

These may be either:

- a conditional discharge or
- an absolute discharge.

A conditional discharge means that the court discharges an offender on the condition that no further offence is committed during a set period of up to three years. It is intended to be used where it is thought that punishment is not necessary. If an offender reoffends within the time limit, the court can then impose another sentence in place of the conditional discharge, as well as imposing a penalty for the new offence. Conditional discharges are widely used by Magistrates' Courts for first-time minor offenders.

An absolute discharge means that, effectively, no penalty is imposed. Such a penalty is likely to be used where an offender is technically guilty but morally blameless. An example could be where the tax disc on a vehicle has fallen to the floor – it is technically not being displayed and an offence has been committed. So, in the unlikely situation of someone being prosecuted for this, the magistrates, who would have to impose some penalty, would most probably decide that an absolute discharge was appropriate.

17.3 Factors in sentencing

When deciding what sentence to pass on a defendant, the courts consider the following matters:

- the offence;
- sentencing guidelines;
- the offender's background.

17.3.1 Aggravating factors in sentencing

In looking at the offence, the most important point to establish is how serious was it, of its type? This is now set out in s 143(1) of the Criminal Justice Act 2003 which states that:

> In considering the seriousness of the offence, the court must consider the offender's culpability in committing the offence and any harm which the offence caused, or was intended to cause or might reasonably forseeably have caused.

The Act goes on to give certain factors which are considered as aggravating factors making an offence more serious. These are:

- previous convictions for offences of a similar nature or relevant to the present offence;
- the fact that the defendant was on bail when he committed the offence;
- racial or religious hostility being involved in the offence;
- hostility to disability or sexual orientation being involved in the offence.

As well as these points in the Criminal Justice Act 2003, there are also other factors which are regarded as aggravating features for specific offences. For example where the defendant has committed an assault, aggravating features include:

- the offender being part of a group attacking the victim;

Activity

If you look back to Figure 17.2 on page 216 you will see the sentencing guidelines for a s 20 offence (Offences Against the Person Act 1861). Use those guidelines to answer the following questions.

Questions

1. What is the maximum penalty for a s 20 offence?
2. The top range of sentences suggested is 2 to 4 years' imprisonment. What factors would lead to a sentence in this range?
3. What factors would lead to a sentence with a starting point of 24 weeks' custody?
4. When the offence was not pre-meditated, what type of sentence do the guidelines give?
5. What additional two mitigating factors might lead to a lower sentence?

- a particularly vulnerable victim, eg a young child or an elderly person;
- a victim serving the public, eg an attack on a nurse in a hospital emergency unit;
- the fact that the assault was premeditated.

Where there is an aggravating factor the court will pass a more severe sentence than it would normally have given.

Magistrates all have a copy of the Sentencing Guidelines issued by the Sentencing Guidelines Council. These give a starting point for an offence, depending on certain factors, in particular whether the magistrates should be thinking of a custodial sentence or a community order. The guidelines also give a sentencing range.

17.3.2 Mitigating factors available in sentencing

A mitigating factor is one which allows the court to give a lighter sentence than would normally be given.

If the offender co-operates with the police, for example helping identify others involved in the crime, then the court can take this into account when deciding sentence.

Other factors taken into account in mitigation include:

- mental illness of the defendant;
- physical illness of the defendant;
- the fact that a defendant has no previous convictions;
- evidence of genuine remorse.

Reduction in sentence for a guilty plea

There will also be a reduction in sentence for a guilty plea, particularly where the defendant made that plea early in the proceedings. The Sentencing Guidelines Council guidelines on this are that the reduction for a guilty plea at the first reasonable opportunity should attract a reduction of up to one-third, while a plea of guilty after the trial has started would only be given a one-tenth reduction. The amount of reduction is on a sliding scale as shown in Figure 17.6.

The only exception is where the evidence is overwhelming and the defendant's guilt is clear. In these circumstances, even if the defendant pleads guilty at the earliest possible opportunity, the judge need only give a 20 per cent discount for that plea of guilty.

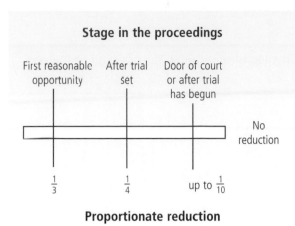

Stage in the proceedings

First reasonable opportunity — After trial set — Door of court or after trial has begun

$\frac{1}{3}$ $\frac{1}{4}$ up to $\frac{1}{10}$

No reduction

Proportionate reduction

Figure 17.6 Reduction in sentence for a guilty plea

17.3.3 Background of the offender

Previous convictions

An important fact about the defendant is whether he has previous convictions or not. Where he has a previous conviction for the same or similar type of offence, then he is likely to receive a heavier sentence.

A defendant who has no previous convictions is usually treated more leniently.

Reports

The courts will often have a report prepared by the probation service on the offender and his background. If the defendant is ill, then the court may also ask for a medical report. These reports will be considered with all other factors in deciding what sentence to impose on the defendant.

Test Yourself

1. Explain what is meant by a tariff sentence?
2. What is the aim of deterrence when sentencing?
3. Name and briefly explain two other aims of sentencing.
4. What is a discretionary life sentence?
5. Give three requirements that can be attached to a community order.
6. What is the most common punishment imposed in the magistrates' courts?
7. What two types of discharge are there?
8. Give two aggravating factors in sentencing.
9. By how much could a sentence be reduced if a defendant pleaded guilty at the earliest opportunity?
10. Give two other mitigating factors in sentencing.

Examination question

See (c) (i) and (c) (ii) in the question at the end of Chapter 14 and c (ii) in the question at the end of Chapter 15.

Examiner's tip

There are three main themes that a question on sentencing may ask. These are:

- aims of sentencing;
- range of sentences available;
- factors the court will consider in sentencing.

As well as knowing these themes, try to link them to the scenario given in the question. For example, question c (ii) at the end of Chapter 15 asks 'Assuming that Andy is found guilty of any offence, outline the range of factors that the court may take into account before he is sentenced'.

Look at the scenario and you will see it states that Andy 'shouted racist abuse'. You must mention this factor as one of the ones that the court will consider.

Chapter 18

The Tort of Negligence

The law of torts is part of the civil law. A tort is a civil wrong. The word 'tort' actually comes from the French word for wrong. The law allows people to claim compensation when they have been injured or their property damaged or interfered with or their reputation harmed. There are a number of different torts. The most important are:

- negligence;
- occupiers' liability;
- nuisance;
- trespass;
- defamation.

For the AS course you only need to study the tort of negligence. This can apply in a wide variety of situations where a person or their property is damaged. One of the most common is a car crash in which the vehicles are damaged and the drivers and passengers injured. When this happens people will want to claim compensation for their injuries and for damage to the car or other property. Other situations include people being injured at work or through medical negligence. In all these situations the tort of negligence is used as the basis of the claim.

The newspaper article at source D in the Activity on page 4, Chapter 1 shows a claim being made under the tort of negligence. In negligence the other person is only liable if:

- they owe you a duty of care;
- they breach this duty; and
- the breach causes damage.

18.1 Duty of care

The idea of a duty of care in the tort of negligence has developed through judges making decisions in cases. The start of our modern law of negligence was the case of *Donoghue v Stevenson* (1932). In this case Mrs Donoghue went to a cafe with a friend. The friend bought her a drink of ginger beer and ice cream. The bottle of ginger beer had dark glass so that the contents could not be seen. After drinking some of it, Mrs Donoghue poured the rest out and then saw that it contained a dead (and decomposing) snail. Because of the impurities in the drink she was taken ill.

She wanted to claim for her illness, but as she had not bought the drink she could not use the law of contract. So she sued the manufacturers claiming that they owed her a duty of care.

In the House of Lords the judges set out a test for when a person would be under a duty. They said:

> 🙶 You must take reasonable care to avoid acts or omissions which you can reasonably foresee would be likely to injure your neighbour. 🙷

They went on to explain this by saying;

> 🙶 Who then, in law, is my neighbour? Persons who are so closely and directly affected by my act that I ought reasonably to have them in my contemplation as being affected when I am directing my mind to the acts or omissions in question. 🙷

This established the broad principles of liability. However, there have been a number of changes to the detail. In *Caparo v Dickman* (1990) the 'neighbour' test was replaced by a three-part test:

- Was damage or harm reasonably foreseeable?
- Is there a sufficiently proximate (close) relationship between the claimant and the defendant?
- Is it fair, just and reasonable to impose a duty?

18.1.1 Reasonably foreseeable

This depends on the facts of the case, though there are some general principles which are used. It is easier to understand by looking at some cases.

In *Kent v Griffiths* (2000) a doctor called for an ambulance to take a patient suffering from a serious asthma attack to hospital immediately. The ambulance control centre replied 'okay, doctor'. The ambulance, without a satisfactory reason, failed to arrive within a reasonable time. The patient suffered a heart attack which could have been avoided if she had been taken to hospital earlier. It was reasonably foreseeable that the claimant would suffer harm from the failure of the ambulance to arrive.

In *Jolley v Sutton London Borough Council* (2000) a boy, aged 14, was paralysed when a boat he was attempting to repair slipped on top of him. The boat had been abandoned on land belonging to the council by a block of flats. The council knew that the boat was in a dangerous condition and that children were likely to play on it. The House of Lords held that attempting to repair the boat was not so very different from normal play, so the injury to the claimant was reasonably foreseeable.

Not foreseeable

In some cases the courts have decided that it is not reasonably foreseeable that the claimant would suffer harm. For example, in *Bourhill v Young* (1943) a motorcyclist going too fast, crashed into a car and was killed. Mrs Bourhill, who was eight months' pregnant, was about 50 yards away. She heard the accident, but did not see it. Afterwards she saw blood on the road and suffered shock and her baby was stillborn. She claimed against the motorcyclist's estate. The court decided that the motorcyclist did not owe her a duty of care as he could not have reasonably foreseen that she would be affected by his negligent driving. He did, of course, owe a duty of care to the car driver with whom he collided.

In *Topp v London Country Bus (South West) Ltd* (1993) a driver left a bus unattended with the

Duty of care	Donoghue v Stevenson (1932)	Must take reasonable care not to injure your neighbour
Basic principles	Caparo v Dickman (1990)	Damage or harm must be reasonably foreseeable There must be a close relationship (proximity test) It must be fair, just and reasonable to impose a duty
Reasonably foreseeable	Kent v Griffiths (2000) Jolley v Sutton London Borough Council (2000)	Ambulance took too long to arrive to take asthma sufferer to hospital Leaving a damaged boat where children might play on it
Not reasonably foreseeable	Bourhill v Young (1943) Topp v London Country Bus (South West) Ltd (1993)	Woman who heard accident and saw blood on road Left ignition key in bus. Bus then stolen and thief's driving caused accident
Proximity	Hill v Chief Constable of West Yorkshire (1990) Osman v Ferguson (1993)	Unknown murder victim not sufficiently proximate Where police knew of risk to specific victim there was proximity
Fair, just and reasonable	Capital & Counties plc v Hampshire County Council (1997)	Fair, just and reasonable where fire officer had ordered sprinkler system to be switched off

Figure 18.1 Case chart for duty of care

keys in the ignition. The bus was stolen and driven dangerously causing an accident in which the claimant was injured. The damage to the claimant was held not to be reasonably foreseeable.

18.1.2 Proximity

Even if the harm is reasonably foreseeable, a duty of care will only exist if the relationship of the claimant and the defendant is sufficiently close. In *Hill v Chief Constable of West Yorkshire* (1990) a serial killer had been murdering women in the Yorkshire area. The claimant's daughter was the killer's last victim before he was caught. By the time of her death the police already had enough information to arrest the killer, but had failed to do so. The mother claimed that the police owed a duty of care to her daughter. It was decided by the House of Lords that the relationship between the victim and the police was not sufficiently close (proximate) for the police to be under a duty of care. The police knew that there might be a

further victim of the killer but they had no way of knowing who the victim might be.

The situation was different in *Osman v Ferguson* (1993) where the police officers knew that there was a real risk of an attack on a schoolboy. The attacker had a fixation about the boy and had been following him and causing concern. There had been complaints to the police about the attacker's behaviour. The boy's father was then murdered by the attacker and the boy was seriously injured. The court held that there was a sufficiently close relationship between the police and the victim and the victim's family. However, the case did not succeed because it was ruled that it was not fair, just and reasonable to impose a duty of care on the police. This is considered in more detail in the following section.

18.1.3 Fair, just and reasonable

This third part of the duty of care tests allows the courts to decide that, even though the harm was foreseeable and the parties were sufficiently close, there is no duty of care. The courts are often reluctant to find that it is 'fair, just and reasonable' to impose a duty of care on public authorities. In the case of *Hill v Chief Constable of West Yorkshire* (see section 18.1.2) it was pointed out that imposing a duty on police could lead to policing being carried out in a defensive way which might divert resources and attention away from the suppression of crime. This would be likely to lead to lower standards of policing, not higher ones.

The European Court of Human Rights has criticised excluding liability in this way, so the extent to which English courts will follow this decision is now in doubt.

Where the police or other authority have through their own actions created a new danger or substantially increased the risk of an existing danger, then the courts are more likely to hold that it is fair, just and reasonable to recognise a duty of care.

In *Capital & Counties plc v Hampshire County Council* (1997), the fire brigade had attended at the scene of a fire. A fire officer ordered that the sprinkler system in the building be turned off. This caused the fire to spread and led to more serious damage than if the system had been left on. In this situation it was fair, just and reasonable to recognise a duty of care against the fire brigade.

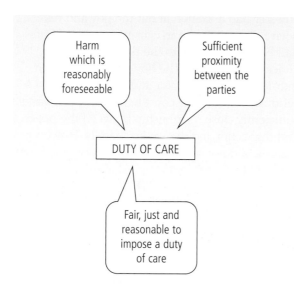

Figure 18.2 Duty of care tests

18.2 Breach of duty

Where, under the three *Caparo* tests, there is a duty of care, the claimant still has to prove that that duty of care has been broken.

18.2.1 Degree of risk

It is important that the risk is foreseeable. If the risk of harm is not known then there is no breach. In *Roe v Minister of Health* (1954) anaesthetic was kept in glass ampoules. At the time it was not known that invisible cracks could occur in the glass and allow the anaesthetic to become contaminated. So, when the claimant was paralysed by some contaminated anaesthetic, there was no breach and he could not claim compensation.

Another way of looking at it is whether there is fault on the defendant's part. In this case the doctors had acted without fault.

Where a risk is small then it is unlikely that there is a duty of care. In *Bolton v Stone* (1951) a cricket ball hit a passer-by in the street. The evidence was that there was a 17-foot high fence around the ground and the wicket was a long way from this fence. Balls had only been hit out of the ground six times in 30 years. Because of the low risk involved there was no breach of the duty of care.

However, where it is known there is a risk and no steps are taken to guard against that risk, there is likely to be a breach of the duty of care. In *Haley v London Electricity Board* (1965) it was known that a particular road was used by blind people. Yet, when the electricity board dug a hole in the road they only put out warning signs; they did not put any barriers around the hole.

18.2.2 The standard of care

If a defendant falls below the standard of care which a prudent and reasonable man would take then there is a breach of duty.

Where the consequences of harm to a particular person are greater than for other people, there is a higher standard of care owed to that person. This is shown in the case of *Paris v Stepney*

Breach of duty	*Roe v Minister of Health* (1954)	If risk of harm is not known then there is no breach, e.g. contaminated anaesthetic used, but risk of this not known
Degree of risk	*Bolton v Stone* (1951) *Haley v London Electricity Board* (1965)	Where risk is small there is no breach, e.g. only occurring 6 times in 30 years Where risk is known there can be a breach., e.g. knowledge that blind people used pathway
Standard of care	*Paris v Stepney Borough Council* (1951) *Latimer v AEC Ltd* (1952)	If consequences of harm are greater than normal then there is a higher standard of care, as with a one-eyed man Only reasonable precautions need be taken, unreasonable to expect closure of a factory after flooding
Standard for experts	*Bolam v Friern Hospital Management* (1957)	Standard is that of a competent expert

Figure 18.3 Case chart for breach of duty

Borough Council (1951) where Mr Paris was known to be blind in one eye. He was given work to do by his employers which involved a small risk of injury to the eyes. He was not given any protective goggles. While doing this work, his good eye was damaged by a small piece of metal and he became totally blind. His employers were held to have broken their duty of care to him. They knew that the consequences of an injury to his good eye would be very serious. They should have taken greater care because of this and provided him with goggles, even though at that time it was not thought necessary to provide goggles for other workers.

Is it practicable to take precautions?

The courts will consider the balance of the risk involved against the cost and effort of taking adequate precautions to eliminate the risk. In *Paris v Stepney Borough Council* the cost and effort of providing goggles was very small compared with the consequences of the risk.

However, in other situations, the cost and effort of taking precautions may be very high or impracticable compared with the risk. For example, in *Latimer v AEC Ltd* (1953) a factory became flooded and the floor was very slippery with a mixture of the water and oil. Sawdust was spread over the floor to minimise any risk of workers slipping. Despite this one workman slipped and was injured. The court held that there was no breach of the duty of care. The only way to completely prevent injury would have been to close the factory. It was unreasonable to expect the owners to do this. They had taken sufficient steps to prevent injury in the circumstances.

Clearly if the risk had been much more serious, perhaps a risk of an explosion which could have killed and injured many people, then there would have been a higher standard of care on the owners. It would have been reasonable to expect them to close the factory.

Standards for experts

Where the defendant has some expertise, for example, he is a doctor carrying out medical treatment, then the standard of care is that which would normally be expected from a doctor. In *Bolam v Friern Hospital Management* (1957) the judge said:

A man need not possess the highest expert skill; it is . . . sufficient if he exercises the ordinary skill of an ordinary competent man exercising that particular art.

Activity

Read the following situations and explain for each whether there is likely to be a duty of care and if that duty has been broken.

1. Homer is driving his car at a speed which is over the speed limit. He loses control and the car goes on to the pavement, hitting Jamil. Jamil suffers a broken leg.

2. Katie is looking after Leo, a child aged six. She takes him to a park and while he plays she reads a book. She does not notice Leo leave the play area and approach a busy road. Leo then runs out into the road and is knocked down by a motorbike. The motorcyclist was going faster than the speed limit. Consider the liability of both Katie and the motorcyclist.

3. Pete fell and hit his head. He suffered a fractured skull and Dr Moon had to operate to remove a blood clot. During the operation Dr Moon removed the clot but Peter was paralysed because of the effects of the clot. Explain whether Dr Moon owes Peter a duty of care and, if so, whether Dr Moon is in breach of that duty.

4. Ryland parks his car at the side of the road while he goes into a shop. He leaves the keys in the ignition. Sam sees the keys and decides to drive the car around the corner for a joke and leave it there. When reversing into a parking spot, Sam hits the next car causing damage to the wing. The owner of this car wishes to claim for the cost of repairing the car.

Explain whether he can claim against:

(i)   Ryland
(ii) Sam.

18.3 Damage

18.3.1 Causation

Even where the claimant has proved that the defendant owed him a duty of care and that the defendant has broken that duty of care, the claimant must still prove that the damage suffered was caused by the breach of duty.

In *Barnett v Chelsea and Kensington Hospitals* (1969) three nightwatchmen went to a hospital accident and emergency department complaining of sickness after drinking tea made by a fourth man. A nurse telephoned the doctor on duty, who did not come to examine the men but instead recommended that they go home and see their own doctors.

> DUTY OF CARE
> Reasonably foreseeable harm
> Proximity between the parties
> Fair, just and reasonable to impose duty

> BREACH OF DUTY
> Defendant falls below standard of care
> appropriate to the degree of risk

> DAMAGE CAUSED
> Defendant's breach causes damage
> Damage is reasonably foreseeable

> LIABLE IN NEGLIGENCE

Figure 18.4 What must be proved for negligence

Damage	*Barnett v Chelsea and Kensington Hospitals* (1969)	The damage must be caused by the breach. Where a man would have died no matter what the doctor did, a breach by the doctor did not cause the death
Remoteness of damage	*The Wagon Mound* (1961)	The damage must be reasonably foreseeable; spilt oil catching fire because of welding was too remote
	Crossley v Rawlinson (1981)	An injury to man by tripping when running to put out a fire was too remote
Thin skull rule	*Smith v Leech Brain* (1962)	If the type of damage is reasonably foreseeable, then defendant is liable even if the damage is more serious because of a peculiarity of the victim
	Hughes v Lord Advocate (1963)	Liable if type of damage is foreseeable, even though it occurs in an unexpected way

Figure 18.5 Case chart for damage and remoteness

One of the men, the claimant's husband, went home and died a few hours later from poisoning by arsenic. His widow sued the hospital claiming that the doctor was negligent in not examining her husband. She was able to prove that the doctor owed a duty of care to her husband and that by not examining him, the doctor had broken that duty of care. However, the evidence showed that by the time the husband had called at the hospital it was already too late to save his life. The arsenic was already in his system in such a quantity that he would have died whatever was done. This meant that his death was not the result of the doctor's breach of duty of care and so the claim failed.

This is known as the 'but for' test. It must be proved that the claimant would not have suffered damage 'but for' the defendant's breach of duty of care.

18.3.2 Remoteness of damage

The damage must not be too remote from the negligence of the defendant. The rule comes from an Australian case *The Wagon Mound* (1961) where fuel oil had been negligently spilled onto water in a harbour. Two days later the oil caught fire because of welding work being done on another ship. The fire spread to the claimant's wharf and burnt it down.

It was decided that although the damage done to the wharf was a result of the oil being spilled, it was not reasonably foreseeable. It was too remote from the original negligent act of spilling the oil. If the oil had seeped into the wharf and damaged it in that way then that would have been reasonably foreseeable. The chances of it catching fire and causing damage in that way were not.

This rule was followed in *Crossley v Rawlinson* (1981) where the claimant in running towards a burning vehicle with a fire extinguisher to put the fire out, tripped, fell and was injured. It was held that as the claimant was only on the way to the danger created by the defendant's negligence, the injury was too remote.

Thin skull rule

This rule means that the defendant must take his victim as he finds him. So, if the type of damage is reasonably foreseeable, but it is much more serious because of something unusual about the claimant, such as a thin skull, then the defendant is liable. In this situation the damage is not too remote.

This is illustrated in the case of *Smith v Leech Brain and Co* (1962) where, because of the defendants' negligence, a man was burnt on the lip by molten metal. The man had an existing pre-cancerous condition. The burn brought about the onset of full cancer and the man died. His widow claimed against the defendants and it was held

Test Yourself

1. What three elements have to be proved to establish the tort of negligence?
2. What are the three parts of the *Caparo* test?
3. Explain using cases/examples what is meant by 'reasonably foreseeable'.
4. Explain using cases/examples what is meant by 'proximity'.
5. Give a case or example in which the risk was not foreseeable.
6. What is the standard of care normally expected from a person?
7. What is the standard of care expected from an expert?
8. Demonstrate using a case/example that the breach of the duty of care must cause the damage.
9. What is meant by 'remoteness of damage'?
10. What is the 'thin skull' rule?

that as a burn was a foreseeable injury, the defendant was also liable for the death.

Type of injury foreseeable

The defendant will also be liable if the type of injury was foreseeable, even though the precise way in which it happened was not. In *Hughes v Lord Advocate* (1963) Post Office workmen left a manhole unattended, covered only with a tent and with paraffin lamps by the hole. The claimant, an eight-year-old boy, and a friend climbed into the hole. On their way out the boys knocked one of the paraffin lamps into the hole. This caused an explosion which badly burnt the claimant.

The boy was able to claim for his injuries since it was foreseeable that a child might explore the site, break a lamp and be burnt. The type of injury was foreseeable, so, even though the explosion was not foreseeable, the defendants were liable.

18.4 Starting a court case

In Unit 1 (see Chapter 6) you will have learnt that the two civil courts are:

- The County Court
- The High Court.

Most people who have been injured do not want to start a court case unless they have to. They will first of all try to negotiate an agreed settlement with the person who caused their injuries or damaged their property. The vast majority of cases are settled and do not go to court.

18.4.1 Alternative Dispute Resolution (ADR)

Using the courts to resolve disputes can be costly, in terms of both money and time. It can also be traumatic for the individuals involved and may not lead to the most satisfactory outcome for the case. It is not surprising, therefore, that more and more people are trying other methods for resolving their disputes.

Alternative methods are referred to as 'ADR', which stands for 'Alternative Dispute Resolution', and include any method of resolving a dispute without resorting to using the courts. There are many different methods which can be used, ranging from very informal negotiations between the parties, to a comparatively formal arbitration hearing. The main methods of ADR are:

- negotiation
- mediation
- conciliation
- arbitration.

These are explained more fully in Chapter 7.

Type of case	The court to start claim in
Personal injury: claim up to £50,000	County Court
Personal injury: claim over £50,000	High Court (Queen's Bench Division) OR County Court
Damage to property: claim up to £25,000	County Court
Damage to property: claim over £25,000	High Court (Queen's Bench Division) OR County Court

Figure 18.6 Which court to start a claim in

18.4.2 Pre-action protocols

Parties are encouraged to give information to each other, in an attempt to prevent the need for so many court cases to be started. So before a claim is issued, especially in personal injury cases, a pre-action 'protocol' should be followed. This is a list of things to be done and if the parties do not follow the procedure and give the required information to the other party, they may be liable for certain costs if they then make a court claim.

The information is usually in a letter explaining brief details of how the claim arises; why it is claimed that the other party is at fault; details of injury or other damage; and any other relevant matters. The defendant is then given three months to investigate the claim and must then reply, setting out if liability is admitted or if it is denied, with the reasons for the denial. If expert evidence is going to be needed, then the parties should try to agree to use one expert. This should lead to many claims being settled, but there will still be some which need to go to court.

18.4.3 Which court to use

If the other person denies liability or refuses to use ADR, then the only way to get compensation for the injuries will be to start a court case.

Once the decision is made to go to court, then the first problem is which court to use. The court to be used will depend on the amount that is being claimed. There are different limits depending on whether the claim is for personal injuries or for damage to property.

For personal injury cases where the claim is for £50,000 or less, the case must be started in the County Court. For cases involving damage to property the case must be started in the County Court if the amount claimed is £25,000 or less.

If the claim is for more than the above amounts (that is over £50,000 for personal injuries or over £25,000 for damage to property), a claimant can choose whether to start the case in the County Court or the High Court. If the case is started in the High Court, then it will be in the Queen's Bench Division of the High Court. These limits are shown in Figure 18.6.

18.4.4 Issuing a claim

If you are using the county court, then you can choose to issue the claim in any of the 230 or so County Courts in the country. If you are using the High Court, then you can go to one of the 20 District Registries or the main court in London. You need a claim form called 'N1' (see Figure 18.7). The court office will give you notes explaining how to fill in the form.

Claim Form	In the
	for court use only
	Claim No.
	Issue date

Claimant

SEAL

Defendant(s)

Brief details of claim

Value

£

Defendant's name and address		Amount claimed	
		Court fee	
		Solicitor's costs	
		Total amount	

The court office at

is open between 10 am and 4 pm Monday to Friday. When corresponding with the court, please address forms or letters to the Court Manager and quote the claim number.

N1 Claim form (CPR Part 7) (01.02)

Printed on behalf of The Court Service

Figure 18.7a Form NI (front)

	Claim No.	

Does, or will, your claim include any issues under the Human Rights Act 1998?   ☐ Yes   ☐ No

Particulars of Claim (attached)(to follow)

Statement of Truth

*(I believe)(The Claimant believes) that the facts stated in these particulars of claim are true.

* I am duly authorised by the claimant to sign this statement

Full name _____

Name of claimant's solicitor's firm _____

signed _____   position or office held _____

*(Claimant)(Litigation friend)(Claimant's solicitor)   (if signing on behalf of firm or company)

*delete as appropriate

	Claimant's or claimant's solicitor's address to which documents or payments should be sent if different from overleaf including (if appropriate) details of DX, fax or e-mail.

Figure 18.7b Form NI (continued)

Court staff can help to make sure that you have filled in the claim form properly, or you may get help from advice centres or a Citizens' Advice Bureau. Once the form is filled in you should photocopy it so that you have a copy for the court, a copy for yourself and a copy for each defendant. Then take the form to the court office. A court fee for issuing the claim has to be paid. This fee varies according to how much the claim is for.

In 2010 the fee for a claim of up to £300 was £30 with the maximum fee for a small claim (under £5,000) being £108. Claims of £5,000 to £15,000 had a fee of £225, while at the top end of the scale claims of over £300,000 had a fee of £1,530.

 Internet Research

Look up court forms such as N1 on the website www.courtservice.gov.uk.

Also use that website to find guidance on starting cases in the County Court.

18.4.5 Defending a claim

When the defendant receives the claim form there are several routes which can be taken. They may admit the claim and pay the full amount. Where this happens the case ends. The claimant has achieved what was wanted. In other cases the defendant may dispute the claim. If the defendant wishes to defend the claim, he or she must send either an acknowledgement of service (Form N9) or a defence to the court within 14 days of receiving the claim. If only an acknowledgement of service is sent, then the defendant has an extra 14 days in which to serve the defence.

If the defendant does not do either of these things, then the claimant can ask the court to make an order that the defendant pays the money and costs claimed. This is called an order in default.

Once a claim is defended the court will allocate the case to the most suitable 'track' or way of dealing with the case.

18.4.6 The three tracks

The decision on which track should be used is made by the District Judge in the County Court or the Master (a procedural judge) in the High Court. To help the judge consider to which track a claim should be allocated, both parties are sent an allocation questionnaire. If it is thought necessary, the judge can allocate a case to a track that normally deals with claims of a higher value. Alternatively, if the parties agree, the judge can allocate a case to a lower-value track.

There are three tracks and these are:

1. **The small claims track**

   This is normally used for disputes under £5,000, except for personal injury cases where the limit is usually £1,000.

   Small claims cases are usually heard in private, but they can be heard in an ordinary court. The procedure allows the District Judge to be flexible in the way he hears the case. District Judges are given training in how to handle small claims cases, so that they will take an active part in the proceedings, asking questions and making sure that both parties explain all their important points. The parties are encouraged to represent themselves. In fact they cannot claim the cost of using a lawyer from the other side, even if they win the case.

2. **The fast track**

   This is used for straightforward disputes of £5,000 to £25,000. Fast track means that the court will set down a very strict timetable for the pre-trial matters. This is aimed at preventing one or both sides from wasting time and running up unnecessary costs.

   Once a case is set down for hearing, the aim is to have the case heard within 30 weeks. The actual trial will usually be heard by a Circuit Judge and take place in open court with a more formal procedure than for small claims. In order to speed up the trial itself, the hearing will be limited to a maximum of one day and the number of expert witnesses restricted, with usually only one expert being allowed.

3. **The multi-track**
   This is for cases over £25,000 or for complex cases under this amount. The case will be heard by a Circuit Judge who will also be expected to 'manage' the case from the moment it is allocated to the multi-track route.

18.4.7 Case management

Under the Civil Procedure Rules judges are expected to manage a case. Case management by judges includes:

- Identifying the issues at an early stage;
- Deciding which issues need investigation and trial;
- Encouraging the parties to use alternative dispute resolution if this is appropriate;
- Dealing with any procedural steps without the need for the parties to attend court;
- Giving directions to ensure that the trial of a case proceeds quickly and efficiently;
- Fixing timetables by which the different stages of the case must be completed.

This is all aimed at keeping the costs of the case as low as possible and making sure that it is heard reasonably quickly.

In all civil cases the judge has to decide if the claim is proved or not. If the judge decides that the claimant has proved their case, then the judge has to decide how much to award the claimant for the injury or damage.

18.5 Burden and standard of proof

The burden of proving the case is on the claimant. This means that to win the case the claimant has to prove all three elements of the tort of negligence (duty of care, breach and damage). However, there is an exception to this normal procedure under what is known as the rule of *res ipsa loquitur* (things speak for themselves). This rule is explained in the next section.

The standard of the proof is 'on the balance of probabilities'. This means the judge decides who is most likely to be right.

18.5.1 *Res ipsa loquitur*

In some situations of negligence it is difficult for the claimant to know exactly what happened, even though it seems obvious that the defendant must have been negligent. An example of this is where, after an operation in hospital, a patient is found to have a swab left inside them. The patient does not know how the duty of care was breached. They would have been unconscious throughout the operation. They only know that afterwards it has been discovered that there is a swab inside them.

In such a situation the rule of *res ipsa loquitur* can be used. This means that the claimant has to show:

- the defendant was in control of the situation which caused the injury, and
- the injury was more likely than not to have been caused by negligence.

If the claimant can show these two things, then the burden of proof moves to the defendant who has to prove that he was not negligent.

An example of a case in which the rule of *res ipsa loquitur* was used is *Scott v London and St Katherine Docks* (1865). The claimant was hit by six heavy bags of sugar which fell from the defendant's warehouse. The claimant did not know what had happened to make the bags fall. They could only prove that the bags had indeed fallen and caused injury to the claimant. The court held that the facts spoke for themselves and it was, therefore, for the defendant to prove that they had not been negligent.

18.6 Compensatory damages

In negligence cases the court will award a successful claimant an amount of money as compensation for the injuries or damage to property they have suffered. This award is known as damages.

The aim is to place the claimant in the same position as if the tort had not been committed. This can be fairly easily done where the claim is for damage to property. However, where the claimant has suffered serious personal injuries, especially where they have been left with a permanent disability, it is difficult to place a financial value on their loss.

18.6 1 Pecuniary and non-pecuniary loss

Pecuniary loss is a loss that can be easily calculated in money terms. For example, if the claimant had to hire a car to use while their own car was being repaired, then the exact amount of the cost of hiring is known. Also the cost of repairing the car is a pecuniary loss and the exact cost will be known.

Non-pecuniary loss refers to claims that are not money-based. This will include the pain and suffering of the claimant due to injuries caused by the other person's negligence. It also includes compensation for future changes in lifestyle which the injuries have caused. This is referred to as loss of amenity. For example, a person may be left unable to walk as a result of their injuries, or they may be able to walk but unable to enjoy the activities they did previously. This would include something like not being able to play football anymore.

An example of non-pecuniary loss is shown in this true life situation. A friend of the author was a keen ice-skater who had trained for many years and reached the standard for the British Championships. She was good enough that she would probably have skated in international competitions. She was knocked down while crossing the road on a pedestrian crossing controlled by lights. The driver who knocked her down had failed to stop at the red light. He was clearly in breach of his duty of care to her. She suffered very serious injuries to her legs. She was eventually able to walk again, but with difficulty, and she was unable to skate. As well as damages for her injuries and the pain and suffering, she was awarded a sum of money for the loss of her

enjoyment of ice-skating. The judge also included an amount as compensation for the fact that she was prevented from representing her country and taking part in international competitions. All this was non-pecuniary loss.

18.6.2 Mitigation of loss

The claimant is entitled to be compensated for his loss, but he or she is under a duty to keep the loss to a reasonable level. This is called mitigation of loss.

For example, where a person has been injured due to the negligence of another person, the injured person cannot claim for private treatment for the injury if there is suitable treatment available under the National Health Service. However, if there is a need for plastic surgery which can only be carried out privately, then the cost of it is allowed as part of the damages awarded to the claimant.

Where there is damage to property, the same principles apply. The claimant cannot claim for expensive items, if the damaged original was not expensive. An example here would be if the claimant's car was damaged and needed repairs before it could be driven. While the car is off the road, the claimant is entitled to the cost of hiring a car. However, the claimant cannot claim the cost of hiring a luxury car at a very high cost when his own car is only a basic small 3-door model.

If some of the claimant's property is lost or damaged beyond repair as a result of the defendant's negligence, the claimant is entitled to the cost of that property as part of the award of damages. But again, the claimant cannot claim the full cost of replacing the item(s) with very much more expensive ones.

18.6.3 Special and general damages

Special damages

This is the term for damages which can be calculated specifically. In other words it is the damages for pecuniary loss. This could be the cost of repairing a car, hiring a replacement, or replacing damaged clothing. It could also include

Examination questions

Having bought herself a cheap sail board, Olga decided to teach herself to windsurf on a lake near her home. After several hours' practice she began to tire and decided to have one last attempt at crossing the lake. She failed to notice Petra who was fishing from a boat on the lake. Unfortunately, Olga crashed into the boat which capsized, and Petra lost her fishing equipment, worth £3000, in the lake.

(a) Negligence requires proof of **duty**, **breach** and **damage**.

   (i) Explain, using examples, the meaning of the term **duty of care**.

   (ii) Explain, using examples, the meaning of the term **breach of duty**.

   (iii) Explain, using examples, the meaning of the term **damage**.

(b) Using the explanations given in your answers to (a), discuss whether Olga has been negligent towards Petra.

(c) Assuming Olga was found to be liable in negligence,

   (i) identify which court would hear Petra's claim and outline the procedure that would be followed before a trial:

   (ii) outline how the court would calculate an award of damages, if appropriate, to Petra in the situation given.

AQA Law Unit 2 Specimen Paper

Examiner's tip

You must know the three elements of negligence thoroughly. Questions are likely to ask you to explain at least one of these elements. They are also important in applying the law to the situation in the question.

Chapter 19

Law of Contract

A contract is an agreement that is legally binding. This means that if there is a dispute over a contract, the courts are prepared to hear the case and give a judgment on it.

In order for the courts to recognise an agreement as a contract, four main elements must be present. These are:

- an offer;
- an acceptance of that offer;
- intention to create legal relations;
- consideration.

The legal rules for each of these are considered in the next sections.

19.1 Offer

An offer is a proposition or suggestion put by one or more persons to another person or persons. The court will only recognise an offer as being a valid offer if it is intended as an offer. An example of an offer is going to a second-hand car garage and saying to the manager 'I will sell you my car for £1,500.' You have put a clear proposition to the manager. He can choose to accept this offer or reject it.

The person making the offer is called the offeror. The person to whom the offer is made is called the offeree.

19.1.1 Distinction between offer and invitation to treat

There must be a legally recognised offer, if the other person is to accept it. What is known as an invitation to treat is not recognised by the law as an offer.

An invitation to treat is where the other person is inviting you to make an offer. The other person can then consider your offer and accept or reject it. Three important situations which are <u>always</u> invitations to treat and <u>not</u> offers are:

- articles for sale on display in a shop window or on a shelf in the store;

- advertisements of items for sale in newspapers, magazines, catalogues or on the internet;
- auction sales.

Articles displayed for sale

The case of *Fisher v Bell* (1961) demonstrates that items displayed in a shop are only invitations to treat, even though there is a price marked on them. In *Fisher v Bell* a shopkeeper had a display of flick knives in his shop window with the price shown. It was held that this was not an offer. The display was an invitation to treat. In this situation a customer who went into the shop and asked to buy a flick knife would be making an offer to buy one. The sales person in the shop could accept that offer and sell the customer a knife or refuse the offer and not sell.

Items in a shop window are not an offer

Another case where it was held that displaying an item on a shelf in a shop is only an invitation to treat is *Pharmaceutical Society of Great Britain v Boots Chemist* (1953). In this case it was decided that drugs on shelves in a chemist shop were not an offer to sell those drugs. It was only inviting customers to offer to buy the drugs. In contract law it was an invitation to treat and not an offer.

This distinction is important as it means that the offer is made by the customer at the checkout and can be accepted or refused by the cashier. This decision is important for self-service stores as it means they can include items on their shelves which have by law to be supervised at the moment the contract for the sale of the item is made. The sale of drugs has to be supervised by a pharmacist. Also sales of alcoholic drinks have to be supervised at the point of the contract of sale to ensure that they are not sold to anyone under 18 years old.

If the rule in contract was that the display of goods on a shelf was an offer, then this would mean that the customer would accept the offer when he or she picked up the item. The contract for sale would be complete at that point and, in order to supervise the sale, the store would need to have a member of staff standing by every customer who picked up a bottle of wine or beer. As the law stands, the offer is made by the customer at the checkout. This decision makes it easier for stores to supervise such sales.

Magazine adverts

All adverts offering items for sale are invitations to treat. This was decided in *Partridge v Crittenden* (1968) where an advert to sell wild birds was printed in a magazine. It was held that this was not an offer but only an invitation to treat.

This decision avoids any problems that could arise if demand exceeded supply. Suppose there was an advert for 'six adorable puppies for sale at £50 each. Apply in writing to . . . '. If this was an offer, then people writing in to buy the puppies would be accepting the offer. So, if 10 people wrote on the same day, it would lead to an impossible situation of 10 contracts but only six puppies. This illustration makes it easier to see why the courts have held that the original advertisement is not an offer. It is only an invitation to treat. The person who responds to the advertisement is making the offer and the advertiser can choose whether to accept that offer or not.

This same rule applies to advertisements made in a catalogue or newspaper and also to items advertised on the Internet. The only exception is what is known as a 'reward poster'. Reward posters can be offers.

Reward posters

A reward poster is a written document which is exhibited so that people can see it. It makes an offer to pay a reward if the person seeing the poster does what is set out in the poster. The most common reward posters are to pay for the return of a missing animal, but there are other situations where it has been ruled that there was a reward poster and, therefore, an offer.

An important case on this point was *Carlill v Carbolic Smoke Ball Co* (1893). In this case a company, which made smoke balls which could be used as an inhaler, published an advertisement poster. This set out that the correct use of a smoke ball could prevent or cure a number of diseases, including influenza. The poster also stated that there was a '£100 reward' to anyone who used a smoke ball in the correct manner but still caught influenza. Mrs Carlill saw this poster, bought a smoke ball, used it as directed but unfortunately still caught 'flu.

She claimed the £100 reward money from the company but they refused to pay. She sued them for the money and the court held that the advertisement poster was an offer. This meant that Mrs Carlill had accepted that offer when she used the smoke ball. There was a contract and Mrs Carlill was entitled to the £100.

Auctions

In *Payne v Cave* (1775) it was held that an auctioneer asking for bids was not making an offer. It was only an invitation to treat. In that case at the auction, the auctioneer asked people to bid. The defendant made a bid, but then withdrew it. The auctioneer claimed that by asking for bids he, the auctioneer, had made an offer and the defendant had accepted that offer by bidding. It was held that asking for bids was only an invitation to treat. It was not an offer and so could not be accepted.

At auctions a bid made by a person at the auction is an offer. This offer can be accepted or rejected by the auctioneer. Also, as an offer can be withdrawn at any time before it is accepted, a bidder can withdraw the bid before the auctioneer accepts it by banging his hammer.

19.1.2 The terms of the offer must be certain

The offer must be certain. That means it must be definite in its terms that if it is accepted both parties know what they have agreed to. An offer to employ a secretary and 'to pay a London salary' is not certain. The salary is not definite enough.

19.1.3 Communication of offer

The offer may be communicated by any method. An offer can be in writing, spoken or even by conduct.

It is not necessary to make an offer in writing. There are many everyday contractual situations where an offer is made orally or even by conduct. An example is where someone wants to buy a pair of jeans.

This can be done by taking the jeans from the sales rack and saying to a sales person 'I'd like these jeans'. That is a verbal offer to buy the jeans at the price on the label. Or it is possible to make an offer without saying anything. This happens where the customer takes the jeans to the checkout and places them on the counter by the till without speaking. Placing the item on the checkout desk is an offer to buy those jeans. In fact the contract can be completed without anyone speaking when the checkout operator accepts the offer by ringing up the price of the jeans on the till.

A common example of making an offer by conduct is at an auction. The person making the bid (offer) will do so by nodding their head or raising a hand or making another signal to show that they are bidding.

The offer can be to anyone

An offer can be made to one specific individual or to a group of people or to the whole world. The person making the offer decides whether to make an offer to only one person or to more than one. For example, if Adam offers to sell his car to Brian for £2,000 and Chris overhears this, the offer has only been made to Brian. Chris cannot accept that offer: it was not made to him.

However, if Adam says to a group of friends, which include Brian and Chris, 'Do any of you want to buy my car for £2,000?', then anyone in the group can accept the offer.

It is also possible to make an offer to the whole world, so that anyone who wishes can accept the offer. This was the position in *Carlill v Carbolic Smoke Ball Co* (1893) (see section 19.1.1) where the advertisement poster was an offer to anyone who read it. Mrs Carlill read it and so could accept the offer.

The offer must be communicated before it is effective

The person doing the conduct needed to accept the offer must know about the offer when he does that conduct. For example, if Mrs Carlill had not seen the advertisement poster offering a reward of £100 before she bought the smoke ball, then the offer would not have been communicated to her and she could not have accepted it.

Another situation would be where someone advertises a reward of £25 for the return of their lost cat. Zita sees the cat some streets away, and knows that it belongs to her friend. She takes the cat back to the owner, but has not seen the poster offering the reward of £25. The offer has not been communicated to Zita, so she cannot claim the £25, even though she has returned the cat.

Offers sent by post

If an offer is sent by post, then it is communicated when it arrives.

19.1.4 Duration of offer

If the offeror sets a time limit for the acceptance of the offer, the offer only exists during the set times. For example, if the offeror says that the offer must be accepted by next Monday, then the offer only exists until Monday. If someone tries to accept it on Tuesday it is too late; the offer no longer exists.

If the offeror does not set a time limit then the offer remains open for a reasonable time. What is reasonable will depend on the type of offer. If it is an offer to buy fresh food, then the courts would probably hold that it was only open for a few days. Where the offer is for more long lasting items then the offer will remain in existence for longer, but it is unlikely to be held that it exists indefinitely.

In *Ramsgate Victoria Hotel Co Lt v Montefiore* (1866) Montefiore offered in June to buy shares which a company was going to issue. The issue of the shares did not happen until November. It was held that Montefiore's offer to buy the shares had lapsed.

19.1.5 Revocation of offer

The person making the offer (the offeror) can withdraw the offer at any time before it is accepted. This is known as revocation of the offer. This is what happened in *Payne v Cave* (1775) (see above) where the bidder withdrew his bid (offer) before the auctioneer accepted it.

However the person to whom the offer has been made (the offeree) must know that the offer has been revoked. This caused problems in *Byrne v van Tienhoven* (1880). In this case the defendants, who were in England, wrote on 1st October offering to sell 1000 boxes of tinplate to the claimants, who were in New York. This offer arrived at the claimants on 11th October. The defendants then changed their mind and wrote on 8th October revoking their offer. This letter

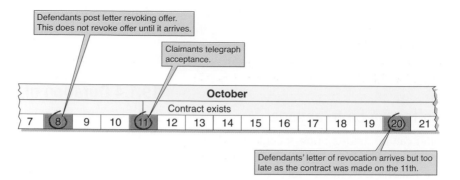

Figure 19.1 *Byrne v van Tienhoven* (1880) date sequence

Defendants post letter revoking offer. This does not revoke offer until it arrives.

Claimants telegraph acceptance.

Defendants' letter of revocation arrives but too late as the contract was made on the 11th.

arrived at the claimants' office in New York on 20th October. In the meantime the claimants telegraphed their acceptance of the offer on 11th October.

This made it important to decide on which date the offer ceased to exist. Was it on the 8th when the letter of revocation was posted or was it on the 20th when the letter of revocation arrived

at the claimants' office. The court decided that the revocation was on the 20th when the letter arrived. So the offer was still in existence on the 11th when the claimants accepted it and there was a contract between the parties.

This complicated date sequence is easier to understand by showing it in diagram form – see Figure 19.1.

Activity

1. Anya receives a mail order catalogue from Look Smart Ltd advertising clothes. Anya orders a pair of combat trousers costing £40. Two weeks later she receives a letter from Look Smart Ltd, returning her cheque and telling her that they do not have the combat trousers in her size.

   Anya believes Look Smart Ltd are in breach of contract.

   Advise Anya.

2. Brendan finds a dog running loose in the street about 5 miles from his home. When he looks at the name tag on the dog's collar, he realises it is his neighbour, Cassie's dog that has been missing for two days. He takes the dog back to Cassie. As Brendan is leaving Cassie's house he sees a notice in her window saying that she will pay £100 for the safe return of the dog. Brendan immediately goes back to Cassie and demands the £100. Cassie refuses to pay.

   Advise Brendan whether he is legally entitled to claim the £100.

3. Darvinder offers to sell a painting to Emily for £600. Emily says she likes the painting but can only afford to pay £500. Darvinder says he will not accept £500. Emily then agrees to pay the full price of £600. Darvinder refuses to sell the painting to her.

   Advise Emily as to whether she has a contract to buy the painting at £600.

4. Ferdinand buys Zap-clean, a new brand of stain remover. Ferdinand has seen an advertisement which states: 'Zap-clean will remove all ink stains. £25 will be paid if it fails to work for you.' Ferdinand uses Zap-clean according to instructions but it does not remove the ink stains from his shirt.

   Advise Ferdinand whether he has a legal claim to the £25.

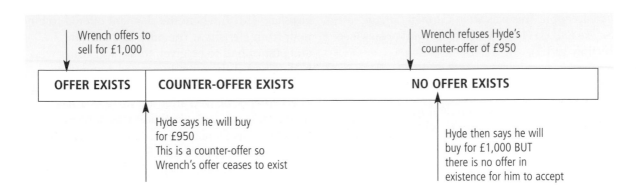

Figure 19.2 Time line of *Hyde v Wrench* (1840)

19.1.6 Rejection of offer

An offer also ceases when it is rejected. So let's look at the example where Adam offers to sell his car to Brian for £2,000. If Brian says no, he does not want to buy the car, then the offer ceases at the moment he says no. If Brian changes his mind and the next day tells Adam that he does want to buy the car, there is no offer for him to accept so there is no contract.

What has happened is that Brian is now making an offer of his own to Adam to buy the car and Adam can accept or reject that offer.

19.1.7 Counter-offer

An offer also ceases to exist if the offeree makes a counter-offer rather than accepting the original offer. For example, in the scenario above, if Brian instead of saying no, had said 'I'll give you £1,800 for the car', this is a counter-offer. Its effect is the same as a rejection: it puts an end to the offer.

A situation like this happened in *Hyde v Wrench* (1840) where the defendant offered to sell his farm for £1,000. The claimant initially counter-offered to buy it for £950. The defendant refused this counter-offer. The claimant then said he would buy the farm for the original asking price of £1,000. The claimant claimed that there was a contract as he had now agreed to the original price.

The court decided that the counter-offer of £950 terminated the offer, so there was no offer in existence when the claimant agreed to pay the original price. Therefore there was no contract.

Figure 19.2 shows this sequence as a time line.

19.2 Acceptance

An acceptance is an agreement to an offer. In order to form a contract, the acceptance must agree to all the terms of the offer. If the acceptance does not agree to all the terms, it is a counter-offer and not an acceptance. We have already seen this in *Hyde v Wrench* (1840) (see section 19.1.7).

However, a person can ask for more information before deciding to accept the offer. This is what happened in *Stevenson v McLean* (1880). The defendant offered to sell iron to the claimant, the offer to remain open until the next Monday. The claimant replied by asking if he might buy the goods on credit. He did not receive a reply from the defendant so on Monday, Stevenson telegraphed a full acceptance. The court held that asking if he could buy the goods on credit was a mere request for information, so the offer remained open and was accepted when the defendant received the telegram on the Monday.

An acceptance must be by the person to whom the offer was made. Another person who hears the offer made cannot try to accept it as the offer was not to them. However, there are situations in which the offer is to the whole world, so any one can accept it. This was so in *Carlill v Carbolic Smoke Ball Co* (1893) with the reward poster (see section 19.1.1).

19.2.1 Method of acceptance

The person who makes the offer can set out a specific way for the offer to be accepted. For example, an offeror may say that the acceptance has to be in writing or that it has to be made in person.

If there is a specific way in which the acceptance has to be made, then only that method will do. This is shown in *Eliason v*

Henshaw (1819) where the claimant offered to buy flour from Henshaw. The offer said that the acceptance had to be given to the waggoner who had delivered the offer. Instead of doing this, Henshaw sent his acceptance by post. The letter of acceptance arrived after the waggoner had returned. The court held that it was not a valid acceptance as Henshaw had not communicated by the method specified by Eliason.

If there is no prescribed way of communicating the acceptance then any effective method will do. The important point is that the method must be effective. For example, if a person telephones the offeror to accept the offer and, just as he is saying

Key facts

	Comment	Cases
Offer	A proposition or suggestion put by one or more persons to another person or persons	
Must be an offer NOT an invitation to treat	The following are only invitations to treat: ● items in a shop window ● goods on shelves in a self-service shop ● adverts in magazines, catalogues etc ● auctions	*Fisher v Bell* *Pharmaceutical Society of Great Britain v Boots Chemist* *Partridge v Crittenden* *Payne v Cave*
An offer can be to the whole world		*Carlill v Carbolic Smoke Ball Co*
The offer must be communicated	If a person is unaware of the offer, then they cannot later claim they have accepted it	
Duration of offer	If the offeror sets a time limit, then the offer ceases at the end of that time If there is no set time, the offer will be open for a reasonable time	*Ramsgate Victoria Hotel Co Lt v Montefiore*
Rejection of offer	An offer ceases to exist if it is rejected, it cannot be later accepted	
Revocation of offer	The offer ceases when the revocation of the offer is communicated	*Byrne v van Tienhoven*
Counter offer	If the offeree makes a counter offer, the original offer ceases to exist	*Hyde v Wrench*

Figure 19.3 Key Facts chart on offer

that he accepts, the telephone line goes dead so that the offeror does not hear the acceptance, then this is not effective acceptance.

19.2.2 Communication of acceptance

The normal rule is that acceptance must be communicated to the offeror. However, the offer can set out that it can be accepted by communication to another person who is acting as agent for the offeror.

Silence

It is not possible to accept an offer by staying silent. This was illustrated in *Felthouse v Bindley* (1862) where the defendant had had a discussion about the possibility of the uncle buying a horse from the nephew for either £30 or 30 guineas (£30.75). The uncle then wrote to his nephew and stated, 'if I hear no more about it I will consider the horse to be mine'. The nephew did not reply but ordered the auctioneer to withdraw the horse from open sale. By error the horse was auctioned and Felthouse sued, claiming that he had a contract with his nephew to buy the horse. It was held that as the nephew had not communicated acceptance of the offer, there was no contract.

19.2.3 Postal rules on acceptance

Postal acceptance is an exception to the rule that acceptance must be communicated effectively. If the use of the post is a reasonable method of accepting, then the acceptance is assumed to have been made at the moment it is posted. This is a very old rule and is illustrated in the case of *Adams v Lindsell* (1818).

On 2 September 1817 the defendants wrote to the claimant offering to sell some wool and requiring an answer in the 'course of post'. Because the letter making the offer was incorrectly addressed, it did not arrive until 5 September. That same evening, the claimant posted his letter of acceptance. This arrived on 9 September. In the normal course a reply would have been expected on 7 September. So, on 8 September, the defendants sold the wool to someone else.

It was held that a contract between the claimant and the defendants came into being on 5 September when the claimant posted his letter of acceptance. This meant that the defendants were in breach of contract when they sold the wool to someone else on 8 September.

The sequence of events is set out as a time line in Figure 19.4.

Posting means placing the letter of acceptance in a post box or into the hands of a Post Office employee authorised to receive letters. Handing a letter to a postman authorised only to deliver letters is not 'posting' and so does not count as a valid acceptance at that point. It can, however, become a valid acceptance when it is received by the offeror.

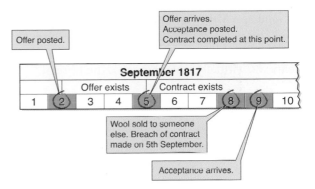

Figure 19.4 Time line for the case of *Adams v Lindsell* (1818)

Letter lost in the post

In *Household Fire Insurance v Grant* (1879) it was decided that even if the letter was lost in the post the postal rule on acceptance would still apply. In this case Grant had made a written offer to purchase shares in a company. A written notice of acceptance was posted to him, but this was never received by him. When the company went into liquidation, Grant claimed that he was not a shareholder as he had never received the acceptance of his offer to buy, and that he was not therefore liable for the value of the shares. It was held that the acceptance was effective when it had been posted. Grant had become a shareholder even though he did not know it.

Test Yourself

1. What is the difference between an offer and an invitation to treat?
2. Give two examples of invitations to treat.
3. Do offers have to be in writing?
4. If an offer is sent by post when is it communicated?
5. Give two ways in which an offer can be revoked.
6. What is a counter-offer and what effect does it have on the original offer?
7. When is an acceptance normally communicated to the person making the offer?
8. Can silence be an acceptance of an offer?
9. What is the rule on an acceptance which is sent by post?
10. If an acceptance is sent by email, when will it be considered to have been communicated to the person making the offer?

19.2.4 Modern methods of communication

In *Entores v Miles Far East* (1955) the dispute was over communication of an acceptance by telex. It was decided that transmission and receipt of a telex was virtually instantaneous. The normal rules of communication of acceptance applied. This meant that a telex was communicated when it arrived. However, in *Brinkibon Ltd v Stahag Stahl* (1982) the situation was that a telex had been received out of office hours. The House of Lords held that the acceptance took effect at the start of the next working day.

Activity

1. Sandeesh emails Tina offering to sell her some jewellery. Sandeesh asks Tina to let her know if she wants the jewellery by 6pm the next day (Tuesday). Tina is having problems with her computer and cannot access her email until Wednesday. When she reads Sandeesh's email she immediately emails back that she will buy the jewellery.

   Advise Sandeesh if she has to let Tina have the jewellery.

2. On Wednesday Victor writes to Umberto offering to sell him an antique clock for £700. Umberto receives the letter on Friday and immediately writes and posts a letter agreeing to buy the clock. On Sunday, while at an antique fair, Victor is offered £800 for the clock by Xavier. As Victor has not heard from Umberto he sells the clock to Xavier.

   On Monday morning Victor telephones Umberto and leaves a message on his answer phone saying that the clock is no longer for sale. Umberto listens to the message that evening. On Tuesday morning Victor receives Umberto's letter.

   Explain to Umberto whether or not he has a contract to buy the clock

3. Yuri and Zahir have had several discussions about the possibility of Yuri buying Zahir's motorbike. In their last discussion they look at an advert for another bike which is exactly the same as Zahir's which is advertised at £1,750. They agree this would be a fair price for such a bike. Later that evening, Zahir texts Yuri saying 'Happy to sell at £1,750. If you don't text back, I assume you will buy'. Yuri does not reply to the text.

   Advise Zahir whether or not he has a contract to sell the bike to Yuri at £1,750.

Key facts

	Comment	Cases
Acceptance	Is an agreement to the offer	
It must agree to all the terms of the offer	If it does not, then it is a counter offer	*Hyde v Wrench*
A request for information is not an acceptance	Nor is it a counter offer: the offer remains in existence	*Stevenson v McLean*
Only the person(s) to whom the offer was made can accept it	If the offer was to the whole world then anyone can accept it	*Carlill v Carbolic Smoke Ball Co*
The offeror can set down a specific method of making the acceptance	If the offeree does not use this method then the acceptance is not effective	*Eliason v Henshaw*
Silence is not an acceptance		*Felthouse v Bindley*
Postal acceptance	If the use of the post is a reasonable method of acceptance the acceptance is effective when it is posted	*Adams v Lindsell*
	The acceptance is effective even if it is lost in the post and not received by the offeror	*Household Fire Insurance v Grant*
Electronic means of acceptance	Acceptance by electronic means (fax email) takes place when the acceptance arrives	*Entores v Miles Far East*
	But if the fax or email arrives out of office hours then the acceptance is effective at the start of the next working day	*Brinkibon Ltd v Stahag Stahl*

Figure 19.5 Key Facts chart on acceptance

The same principles will apply to acceptance by email or fax. That is, the acceptance is normally communicated when it arrives. But if the communication is to a business and it arrives out of office hours, it will be communicated at the start of the next working day.

19.3 Intention to create legal relations

There are some agreements where, even though there is a valid offer and acceptance and consideration (see section 19.4), the courts may still decide that the agreement is not enforceable.

This is because at the time the parties made their agreement they did not intend it to be legally binding. In order to decide whether an agreement was intended to be legally binding the courts have different rules for social/domestic agreements and for business/commercial agreements.

19.3.1 Commercial agreements

If the agreement is a business one, then the courts start by presuming that the agreement is legally binding. This means that the courts assume that the parties intended to enter into a legally binding contract, unless there is evidence to the contrary.

In *McGowan v Radio Buxton* (2001) the claimant entered a radio competition for which the prize had been stated to be a Renault Clio car. The claimant was told she had won the competition but was given a four-inch scale model of a Clio. The defendants argued that there was no legally binding contract. The judge held that there was intention to create legal relations. The claimant had entered the competition as a member of the public and that 'looking at the transcript of the broadcast, there was not even a hint that the car would be a toy'.

However, if one of the parties can show that this was not meant to be the situation, then the court may decide that there is not a binding contract. This occurred in *Rose & Frank Co. v Crompton* (1925) where the parties had included in their written agreement the words 'this agreement is not entered into as a formal or legal agreement and shall not be subject to legal jurisdiction in the law courts'. It was held that these words made it quite clear that the parties had not intended their agreement to be a legally binding contract.

The courts have also held that using the words 'binding in honour only' means that the agreement is not intended to be legally binding. This phrase is usually used on football pools entry forms. This means that when a person enters the football pools competition, he is agreeing that there is no legally binding contract between him and the pools company. This means that if he correctly forecasts the results of the football matches, the company is not obliged to pay him any winnings. The person cannot sue the company as the words *binding in honour only* show there is no intention to enter in to legal relations. This happened in *Appleson v Littlewood Pools* (1939).

19.3.2 Social and domestic agreements

Where the agreement is between family members the courts start by presuming that it was not intended to be legally binding. An example is *Balfour v Balfour* (1919) where a husband, who worked in Sri Lanka, agreed to pay his wife £30 a month when she was unable to go to Sri Lanka with him due to illness. When the husband stopped paying the £30, the wife was not able to enforce the agreement in the courts. It was held it was a purely domestic arrangement and the parties, when the agreement was made, did not intend it to be a legally binding contract.

Similarly, in *Jones v Padavatton* (1969) a daughter was unable to enforce an agreement with her mother. The daughter had agreed to give up her highly paid job in New York and study to become a barrister in England. The mother promised to give the daughter an allowance during her studies. The daughter found it difficult to manage on the allowance, so the mother bought a house for her to live in part of it and let the other part for extra income. When the mother and daughter later quarrelled, the mother sought to repossess the house. The daughter's case was that the agreement over the house was legally binding: the courts held that it was not: there was no intent to create legal relations.

However, if one of the parties can show that the agreement was intended to be legally binding then the courts will accept that and there will be a valid contract. This happened in *Merritt v Merritt* (1970) where a husband had deserted his wife for another woman. The husband and wife agreed that the husband would pay income to the wife if she paid the mortgage on their former

Key facts

	Comment	Cases
Business agreement	Presumption that the parties DO intend to be legally bound	*McGowan v Radio Buxton*
	If there is evidence that the parties did NOT intend to be legally bound, the court will NOT enforce the contract	*Rose & Frank Co. v Crompton*
	Binding in honour only means that it is not intended as a legally binding contract	*Appleson v Littlewood Pools*
Domestic or social agreement	Presumption that the parties do NOT intend to be legally bound	*Balfour v Balfour* *Jones v Padavatton*
	If there is evidence that the parties DID intend to be legally bound, the court will enforce the contract	*Merritt v Merritt* *Simpkin v Pays*

Figure 19.6 Key Facts chart on intention to create legal relations

home. It was held that this was intended to be a legally binding agreement.

Also in *Simpkin v Pays* (1955) the defendant, her granddaughter and the claimant, who was a lodger in the house, jointly entered a competition. The entry, which was sent in under the defendant's name, won £750, but the defendant refused to give the claimant any of the prize money. She sued for one-third of the prize and the court held that the arrangement had been intended as a legally binding contract, so she could get her share.

Chapter 1 at Source E shows an article about an agreement to enter the lottery. A court case was started, but the parties settled the case, so the court did not have to make a decision.

Activity

Read Source E on page 5 and decide if there was a legally binding agreement or not. Explain your reasons for your answer.

19.4 Consideration

Consideration is what the parties put into the contract. It is what they contribute to the bargain. Both parties must contribute something to the agreement. It must be certain: a vague promise is not enough. It must be real and have some value, though that value can be very small.

Clear examples of good consideration are:

- money;
- goods;
- performing a service;
- stopping doing something.

19.4.1 Nature of consideration

The consideration has to be real. It must have some value, but it need not match the 'value' put in by the other person. An example of the value not matching is in this invented scenario. If Matt promises to pay Nina £100 if she will give him a can of lager, then both are contributing something to the bargain. There is real consideration from both parties. Nina is going to give Matt a can of lager and Matt is going to pay Nina £100 for it. It does not matter that the value of the lager is much less than £100.

This point was considered in *Chappell & Co v Nestle Ltd* (1960). The House of Lords held that three chocolate bar wrappers could be valuable consideration in the situation where a customer sent in the three wrappers (and money) in return for a music record.

Also, in *Thomas v Thomas* (1842) a husband, before his death, expressed the wish that his wife should be allowed to remain in their home. He had not put this into his will but, when he died, his executors carried out this wish and charged the widow a nominal ground rent of £1 a year. Later the executors tried to get the widow out of the house. It was held that the £1 she was paying was consideration and there was a valid contract between the executors and the widow.

So, if the parties are agreed on the matter, it does not matter that the consideration is of very low value, provided it is tangible and has some value.

19.4.2 Intangible matters cannot be good consideration

The consideration must be real and tangible. In *White v Bluett* (1853) it was held that there was no consideration. In this case a son owed his father money. When the father died his executors tried to recover the debt. The son claimed that he did not have to pay the debt as he had had an agreement with his father that the debt would be forgotten in return for the son's promise not to complain about the distribution of the father's assets in his will. The court held that the son's promise was too intangible to be consideration, so he had to pay the debt to the executors.

However, in the case of *Ward v Bytham* (1956) it was held that a promise to keep a child well looked after and happy was good consideration. The child's father had promised the mother money towards the upkeep of the child if she would keep the child 'well looked after and happy'. When the father stopped paying the mother sued him for the money. The father argued that the mother was doing no more than

Activity

1. Louie needs a law textbook for his course. The local bookshop has run out and so Louie asks a fellow student, Monique, who has a car, if she will drive to the bookshop in the next town and get the book. Monique does this and when she returns gives the book to Louie. He gives Monique the cost of the book and says that when he gets his wages for his weekend work, he will pay her another £10 for the cost of her petrol. Louie does not pay Monique the £10.

   Advise Monique whether there is a legally enforceable agreement in respect of the £10.

2. Nigella rents a flat belonging to Omar. Nigella redecorates all the rooms. Omar is pleased when he sees the rooms and promises Nigella that he will pay her £40 towards the cost of the paint. Two months later Omar has still not paid the £40 to Nigella.

   Advise Nigella whether she is entitled to claim it from Omar.

3. Paul wants his son, Richard, to give up smoking. Paul promises to buy Richard a motorbike, costing £4,000, if Richard does not smoke for two months. Richard does stop smoking for two months, but his father then says the motorbike is too expensive and gives him £500 instead.

   Advise Richard whether he can claim the extra cost of the bike.

Key facts

	Comment	Cases
Consideration	What the parties put into the contract: what they contribute to the bargain	
Consideration must have some value	But the parties' consideration need not match in value	*Chappell & Co v Nestle Ltd* *Thomas v Thomas*
Consideration must be tangible	A promise not to complain about the distribution of the father's assets was NOT good consideration	*White v Bluett*
	A promise to keep a child happy was good consideration	*Ward v Bytham*
Past consideration	This is NOT good consideration *Exception* If one party has asked the other to act and later promised to pay this may be good consideration	*Re McArdle* *Lampleigh v Braithwaite*

Figure 19.7 Key Facts chart on consideration

she was already obliged to do in looking after her child. The court was prepared to enforce the agreement since there is no obligation in law to keep a child happy. The promise to do this was good consideration.

19.4.3 Past consideration

Where the thing that you are offering to put into the contract has already occurred, then it cannot be good consideration for a contract you make now.

This is shown by *Re McArdle* (1951) in which a widow had been left a house for her to live in during her lifetime. She repaired and decorated the property. After she had done this her children, who were the ultimate beneficiaries (that is they were to inherit the house when the widow died) promised to pay towards the improvements. But they did not keep this promise. It was decided that the payment could not be claimed as the widow had already finished the work when the promise was made. This meant that it was in the past when the agreement was made. It was not, therefore, good consideration.

There is an exception to this rule. This occurs when one party has asked the other to act and, although payment is not specifically mentioned at the time, it is implied that the work or service will be paid for. If the other party later promises payment for what has just been done at his request, then the courts will enforce that promise. This idea comes from the old case of *Lampleigh v Braithwaite* (1615).

In that case Braithwaite, who had been tried and sentenced to death, asked Lampleigh to travel to the King and seek a pardon for him. Lampleigh did this successfully. Braithwaite was so pleased that he promised to pay Lampleigh £100. He failed to make this payment and Lampleigh sued him. The court decided that Lampleigh should receive the money even though he had already got the pardon for Braithwaite when the promise was made. This was because he acted at Braithwaite's request.

19.5 Breach of contract

Breach of contract can be either an actual breach or an anticipatory breach.

An actual breach of contract occurs where one party either fails to perform his or her side of the contract or performs it improperly. An anticipatory breach is where one party is due to perform their part of the contract in the future and, before the date for performance, they inform the other party they will not be performing the contract.

19.5.1 Actual breach

An actual breach can be either through:

- non-performance or
- improper performance.

Non-performance

An obvious example of this is where one party is due to sing at a concert and will be paid by the other party for this. If the singer fails to come to the concert, then this is an actual breach.

There can also be an actual breach where it is not quite so obvious. An example is the case of *Pilbrow v Pearless de Rougemont & Co* (1998). In this case a man arranged to see a solicitor for advice on a legal point. When he went to the solicitor's office, his case was not dealt with by a solicitor (or even by a legal executive). When he realised the case had not been handled by a solicitor, the man refused to pay the full bill. The solicitors' firm sued him for the balance of the bill. The Court of Appeal held that the contract was to provide the services of a solicitor. So, even though the advice was correct, there was an actual breach of contract. The contract had not been performed.

Improper performance

This occurs where the contract is performed but not quite as agreed in the contract. An example is *Bunge Corporation v Tradax Export SA* (1981) where a buyer was required by the contract to give at least 15 days' notice of readiness to load a ship. In

fact the buyer only gave 13 days' notice. This was improper performance of the contract.

19.5.2 Anticipatory breach

In some contracts there is an agreement to do something in the future, for example a band may agree to perform at a rock festival on 15 June next year. If, in April, two months before they are due to perform the band splits up and says that they will not do the concert, this is an anticipatory breach. The contract is not due to be performed until 15 June but the other person need not wait until then to claim for breach of contract. He can claim once it has been made clear that the band will not perform, that is in anticipation of the breach.

A case example is *Hochster v de la Tour* (1853) where a man was hired to work as a courier. The work was due to start two months after the contract was made. One month after the making of the contract, the defendants wrote to the man cancelling the contract. This was an anticipatory breach of contract and the man was entitled to sue the defendants straight away.

An important point in anticipatory breach cases is that the innocent party can sue for breach of contract immediately once the breach has occurred. It is not necessary to wait until the date the contract was due to be performed.

19.6 Compensatory damages

If there is a breach of contract, the innocent party can sue in the courts for damages. Being awarded damages means that the court states the amount of money that the defendant must pay the successful claimant. The aim is to place the claimant in the same position as if the contract had not been broken. The court is compensating the claimant for his loss.

Loss

Take the example where the claimant had a contract to buy parts for use in machines he was making and the defendant failed to deliver the parts. As a result, the claimant had to buy the parts at a higher price from another supplier. Here the loss is the difference in price between the price in the contract with the defendant and the higher price that the claimant had to pay.

Loss can arise in various ways. If you look at the case of *Stansbie v Troman* (1948) in the next section (19.6.1), you will see that the loss was the value of goods stolen as a result of the defendant's breach of contract. In *Anglia Television v Reed* (1972) (see section 19.6.2) the loss was the cost of doing preparatory work for a television film. While in *Victoria Laundry v Newman Industries Ltd* (1948) (see section 19.6.2), the loss was loss of profits.

19.6.1 Causation

This is a question of fact as to whether the breach has been the main cause of the loss.

If the loss arises partly from the breach and partly as the result of intervening events, the party in breach may still be liable provided that the chain of causation is not broken.

In *Stansbie v Troman* (1948) a decorator was entrusted with the keys to the premises where he had a contract to decorate. When he left the premises unlocked a thief entered and stole property. It was held that the decorator was liable for the loss as it had resulted from his failure to comply with his contractual duty to lock the premises when he left.

19.6.2 Remoteness of damage

The law does not allow a claim for loss which is considered to be too remote a consequence of the breach. This rule comes from *Hadley v Baxendale* (1854). The claimant owned a mill and ordered a new driving shaft for it. This was to be delivered by the defendant. The defendant was late in delivering the shaft and the claimant sued for breach of contract.

The claimant tried to claim for loss of profit as the mill had been out of action while waiting for the new shaft. It was held that as the defendant did not know that the mill could not operate without the shaft, the loss of profits was too remote.

The case decided that damages should be awarded where:

(a) they arose naturally from the breach of the contract; or
(b) they were reasonably in contemplation of both parties when the contract was made.

If the mill owner had told the defendant that a quick delivery was necessary because the mill could not operate without the shaft, then he would have been able to claim his loss of profit. The loss of profit would have been 'reasonably in contemplation of both parties'.

In *Anglia Television v Reed* (1972) an American actor made a contract with the claimants to play the leading role in a television film. The claimants had already spent money on preparing for the filming and after the contract was made they spent more. The actor then broke the contract and the claimants were unable to find a suitable replacement.

The TV company sued the defendant, claiming all the wasted money, including that spent before he had entered into the contract. The court ordered the defendant to pay for all the cost of preparation. The court said that the actor must have contemplated that, if he broke the contract, all the money spent would be wasted, whether it was spent before or after the contract.

In *Victoria Laundry v Newman Industries Ltd* (1948) part of the damage was foreseeable and part was not. The claimants ordered a new boiler from the defendants. The defendants were five months late in delivering the boiler and the claimants sued them for loss of profits during that five months. The court held that they could claim for loss of normal profits during this time as these were reasonably foreseeable.

However, they could not claim for loss of extra profits which would have been made from special dyeing contracts. They had not told the defendants about these contracts and the defendants could not have been expected to foresee this extra loss.

Test Yourself

1. What is the presumption about intention to create legal relations in:
   (a) a commercial agreement
   (b) a domestic agreement?
2. What words can be used in a commercial agreement to show that it is not intended to be legally binding?
3. Give an example/case of a domestic agreement where it was held that the parties did <u>not</u> intend to create legal relations.
4. Give an example/case of a domestic agreement where it was held that the parties <u>did</u> intend to create legal relations.
5. Explain what is meant by consideration in a contract?

6. Does the consideration given by one side in the contract have to match in value the consideration given by the other side? Give a case or example to illustrate your answer.
7. What is meant by past consideration? Give a case or example to illustrate your answer.
8. Are there any circumstances in which past consideration can be good consideration?
9. What is an 'anticipatory breach' of contract?
10. Give an example of when damage caused by breach of contract may be too remote to claim for.

19.6.3 Mitigation of loss

Where there has been a breach of contract, the innocent party must take reasonable steps to minimise his loss. This is known as mitigation of loss.

If a contract is to buy goods and the defendant fails to deliver the goods, the claimant must try to find an alternative source. If he can, then his loss is the extra cost of the replacement goods together with any loss of profit while searching for the replacements. If the claimant cannot find suitable replacements, then any loss of profit or other expenses caused by the breach can be claimed.

In *British Westinghouse and Manufacturing Co Ltd v Underground Electric Railways of London Ltd* (1912) British Westinghouse had contracted to supply turbines to Underground Electric Railways. When the turbines were delivered it was found that they did not match the specifications in the contract. As a result Underground Electric Railways had to replace them by buying more expensive turbines from another supplier.

Normally, it would be possible to claim the extra cost of having to buy turbines from another supplier. In fact the new turbines were so efficient

that they saved money on running them and this soon paid for the difference in price. The court held that only losses caused before the new turbines were installed could be claimed. There was no loss after their installation.

Anticipatory breach

Where there is an anticipatory breach, the innocent party has a choice. We have already seen (in section 19.5.2) that they can immediately consider the contract at an end and sue for damages.

Alternatively they can choose to continue with the contract and continue to fulfil their obligations under it. In this situation they can claim for loss caused after the other party breached the contract.

In *White and Carter Ltd v McGregor* (1962) the defendant owned a garage and entered into a contract for advertising of his business to be placed on litterbins for a local council for a three-year period. Later the same day he changed his mind and told the claimants that he did not want the adverts. The claimants could have claimed anticipatory breach and sued the defendant at that point, but they did not. Instead they chose to go on with the contract and prepare the adverts.

The House of Lords held that the claimants were entitled to claim the cost of all the work on the adverts, even though the cost of it had been incurred after the defendant told them he was not going ahead with the contract.

19.7 Starting a court case

In Unit 1 (see Chapter 6) you will have learnt that the two civil courts are:

- The County Court
- The High Court.

Most people who have been injured do not want to start a court case unless they have to. They will first of all try to negotiate an agreed settlement with the other party to the contract. The vast majority of cases are settled and do not go to court.

19.7.1 Alternative Dispute Resolution (ADR)

Using the courts to resolve disputes can be costly, in terms of both money and time. It can also be traumatic for the individuals involved and may not lead to the most satisfactory outcome for the case. It is not surprising, therefore, that more and more people are trying other methods for resolving their disputes.

Alternative methods are referred to as 'ADR', which stands for 'Alternative Dispute Resolution', and include any method of resolving a dispute without resorting to using the courts. There are many different methods which can be used, ranging from very informal negotiations between the parties to a comparatively formal arbitration hearing. The main methods of ADR are:

- negotiation
- mediation
- conciliation
- arbitration.

These are explained more fully in Chapter 7.

19.7.2 Which court to use

If the other person denies liability or refuses to use ADR, then the only way to get damages of another remedy for the breach of contract will be to start a court case.

Once the decision is made to go to court, then the first problem is which court to use. The court to be used will depend on the amount that is being claimed. If the amount claimed is £25,000 or less then the case must be started in the County Court. If the claim is more than £25,000 then the claimant can choose whether to start the case in the County Court or the High Court. If the case is started in the High Court, then it will be in the Queen's Bench Division of the High Court. These limits are shown in Figure 19.8.

19.7.3 Issuing a claim

If you are using the County Court, then you can choose to issue the claim in any of the 230 or so County Courts in the country. If you are using the High Court, then you can go to one of the 20 District Registries or the main court in London. You need a claim form called 'N1' (see section 18.4.4). The court office will give you notes explaining how to fill in the form.

Court staff can help to make sure that you have filled in the claim form properly, or you may get help from advice centres or a Citizens' Advice Bureau. Once the form is filled in you should photocopy it so that you have a copy for the court, a copy for yourself and a copy for each defendant. Then take the form to the court office. A court fee for issuing the claim has to be paid. This fee varies according to how much the claim is for.

In 2007 the fee for a claim of up to £300 was £30 with the maximum fee for a small claim (under £5,000) being £108. Claims of £5,000 to £15,000 had a fee of £225, while at the top end of the scale claims of over £300,000 had a fee of £1,530.

@ Internet Research

Look up court forms such as N1 on the website www.courtservice.gov.uk.

Also use that website to find guidance on starting cases in the County Court.

19.7.4 Defending a claim

When the defendant receives the claim form there are several routes which can be taken. They may admit the claim and pay the full amount. Where this happens the case ends. The claimant has achieved what was wanted. In other cases the defendant may dispute the claim. If the defendant wishes to defend the claim, he or she must send either an acknowledgement of service (Form N9) or a defence to the court within 14 days of receiving the claim. If only an acknowledgement of service is sent, then the defendant has an extra 14 days in which to serve the defence.

If the defendant does not do either of these things, then the claimant can ask the court to make an order that the defendant pays the money and costs claimed. This is called an order in default.

Once a claim is defended the court will allocate the case to the most suitable 'track' or way of dealing with the case.

19.7.5 The three tracks

The decision on which track should be used is made by the District Judge in the County Court or the Master (a procedural judge) in the High Court. To help the judge consider to which track a claim should be allocated, both parties are sent an allocation questionnaire. If it is thought necessary, the judge can allocate a case to a track that normally deals with claims of a higher value. Alternatively, if the parties agree, the judge can allocate a case to a lower-value track.

There are three tracks and these are:

1. **The small claims track**
   This is normally used for disputes under £5,000, except for personal injury cases where the limit is usually £1,000.

   Small claims cases are usually heard in private, but they can be heard in an ordinary court. The procedure allows the District Judge to be flexible in the way he hears the case. District Judges are given training in how to handle small claims cases, so that they will take an active part in the proceedings, asking questions and making sure that both parties explain all their important points. The parties are encouraged to represent themselves. In fact they cannot claim the cost of using a lawyer from the other side, even if they win the case.

2. **The fast track**
   This is used for straightforward disputes of £5,000 to £25,000. Fast track means that the court will set down a very strict timetable for the pre-trial matters. This is aimed at preventing one or both sides from wasting time and running up unnecessary costs.

   Once a case is set down for hearing, the aim is to have the case heard within 30 weeks. The actual trial will usually be heard by a Circuit Judge and take place in open court with a more formal procedure than for small claims. In order to speed up the trial itself, the hearing will be limited to a maximum of one day and the number of expert witnesses restricted, with usually only one expert being allowed.

3. **The multi-track**
   This is for cases over £25,000 or for complex cases under this amount. The case will be heard by a Circuit Judge who will also be expected to 'manage' the case from the moment it is allocated to the multi-track route.

Amount claimed	Court	
Up to £5,000	County Court	Will usually be dealt with as a small claim
£5,000 to £25,000	County Court	Will usually be dealt with as a fast track case
Over £25,000	County Court or High Court (Queen's Bench Division)	In either court it will be dealt with as a multi-track case

Figure 19.8 Case chart for damage and remoteness

19.7.6 Case management

Under the Civil Procedure Rules judges are expected to manage a case. Case management by judges includes:

- Identifying the issues at an early stage;
- Deciding which issues need investigation and trial;
- Encouraging the parties to use alternative dispute resolution if this is appropriate;
- Dealing with any procedural steps without the need for the parties to attend court;
- Giving directions to ensure that the trial of a case proceeds quickly and efficiently;
- Fixing timetables by which the different stages of the case must be completed.

This is all aimed at keeping the costs of the case as low as possible and making sure that it is heard reasonably quickly.

In all civil cases the judge has to decide if the claim is proved or not. If the judge decides that the claimant has proved their case, then the judge has to decide how much to award the claimant for the breach of contract or whether another remedy should be awarded.

19.8 Burden and standard of proof

The burden of proving the case is on the claimant. This means that to win the case the claimant has to prove that there was a contract and that it should be enforced or that there was a breach of contract.

The standard of the proof is 'on the balance of probabilities'. This means the judge decides who is most likely to be right.

Test Yourself

1. Which two courts deal with breach of contract cases?
2. Give two methods of alternative dispute resolution which could be used to settle a breach of contract claim.
3. How does a claimant start a court case?
4. What are the three tracks and what are their financial limits?
5. What is meant by 'case management'?
6. Who has to prove the case under the burden of proof?
7. What is the standard of proof in a civil claim?

Examination questions

Matt owned a number of computer game shops. On 1 September, he contacted his supplier, CGQ Ltd, by email, requesting a price for 1000 of the eagerly-anticipated Mark Six consoles and 5000 games designed to work on the console. He wanted them to be delivered in time for the release date of 7 November. CGQ Ltd replied immediately, giving a price of £270,000. Matt then telephoned CGQ Ltd and offered £250,000, which they refused. He then asked for prices from other suppliers, but all of them quoted a higher price.

On 8 September, he sent an email to CGQ Ltd stating that he was willing to pay £270,000. CGQ Ltd emailed back, agreeing to deliver the goods by 6 November for £270,000. By that date, none of the goods had been delivered to him and Matt had to buy them from another supplier for £350,000 in order to fulfil his existing orders from his own customers.

(a) A valid contract requires an offer and acceptance, an intention to create legal relations and consideration. If one party to the contract does not do what has been agreed, there is likely to be a breach of contract.
  (i) Explain the ways in which an offer can come to an end.   (7 marks)
  (ii) Explain the meaning of 'intention to create legal relations'.   (7 marks)
  (iii) Explain the difference between **actual** breach and **anticipatory** breach of contract.   (7 marks)

(b) (i) Discuss whether Matt has a valid contract with CGQ Ltd and, if so, when that contract came into existence. (7 marks)
  (ii) Assuming there was consideration between Matt and CGQ Ltd, briefly explain what is meant by consideration, and identify the consideration in this situation.   (7 marks)

(c) Assume that CGQ Ltd had breached its contract with Matt.
  (i) Identify which court would probably hear Matt's claim, and which track the case would be allocated to. Outline **one** opportunity there would be for settlement of the dispute without going to court.   (5 marks)
  (ii) Assuming CGQ Ltd is found liable, outline how the court would calculate an award of damages and briefly explain how much Matt might be awarded as damages.   (5 marks)

Examiner's tip

In most contract questions there will be a series of events happening on different dates. In order to help you work out whether there is a contract, write these dates down in sequence and try to work out what legal effect each event has. Look at the chart in Figure 19.9 below.

Date	Event	Legal effect
1 Sept	Matt emails CGQ requesting a price	
later on 1 Sept	CGQ email Matt giving a price of £270,000	
later on 1 Sept	Matt telephones CGQ offering £250,000	
After Matt's counter-offer on phone	GCQ refuse Matt's counter-offer of £250,000	
8 Sept	Matt emails GCQ saying he is willing to pay £270,000	
8 Sept	GCQ email agreeing to deliver goods	

Figure 19.9 Time chart for examination question

Doing this should make it easier to answer questions about when a contract was formed. See question (b)(i) above. Try writing in the legal effect of each of these events. Check what you have written by looking at the chart on page 267.

Appendix

This appendix gives help with the activities on pages 5, 51, 204 and 265.

Distinguishing between civil and criminal cases (page 5)

Question 1 answer

Sources A and C are criminal cases. Sources B, D and E are civil cases. This information helps with the remainder of the questions in the activity.

Statutory interpretation and the case of *Fisher v Bell* (page 51)

The court used the literal rule in coming to the decision in this case. The court considered a technical legal meaning of 'offer for sale' and used this meaning in its literal sense. This meant that literally displaying knives in the window was not offering them for sale. As a result the court came to the decision that the knives were not 'offered for sale', and since they had not been sold or hired or lent either, the shopkeeper had not committed any offence under the Act. He was found not guilty.

Completed chart for examination question at end of Chapter 15

Actions	Injuries	Possible offence
Andy ran over to Bilal in an aggressive manner, shouting	No injuries	Assault
Andy hit Bilal repeatedly with a rubbish bin	Fractured cheekbone and jaw, and severe cuts	s 18 or s 20

Completed chart for examination question at end of Chapter 19

Date	Event	Legal effect
1 Sept	Matt emails CGQ requesting a price	Merely a request for information
later on 1 Sept	CGQ email Matt giving a price of £270,000	Offer by CGQ to Matt
later on 1 Sept	Matt telephones CGQ offering £250,000	Counter-offer by Matt. This brings the offer by CGQ to an end
After Matt's counter-offer on phone	GCQ refuse Matt's counter-offer of £250,000	No contract
8 Sept	Matt emails GCQ saying willing to pay £270,000	Offer by Matt to GCQ
8 Sept	GCQ email agreeing to deliver goods	Acceptance by GCQ of Matt's offer. Contract formed at this point

Index

Notes: page references in **bold** indicate Key Facts tables